GOD'S GREENHOUSE

HOW TO GROW PEOPLE GOD'S WAY

TOM SWARTZWELDER

SAGE

WORDS

Robinson, Illinois

God's Greenhouse: How to Grow People God's Way

Ron DeMarco, "Heaven's Grocery Store," Bible.org, January 15, 2019, https://bible.org/illustration/heavens-grocery-store.

Susan Soria, "Preach On," New Hope Baptist Church Plano, Illinois, January 15, 2019, http://www.findglocal.com/US/Plano/132011994985/New-Hope-Baptist-Church.

Published by Sage Words
ISBN: 978-1074823887

Cover Design: Paula Wiseman

To Ruth Ellen,

my wife and co-worker
in the gospel since 1976.

Eternity holds your reward.

Contents

INTRODUCTION

One of the greatest English preachers of all time was Charles Haddon Spurgeon (1834-1892). Oh, how he could preach! Despite the distance and that era's poor means of communication, his sermons were often printed in our own newspapers! It would not be an understatement to say that everyone had heard of Spurgeon, the man who was appropriately described as "The Prince of Preachers."

Spurgeon pastored the Metropolitan Tabernacle in London for thirty-eight years. At the peak of his ministry, the church experienced the salvation of hundreds of people *every* year.

There were no motor vehicles in that day. The main source of travel was still horse and carriage.

(And this is where our Greenhouse study begins!)

It was, therefore, quite common for the hack drivers (also known as carriage drivers) to meet tourists from throughout the world. These tourists came to London to hear Spurgeon in person. After all, Spurgeon's sermons were printed in newspapers on every continent.

This is how the conversation would often go. The tourists would say, "We want to see Spurgeon's Tabernacle."

The hack drivers would respond, "Aye, laddie, for a fee I'll take you across the Thames River and show you the Tabernacle. But I warn you, it's a soul trap. If you hang around that place for very long, you're liable to get converted."

Let those words sink into your mind, and most of all, your spirit!

"But I warn you, it's a soul trap. If you hang around that place for very long, you're liable to get converted."

Consider this question: does that kind of church happen by accident? A church where people get saved and then grow and grow and grow and keep growing into what God wants them to be?

There are over 300 Bible-believing churches in my own Tri-State area of Ohio, West Virginia, and Kentucky. What are the chances that all of those Bible-believing churches are on the same spiritual level? Probably zero, or if you're a real pessimist, even less than zero. Wonder why zero is the logical answer?

Let's take this matter one step further and ask even more specific questions. For example, why are some churches more blessed than others? Then again, why do some churches struggle while others seem to thrive? Why do some church congregations get along better than others? Why do some churches produce preachers by the bucketful and other churches can't even produce good teachers? Why do some churches attract new members, but others rarely see a new member? Why do some churches maintain a baptistery full of water while others utilize the baptistery as a storage area? Plus (this is one of my favorites), why do some churches seem to succeed with a pastor who is just a mediocre preacher and maybe even a poor administrator? That last question is a really good one because it happens more often than one would expect.

In Chapter One we will start answering those questions, and perhaps add a few questions, too. Suffice it to say that those situations—both pro and con—do not happen by accident. They are the result of a long-term pattern of sowing and reaping.

With that in mind, it is a good time to add some color as to why and how this Greenhouse project came into being. In a nutshell, it came into being as **God's effort to turn an unhealthy church into a healthy church**.

Here is what happened. I remember when a church (the name is unimportant; a similar church likely exists in your own neighborhood) contacted me about becoming its pastor. It was just a get-acquainted call. During the call, I asked the chairman of the pastor search committee, "How many deacons do you have?" The chairman told me eleven. I was surprised that a church with a Sunday morning attendance of one hundred and eighty people had eleven deacons. My first thought was that several of those deacons were likely deacons in name only. Based on prior experience that thought seemed logical! I asked, "How many of them are active, really active and involved in the church?" The chairman proudly answered, "Every one of them. If they weren't involved, they would not be a deacon in our church!"

Sure enough, he was telling the truth! One of those deacons had walked ninety years upon this earth, and yet he would often be seen visiting the sick in the hospital. He was amazing and was one of those special saints who had aged with grace, even abundant grace!

Sometimes the deacons can be a serious problem (hence Wake Forest's nickname of Demon Deacons), but that was not so in this church. The problem was in the membership. Quite honestly, the members simply did not like one another.

It had reached a point where the state convention actually sent a representative urging me **not** to accept the call to pastor the church. I recall sitting with the representative in the church's elegant reception room one week before the pastor election! He kindly said, "We don't want you to take this church. You don't know how bad this situation is. It's one of the worst situations in the state. We instead want to bring in a pastor with experience in conflict resolution. The people in this church do not get along. They need help on a very high level. Unfortunately, you are not trained on that level. We would like to sign a two- or three-year contract with the church and place our man here in the hope of getting this church back on the right path, to help the members start trusting one another and working together."

I was stunned by his words. At that time, I was quite naïve, too. I had never heard of such an outside consultant. Imagine a pastor specializing in conflict resolution! The concept was foreign to my way of thinking. The church rejected the consultant suggestion. I thought the convention representative was overstating the problem, so I accepted the call to be the church's next pastor.

Within thirty days I realized the representative's opinion of the church was correct. The church was actually more a collection of groups than an actual church. One of their oft-repeated sayings was, "We have too many chiefs and not enough Indians." Of course, those words usually came from the chiefs!

If one group got a new idea, the other groups (who did not usually get along) would band together to squash that new idea. In my first month, the three youngest deacons made it known they were exasperated with the situation; they would leave the church if my pastorate did not succeed. (And they did indeed leave three years later.) To paraphrase their words, "Enough is enough!"

This had gone on for decades. During the church's seventy-five-year history, only one pastor had left the church on good terms with the majority of the membership. Just one! This internal conflict existed regardless of who was selected as pastor or what the pastor's style happened to be. It existed regardless of who the deacons happened to be. The conflict was so deep in the church that it would be correct to say the conflict had become ingrained within the people.

Perhaps in hindsight, the church should have gone the outside consultant route, but I am uncertain it would have truly resolved the conflict. Interestingly, the largest Bible-believing church in our city actually tried the outside consultant solution at the very same time. (Was there something in the water supply?) However, that solution did not work, and the church closed its doors fifteen years later.

We must never forget that our opponent is a very smart devil. He knows how to wage both open warfare and guerilla warfare against God's church. Once warfare begins, it is difficult to end the battle on terms agreeable to all of the parties. Usually, someone wins. That means someone else loses, and losers don't like losing. The church is then faced with the difficulty of trying to put Humpty Dumpty back together again. It would have been much easier to have kept Humpty together in the first place!

It is true that every church has some degree of conflict, but we don't want the conflict to rise to a level where the very soul of the church is at risk. The Bible says in Ephesians 4:3 that we are to "diligently or strenuously keep . . . maintain . . . preserve the unity which has been created by the Holy Spirit." This verse will be examined closely in a later chapter, but let's be sure we understand that we are not—absolutely not—responsible for creating the unity. It is the Holy Spirit's work to create the unity! Our responsibility is to do nothing to hinder His work of creating the unity! It is by surrendering our will to His will that such unity is maintained!

Experience teaches us there are at least three ways to resolve conflict inside a church. One way to resolve conflict is for people to leave. It may occasionally be necessary to undergo the process known as "blessed subtractions," but our focus should be on the "blessed additions" and "gaining your brother" as Jesus described in Matthew 18:15. A gain is healthier than a loss!

The second way to resolve conflict is by death or old age. An American tourist visited the bush in Africa. One morning he stepped out of the tent and found himself face to face with a large lion. He immediately screamed for help! A nearby native laughed and said, "Don't worry! That lion's old and his teeth have all rotted out!" Sometimes conflict never truly gets resolved—it just dies a long death as people become old ("I can't remember what we argued about, but I know I was right!") or even die. Unfortunately, the church may be too far gone at that point to recover from the years of damage.

But the third way to resolve, or even avoid conflict, is the biblical way of having all of the parties agree on God's purpose for the church. This view is presented in the following pages. Re-discovering God's purpose for God's church can be an eye-opening experience for many church members! Such a discovery is much more than an easy to memorize seven-word slogan which fizzles within a year. On the contrary, this discovery unveils deep, abiding truths that transform how we think at the very core of our ministry. It is not an overstatement to say this discovery can transform our total approach to ministry.

God's Greenhouse: How to Grow People God's Way came from this background. I was serving as pastor in a dysfunctional church and had no solutions. Quite honestly, I was in over my head in this area of conflict resolution. I suspect many of you would admit the same weakness regarding your own abilities. It was then that God opened my eyes to the Greenhouse concept—that God intends every church to be a spiritual greenhouse which grows people into what God intends them to be. That concept provided me with our identity as well as our purpose.

The next question became one of how to best present this material in an easy-to-understand fashion. One of my faithful men constructed a small greenhouse consisting of a wooden frame and a thin, see-through plastic covering. The pulpit was replaced with a small table. The greenhouse fit perfectly on the table! The greenhouse was large enough that even the people on the back row could see the greenhouse as well as the plants we would later place inside the greenhouse.

When I was a small child, I learned spiritual truth by seeing or visualizing Bible truth on a flannelgraph. Many years later I had now moved upscale! I had a miniaturized greenhouse!

The second step involved populating the greenhouse. After graduating from Chattanooga's Tennessee Temple University in 1979, my wife and I returned home and rented a house from the owners of the largest greenhouse in southeastern Ohio. Not everyone can say this, but we had five enormous greenhouses in our backyard! We gained an eyeful of appreciation for the greenhouse concept. (Perhaps God was already preparing my mind for this study, even though it was some ten years in the future!) For example, I learned snow might be on the greenhouse roof, but the plants were still able to grow inside this incubator!

My goal was to duplicate what was happening in the five greenhouses. I enlisted one woman to recruit flowers from the other women of the church. For weeks upon weeks, the women brought flowers on Sunday morning and Sunday evening to put in my miniature greenhouse. (The flowers were absolutely beautiful and became a discussion/fellowship item!) Of course, each flower represented a person. This process made everything very personal to the viewers and especially to the women!

That brought us to the key question: what is necessary to grow this plant/person inside our greenhouse?

It is too simplistic to say this concept is simple enough for everyone to understand. Seeing and understanding are often separated by what we Ohioans like to call "a country mile." Country measurements are longer than city measurements, or so they say. Jesus said in Matthew chapter thirteen that people have the ability to see and yet not see, to hear and yet not hear or understand. Then He added these very important words, "He that has ears to hear, let him hear." In other words, "If you have ears, listen and understand!"

Thus, my approach in presenting this material to the church as well as to you is slow and prayerful and as simple as I can make it.

One final comment needs to be added before we move into the actual material. How should you as a church leader view this material? One way to prevent a small fire from becoming a deadly forest fire is to limit the potential fuel for such an explosive fire. **Therefore, it seems best to approach this Greenhouse concept as a preventive measure.** It is best to prevent the fire from ever beginning or to nip it in the bud while it is still small! Such an effort requires time, effort, resources, money, training, etc. I believe all of us would agree, though, that the long-term results are well worth the investment!

Second, this material will provide a fresh way for you to present your purpose to the church or your leadership team. The greenhouse itself is unique. The required level of participation is unique. The skits are unique. The handouts are unique. Last, the material is unique in that it is a combination of solid Bible doctrine (which your people need to hear) and practical application.

Church health is perhaps the biggest issue we face as God's church. It is a much bigger subject than my feeble mind can develop. However, this book will provide an excellent starting point for many of you. The Greenhouse concept provides a unique means of presenting church health to your entire congregation or to just a small leadership team! In addition, it can easily be adapted to an occasional refresher course throughout your ministry. Simply pull out one chapter and plug it into your ministry!

It is not a tell-all-end-all because you will need to continually circle back to this issue of church health. Above all, keep the issue of church health constantly in front of you!

You may never do this particular study with your church. It may sound too simplistic to you. Fine! But if you can use its concepts in helping develop a purpose that everyone can buy into . . . well, you get my meaning.

Let's begin!

SECTION ONE: CONCEPTUALIZING GOD'S GREENHOUSE

1

FOUNDATIONAL PRINCIPLES

It's Who We Are. It's What We Do.

Where should one begin in the construction of a new building? Everyone knows to begin with the foundation! But far too often we ignore the importance of the foundation in our churches. Perhaps it occurs because we employ so many unpaid staff members. Our staff members simply don't have the time to "do the theoretical stuff" and their time has to be devoted to pure ministry, not to thinking or planning! Perhaps it is because the foundation occurs below the surface, where no one can see the results, and such effort is not considered worthwhile.

But one truth stands regardless of how we think or behave! That truth states no building can survive for long if it has a faulty foundation, or no foundation at all!

Jesus expressed the principle of a solid foundation in the story of the two houses.

"Therefore, everyone who hears these words of Mine and acts on them will be like a sensible man who built his house on the rock. The rain fell, the rivers rose, and the winds blew and pounded that house. Yet it didn't collapse because its foundation was on the rock. But everyone who hears these words of Mine and doesn't act on them will be like a foolish man who built his house on the sand. The rain fell, the rivers rose, the winds blew and pounded that house, and it collapsed. And its collapse was great!" (Matthew 7:24-27, HCSB)

I have often visualized that both houses used the same building plan and they were equally beautiful! One house, though, was built upon the rock, and the second house was built upon the sand. Eventually, the storms of adversity came against both houses. The house built upon the sand crashed, but the house built upon the rock survived.

What was the difference? Jesus emphasized, "the second house fell *because* its foundation was *not* built upon a rock." The rock was the difference! The rock was the reason that the foundation did not crumble and collapse.

Jesus said in Luke 6:48 that the contractor dug *below* the sand and *kept digging* until he found the rock that was unshakeable. But that did not happen for the house which was built upon the sand.

Consider these basic thoughts:

It took more *foresight* to build the house upon the rock than the house upon the sand.

It took more *planning* to build the house upon the rock than the house upon the sand.

It took more *resources* (including time, training, and money) to build the house upon the rock than the house upon the sand.

It took more *persistence* to build the house upon the rock than the house upon the sand.

Conclusion: It took more of everything to build a house which would accomplish its purpose of being a house (and a home) for years to come!

Thus, much of *everything* needs to be allocated to make certain the foundation is a solid foundation which can support growth. Otherwise, cracks will appear very quickly! And then something even worse may occur!

Chapter One is a foundational chapter for everything in the pages which follow. I mentioned in the Introduction that there are at least three ways to resolve conflict in a church. The first is for people to leave, the second is for people to grow old or die, and the third is for ***people to agree upon a purpose***. The third option, of course, is the much-preferred option! The agreed-upon purpose drives everything in the church. We evaluate every church activity by asking, "Does this activity fulfill our purpose?"

This is where our study begins. It begins with the foundation, for if the foundation is shaky, uncertain, or even crumbling what can the righteous do? (Psalm 11:3) Such a purpose must be clearly and boldly stated. Such a purpose must also be understood and accepted by the staff *and* the congregation.

When I retired from secular work, I allocated time to just relax and get caught up on my reading. The author, Douglas Reeman, attracted my attention. Reeman wrote over fifty fictional books about war involving the British people. I read the books one after another and, therefore, certain repetitive lines stood out to me. One of those lines was spoken over and over again by brave men facing a difficult assignment. These men would look into the abyss of war, count the cost of possible death or mutilation, and then say, *"It's who we are. It's what we do."* Those words were words of purpose for the soldiers. Those words established their identity just as much as their uniform.

The same words could be printed in every church bulletin, appear on banners throughout the classrooms and auditorium, and be repeated in unison in every service.

"It's who we are. It's what we do." In other words, this is why our organization (church) exists. God has identified who we are and what we are to do with our available resources.

In recent years there has been a renewed emphasis upon the biblical purpose of God's church. Hallelujah! Such an emphasis is long overdue. (Unfortunately, it is probably too late to make a difference for many churches.) I am personally fond of Rick Warren's approach in *The Purpose Driven Church* and *The Purpose Driven Life*. I am confident those texts will stand the test of time. Some criticize those texts as being too shallow; however, it is my experience that one must start somewhere! Sadly, too many churches have not even been able to get to first base in the purpose-driven strategy, let alone get to the "deep" level promoted by some so-called experts.

This chapter goes beyond the simplicity or catchiness of a seven-word purpose statement. This chapter develops an understanding of what God's church is supposed to be, and what is essential to such development. It is *a sermon in action*—a sermon the members can see with their own eyes and easily comprehend.

The concepts in Chapter One are very elementary. They may actually seem *too* elementary. However, we must remind ourselves that a church consists of sheep—not giraffes. Sheep need truth presented in simple ways. This study presents these truths in a way that the sheep can understand, accept, and make work.

I suggest employing your church leaders to present this material. Why? First, leaders enjoy leading and being in front of the people. This method is an easy way to encourage them! Chapter One is a very uplifting, positive message. Leaders enjoy saying "Yes!" much more than saying that other word we won't mention here.

Second, building the right kind of church requires substantial buy-in across the entire church. The leadership team will gain a much better understanding of the church's overall purpose if the team is involved in presenting the material. After all, the teacher is always the one who learns the most from any lesson! Don't forget you are teaching your leaders just as much as you are teaching others!

Third, the method of presenting all of the Greenhouse material will be quite unique. This type of presentation is not normally done in a Baptist church. As a matter of fact, this entire Greenhouse series is quite un-orthodox. The church critics will likely do what they do best: criticize anything that has not been done this way before. This will be especially true if only the pastor does all of this chapter's presentations as well as those presentations in the following chapters. *So, involve others as much as you can!* Their involvement sends a signal that the leaders have already adapted to this new approach and so should the critics!

The presentation for Chapter One's "Foundational Principles" includes two items. First, each deacon or leader will read (the vocal part) a short script that provides one aspect regarding our purpose. That's the easy part! Second, the deacon/leader will hang a sign (the visual part) which the audience can see. That's the almost-easy part!

In the pre-PowerPoint days, we hung a fishing line across the auditorium. The leader used clips to hang his sign on the fishing line then moved to a microphone to read his script. That was very easily done! I still like the primitive idea of using a fishing line even though we have now graduated to PowerPoint. The size of the auditorium, of course, will have something to say about your method of displaying the visual. I still suggest doing an actual sign (perhaps arranged in a collage to illustrate multiple pieces of the puzzle coming together as one) **plus** displaying a picture of the sign on the overhead screen. It is best to keep all of the signs visible at all times so the people can see the whole picture at all times.

"It's who we are. It's what we do."

So, who are we and what are we to do?

Let me share with you my script for the opening message.

Pastor: Our deacons (church leaders) are going to help me. No, this is not team tag preaching. Our deacons want to share what they believe our church ought to be for every single one of us. The fact is our church exists for a purpose, and that purpose is supposed to be God's purpose rather than our own purpose.

Think of God's purpose like a bull's-eye in a target. The bull's-eye tells you where you should shoot the arrow. If you hit the bull's-eye, you have succeeded. But if you miss the bull's-eye, you have failed and have wasted your time. I don't want to waste my time, how about you? Our leaders don't want to waste their time, or your time, or their money, or your money.

So today we want to learn what our church ought to be for every single one of us. Look at your study sheet and get ready to write.

What does God expect our church to be? Let's find out!

(Note: the deacons/leaders will first hang their signs then read the following scripts. The sign inscriptions can be found in the Study Material at the conclusion of this book. I suggest staggering the deacons/leaders on each side of the auditorium.)

DEACON/LEADER #1

(Deacon/Leader #1 hangs the sign bearing "TEMPLE OF GOD" and reads his script.)

Our church, known as <u>insert your church's name</u> Church, is made up of people just like you and me. It is more than just an organization. It is more than just a fellowship. It is something which rises far above any of that because it includes, and even requires, the presence of Almighty God in order for our church to exist. There are many different aspects of the church of God which we will present in the next few minutes. You will probably want to write them down.

The one aspect which I would most like to emphasize is found in the book of John, chapter four. Jesus said, "The hour will come, and even now has come, when the true worshippers shall worship the Father in spirit and in truth: The Father desires people to worship him in that manner. God is a Spirit; those who worship God must worship Him in spirit and in truth." (John 4:23-24)

Yes, our church should be a *people* of worship in a unified *place* of worship—a place where people can forget the problems of the world, a place where we can come together and worship the Lord in spirit and in truth.

The Bible says in the book of 1 Corinthians chapter three, "Do you not understand that you collectively as a group are the ***temple*** of God, and that the Holy Spirit of God dwells in you? If any person defiles or injures the temple of God, that person shall be destroyed by God. Why? Because the temple of God is holy, and you yourselves at _____ Church are such a temple." (1 Corinthians 3:16-17)

> *"For we as God's people are built upon the foundation of the apostles and prophets, and Jesus Christ Himself is the chief cornerstone! In Him and Him alone this entire body of believers has been joined together. This church is now growing heavenward into a holy temple both in the Lord and for the Lord. In Jesus Christ, we are being built together into God's temple on earth in His Holy Spirit."* (Ephesians 2:20-22)

Yes, when we come together, we are to worship our God, our Creator, and most important of all, our magnificent Savior. Let us never forget that we are the temple of God!

DEACON/LEADER #2

(Deacon/Leader #2 hangs the sign bearing "TRUTH OF GOD" and reads his script.)

Yes, our church is made up of people just like you and me—people who need guidance in each of our daily lives. Our world needs to know what to do and what not to do, what is true and what is false, what is right and what is wrong, what is acceptable to God and what is not acceptable to God.

The Bible teaches us that, "Righteousness or being committed to doing what is right lifts up a nation, but sin and doing what is wrong is a disgrace, even an embarrassment to any people or society." (Proverbs 14:34) Furthermore, the Bible says, "There are many ways which seem right to a man, but those ways ultimately end in death." (Proverbs 14:12) Jesus cautioned, "There is a wide gate and a broad road that leads to destruction, and many choose to go down that road. But there is a small gate and a narrow road that leads to eternal life, and only a few find that narrow road to eternal life." (Matthew 7:13)

Well, guess who happens to be God's means of educating the world regarding what is right and what is wrong? It is _____ Church.

This is exactly what the Apostle Paul calls us not only to do, but also to be, in our daily life. Paul says, "These things I write to you at _____ Church so you can know how you ought to conduct yourself in the house of God, which is the church of the living God, and this church is to be the pillar and foundation of the truth." (1 Timothy 3:15)

"God's purpose has been to use the church to display his wisdom. This was His eternal plan, which He carried out through Christ Jesus our Lord." (Ephesians 3:11) That means _____ Church is part of God's eternal plan to display His truth and wisdom!

Yes, the world may believe the devil's lies about our origin, about our destiny, even about our textbook called the Bible, but God has revealed the truth about each of these items to His church—to you and me both.

Let us as a church never forget that we are the pillar and foundation of the truth of God.

DEACON/LEADER #3

(Deacon/Leader #3 hangs the sign bearing "FAMILY OF GOD" and reads his script.)

A few years ago, our church authorized the creation of a new church directory. This directory had a beautiful picture of our church on the front cover, but it had something even more important on the inside. Do you remember what was on the inside? On the inside were the pictures of all of us who make up our church family.

There is a picture of the Smiths and the Browns, of the Joneses and the Greens, of the Adamses and the Berrys and the Roberts, too.

Each picture represents one part of our church family—not merely a part of our church organization but actually a part of our family. God's church is to be a family of brothers and sisters in Jesus Christ. It is to be just as much a family as our own individual family. You may not have a brother or sister in your earthly family, but I want you to know you have plenty of brothers and sisters in our church family.

The Bible says in the book of Ephesians chapter three, "For this cause I bow my knees unto the Father of our Lord Jesus Christ, Of whom the whole family in heaven and earth is named." (Ephesians 3:14-15) Our church family includes mere babes in Christ such as our recently born-again new members; our church family also includes those who have been saved for many years. The key is we have been spiritually born again into the family of God the Father, God the Son, and God the Holy Spirit.

God wants His church to behave like a family! The Bible gives us our goal when it says, "that there may be no division in the body, but that the members may have the same care for one another. If one member suffers, all suffer together; if one member is honored, all rejoice together." (1 Corinthians 12:25-26, ESV) Just like in a normal family!

Our music director will come at this time and lead us in singing one of our favorite songs. Bill Gaither wrote some very powerful words when he wrote this song. We want to put these words into practice throughout our church. The song is "The Family of God." Aren't you glad you're a part of the family of God? And aren't you glad you're a part of our church family, too?

(Note: the congregation sings "The Family of God" at this time.)

Yes, the name over our door may identify us as a church, but let us never forget that being a part of this church means we are also a part of a family—the family of God.

DEACON/LEADER #4

(Deacon/Leader #4 hangs the sign bearing "PRIESTHOOD OF GOD" and reads his script.)

Have you ever wondered what it was like to be a priest in the Old Testament? To offer sacrifices to God and to intercede for the people? Believe it or not, that is exactly what God expects His New Testament church to be: to be the priesthood of God where each and every believer is also a priest and can do priestly service for our own High Priest, Jesus Christ.

The Bible says in the book of 1 Peter chapter two that you and I are *living* building blocks. We aren't dead like those building blocks our children receive at Christmas or like the concrete blocks in this building. The Bible views us as building blocks which are spiritually alive! God then takes us as His building blocks to construct a spiritual house.

The Bible name for that spiritual house is a holy priesthood. That means we are now God's priests, and we now have the opportunity to offer up spiritual sacrifices which God finds acceptable through Jesus Christ. Another Bible verse points out that we are a royal priesthood—priests of Almighty God—and we are proclaiming both far and wide "the praises of our God who has called us out of spiritual darkness into His marvelous light." (1 Peter 2:9)

The Bible urges us as God's priests to now "present our bodies as a living sacrifice, holy, acceptable to God, which is our reasonable service." (Romans 12:1) Then we can "continually offer the sacrifice of praise to God, that is, the fruit of our lips," and continually give thanks to Him who has so freely given us so many things. The Bible adds that we should not forget to do good and to share with others because God considers doing good and sharing to be two more sacrifices, also.

It is for this reason that the church bulletin often speaks of our worship in terms of giving or sacrificing our tithes and offerings. It is why we sing songs like, "Is Your All on the Altar of Sacrifice Laid?" It is why we sing "I Surrender All" and "Have Thine Own Way, Lord." It is why we lift up holy hands unto the Lord in our act of worship. It is why we praise His name in song even if we don't have the best singing voice in our church. It is why we intercede for one another in prayer, and what a wonderful privilege that is!

Let us as God's church never forget that we are the priesthood of God.

DEACON/LEADER #5

(Deacon/Leader #5 hangs the sign bearing "SCHOOLMASTER OF GOD" and reads his script.)

Thank God for what we have already heard about our church, but the Bible teaches that God's church is more than just these items. In addition, the church is also the schoolmaster of God. Quite often we hear that we are to love one another, but what we often fail to understand is that true love also works as a schoolmaster in our lives.

True love establishes order in the classroom when there is disorder. True love restores right behavior when we do wrong. True love brings us back into line so that we might become everything that God would have us to be. God did not call us as His church to tolerate every form of behavior, but He said in the book of 2 Thessalonians chapter three:

21

> *Now we command you, brothers, in the name of our Lord Jesus Christ, to keep away from every brother who walks irresponsibly and not according to the tradition received from us. For you yourselves know how you must imitate us: We were not irresponsible among you; we did not eat anyone's food free of charge; instead, we labored and struggled, working night and day, so that we would not be a burden to any of you. It is not that we don't have the right to support, but we did it to make ourselves an example to you so that you would imitate us. In fact, when we were with you, this is what we commanded you: "If anyone isn't willing to work, he should not eat." For we hear that there are some among you who walk irresponsibly, not working at all, but interfering with the work of others. Now we command and exhort such people by the Lord Jesus Christ that quietly working, they may eat their own food. Brothers, do not grow weary in doing good. And if anyone does not obey our instruction in this letter, take note of that person; don't associate with him, so that he may be ashamed. Yet don't treat him as an enemy, but warn him as a brother. (2 Thessalonians 3:6-15, HCSB)*

The last two verses of James remind us, "My brethren, if any among you strays from the truth and one turns him back, let him know that he who turns a sinner from the error of his way will save his soul from death and will cover a multitude of sins." (James 5:19-20, NASB)

It may not be an easy thing to do, but let us never forget that we are also the schoolmaster of God. You need it, and so do I.

DEACON/LEADER #6

(Deacon/Leader #6 hangs the sign bearing "HOSPITAL OF GOD" and reads his script.)

Through the years, our family, like many of yours, has known a great deal of sickness. We have needed doctors and medicine and even hospitals so that our illness might be cured, that our broken bones might be restored, and that our wounded spirits might be healed.

Sure enough, the Bible says that our church should also be a hospital—a hospital for those who are spiritually sick, who have been broken by sin, who are burdened with a heavy load, who cannot see which way to turn.

The Apostle Paul said to the church at Rome in chapter fifteen, "Now we who are strong ought to bear the weaknesses of those without strength and not just please ourselves. Each of us is to please his neighbor for his good, to his edification. For even Christ did not please Himself . . . " (Romans 15:1-3, NASB)

Then listen also to these other words from the Bible, "Brothers, if anyone is caught in any transgression, you who are spiritual should restore him in a spirit of gentleness. Keep watch on yourself, lest you too be tempted. Bear one another's burdens, and so fulfill the law of Christ. For if anyone thinks he is something, when he is nothing, he deceives himself." (Galatians 6:1-3, ESV)

"Religion that is pure and undefiled before God, the Father, is this: to visit orphans and widows in their affliction, and to keep oneself unstained from the world." (James 1:27, ESV)

You see, the Christian life is not one of getting but rather one of giving. As a matter of fact, those words are one of the finest definitions of Christianity that you will ever hear because the spirit of Christianity is never one of getting but always one of giving.

The Bible says in the book of Matthew chapter twenty-five:

> *Then the King will say to those on His right, 'Come, you who are blessed of My Father, inherit the kingdom prepared for you from the foundation of the world. For I was hungry, and you gave Me something to eat; I was thirsty, and you gave Me something to drink; I was a stranger, and you invited Me in;naked, and you clothed Me; I was sick, and you visited Me; I was in prison, and you came to Me.' Then the righteous will answer Him, 'Lord, when did we see You hungry, and feed You, or thirsty, and give You*

something to drink? And when did we see You a stranger, and invite You in, or naked, and clothe You? When did we see You sick, or in prison, and come to You?' The King will answer and say to them, 'Truly I say to you, to the extent that you did it to one of these brothers of Mine, even the least of them, you did it to Me.' (Matthew 25:34-40, NASB)

I do not know what the rest of you think, but that is the kind of hospital our city needs, my family needs, and I myself need.

Let us never forget that it is you and I together who are the hospital of God. God help us to be a spiritual bandage to someone today.

DEACON/LEADER #7

(Deacon/Leader #7 hangs the sign bearing "WITNESS OF GOD" and reads his script.)

One of the saddest verses in all of the Bible is the verse which says, "No man cares for my soul." (Psalm 142:4) We see that verse portrayed in the case of the homeless person who has nowhere to go, but if we opened our eyes, we would also see the same situation in the case of people up and down our street, people with whom we work, people who are even members of our own family. They are people who need someone to tell them that Jesus loves them, that Jesus died on the cross for their sins, and that they can be saved by humbly receiving Jesus Christ as their personal Lord and Savior.

But these people will never know unless we as God's people tell them and witness to them.

Just before Jesus went back to heaven, He said, "Go therefore and make disciples of all the nations, baptizing them in the name of the Father and the Son and the Holy Spirit, teaching them to observe all that I commanded you; and lo, I am with you always, even to the end of the age." (Matthew 28:19-20, NASB)

On another occasion, Jesus said, "As my Father hath sent Me, even so send I you." (John 20:21, KJV)

The book of Mark ends with Jesus telling us, "Go ye into all the world, and preach the gospel to every creature." (Mark 16:15, KJV) Those words "all the world" mean every continent, every country, every city, and every house. It is a worldwide commission.

We must remember:

> *"How then will they call on Him in whom they have not believed? How will they believe in Him whom they have not heard? And how will they hear without a preacher? How will they preach unless they are sent? Just as it is written, 'How beautiful are the feet of those who bring good news of good things!' However, they did not all heed the good news; for Isaiah says, 'Lord, who has believed our report?' So, faith comes from hearing, and hearing by the word of Christ." (Romans 10:14-17, NASB)*

I remember my own salvation. It took place at _____ (location). The date was _____. I now have Jesus in my life for not only today and tomorrow, but also for all of eternity, too. None of that would have been possible if someone did not witness to me about Jesus Christ.

The reason I am saved today is because someone told me about an old rugged cross, about a perfect Savior, about a glorious resurrection and a soon coming King. I hope you can say the same!

It has been well said that you cannot spell the word "gospel" without the first two letters "g" and "o"—in other words, GO! Go and keep going!

Jesus said, "But you shall receive dynamite power when the Holy Spirit comes upon you; you shall be witnesses of Me in Jerusalem, Judea, and Samaria, and to the uttermost parts of the earth." (Acts 1:8)

He says we are to go! Go into our own Jerusalem of this city, go into our own Judaea of this county, go into our own Samaria of this state, and do not stop going until we go unto the uttermost part of the earth.

Let us never forget that we as God's church are the witness of God.

DEACON/LEADER #8

(Deacon/Leader #8 hangs the sign bearing "SALT OF GOD" and reads his script.)

Everyone who has ever fixed a meal or eaten a meal knows the importance of salt. As a boy, I learned that everything tasted better with salt! I did not know why, but I just knew that it was so!

Sure enough, this world of ours tastes bad— what our world needs is some salt applied to it, also! This world needs something to add flavor to it and preserve it from rotting! This is so in our schools, our entertainment, our businesses, our politics, our culture, and the list goes on and on.

The Bible says that we as _____ Church are to be that salt. Jesus said in the book of Matthew chapter five:

> *You are the salt of the earth, but if salt has lost its taste, how shall its saltiness be restored? It is no longer good for anything except to be thrown out and trampled under people's feet.*
> *You are the light of the world. A city set on a hill cannot be hidden. Nor do people light a lamp and put it under a basket, but on a stand, and it gives light to all in the house. In the same way, let your light shine before others, so that they may see your good works and give glory to your Father who is in heaven. (Matthew 5:13-16, ESV)*

We need to give this world a conscience about abortion, about crime and morality, about the sacredness of marriage between a man and a woman, about raising families, about ethics and patriotism, about doing what is right, and especially about someday meeting God in the judgment.

Let us never forget that we are the salt of God!

DEACON/LEADER #9

(Deacon/Leader #9 hangs the sign bearing "SERVANT OF GOD" and reads his script.)

The Bible says, "Let this mind or attitude be in you which was also in Christ Jesus." (Philippians 2:5) One of our Lord's characteristics was that He never forgot His identity! He always remembered that He was the Servant of His heavenly Father. From the cradle to the grave, Jesus showed us by His everyday activities what God was really like. His religion was a religion of everyday service no matter whether God wanted Him to serve the richest of the rich or even the poorest of the poor.

As a matter of fact, the story of the Good Samaritan is really the story of Jesus Christ! Listen closely to the conversation between a young man and Jesus. The story begins with the young man asking a question of Jesus.

> *But he, desiring to justify himself, said to Jesus, "And who is my neighbor?" Jesus replied, "A man was going down from Jerusalem to Jericho, and he fell among robbers, who stripped him and beat him and departed, leaving him half dead. Now by chance a priest was going down that road, and when he saw him he passed by on the other side. So likewise a Levite, when he came to the place and saw him, passed by on the other side. But a Samaritan, as he journeyed, came to where he was, and when he saw him, he had compassion. He went to him and bound up his wounds, pouring on oil and wine. Then he set him on his own animal and brought him to an inn and took care of him. And the next day he took out two denarii and gave them to the innkeeper, saying, 'Take care of him, and whatever more you spend, I will repay you when I come back.' Which of these three, do you think, proved to be a neighbor to the man who fell among the robbers?" He said, "The one who showed him mercy." And Jesus said to him, "You go, and do likewise." (Luke 10:29-37, ESV)*

Let us never forget that we are the servant of God. Jesus was our Good Samaritan, and now we can be a Good Samaritan to someone else.

DEACON/LEADER #10

(Deacon/Leader #10 hangs the sign bearing "FLOCK OF GOD" and reads his script.)

Yes, our ministry as a church reaches upward in worship of our God; it reaches inward in caring for one another; it reaches outward in ministering to those who do not know our Lord and Savior Jesus Christ.

But all of this depends upon us as a church understanding just how much we need to come together—come together not only to find the will of our Father, but also to do the will of our Father.

The Bible describes us over and over again as sheep. All of us know a sheep is an ignorant animal. A sheep cannot find its way home unless it has someone to guide it. A sheep cannot protect itself unless it has someone to protect it. A sheep will make a mess of things if it goes its own way.

Sometimes we as a church forget that we are actually sheep . . . sheep who will make a mess of the church if we do it our own way . . . sheep who say, "Baa!" so loudly that we cannot hear the voice of our gracious Shepherd . . . sheep who need direction and love and protection . . . sheep who need someone to call us by our own name and lead us all the way home.

The Bible says, "The Lord is My shepherd; therefore, I shall not want or lack for any good thing," and that is just as true for our church as it is for you and me.

Let us always remember that the Shepherd calls His own sheep by name and He wants—He truly wants—to lead them out, out into green pastures, out into blessings which are more than we can count, out into a vision to do things we have never done before, out where there are people to be ministered to and souls to be saved and lives to be changed.

Would you pray for me that I will set the right example in listening to the voice of my Shepherd? Not only that, but would you pray for all of us as your leaders that we will also set the right example in listening to the voice of our Shepherd? And would you also pray for our pastor that he will always remind us that we are sheep, that God alone is our Shepherd, and that we need to always follow the voice of the Shepherd?

Let us never, ever forget that we are the flock of God.

(Note: The Pastor now speaks to the church.)

Do you as a church agree this is the kind of church God will bless? We know the answer is yes because every sign is supported by many verses in the Bible. But how can such a church come into being?

Many of our women have brought flowers from home for this service. At this time, I would like for them to set their flowers around the front of our church.

(Note: this activity had been previously announced for the past two weeks. Each of the women had been encouraged to bring one potted plant to this service. My only rule was this: any plant qualifies as long as it can be carried— not carted! The women will now come forward and set their flowers across the front of the church. The women may then return to their seats. It would be wise to have someone take pictures of this flower display while the service continues.)

Pastor: Isn't this a beautiful display? This beautiful display did not happen by accident. I want you to notice that our women brought healthy plants to this service. We know that is so because healthy plants can become beautiful plants and make everything look so very special.

Likewise, I want you to know that people in a church **cannot grow** unless the church is alive and healthy. If the plant is diseased, it won't grow. If it is given the wrong food, it won't grow. If it is given no water, it won't grow. If it is given no sunshine, it won't grow.

That brings us to our chief text for this new study we are calling *God's Greenhouse: How to Grow People God's Way.*

29

Our main text is taken from 1 Corinthians chapter three and verse nine. Some of you may remember the old-time skill known as writing in shorthand. Let me do the opposite. Let me give you the verse in long-hand so we get the full picture. "For we are God's fellow workers, also known as God's coworkers. You, as God's people, are God's <u>field</u>. You are God's <u>farm</u>. You are God's <u>garden</u>. You are the place where God grows things. You are also God's building."

I have underlined three words. Field. Farm. Garden.

The King James Version uses a fourth word—the word "husbandry." A husbandry can be defined as the practice of cultivating crops. Let's add that word to our list. I now have four words: field, farm, garden, and husbandry which is the practice of cultivating crops.

Do you get the idea we are talking about a place where we grow plants?

Let me suggest to you that a modern-day greenhouse is a good way to imagine this verse. *We can't turn this auditorium into a farm or a garden, but we can create a greenhouse.*

Let me read verse nine again. "For we are God's coworkers and you are God's greenhouse . . . a place where God specializes in growing people."

Let those words sink in! Our church is a place where God grows people!

It's time to make this lesson very personal. Our Primary Sunday School class contains some of our most precious flowers. They are now marching in with their own flower. (Note: this class of children is led to the greenhouse by their teacher.) Each student is holding a flower which represents that student. Young people, hold up your flower so everyone can see your flower. That flower represents you. I want the adults to notice that every boy has a flower and every girl has a flower.

Here is the question: where should we place these children? Remember, these children are represented by the flower in their hands.

We have several choices.

We can place these children in the Sahara Desert. How long would they last in that environment? Not long. Why? There is no water in the desert.

We can place these children on the moon. How long would they last on the moon? Not long. Why? There is no air on the moon.

We can place these children outside in the world of a Christless humanity. The Bible describes our world as lying in wickedness, in the hands of the wicked one. Our world is full of people who do that which is right in their own eyes but is not right in God's eyes. Is that where we want to place these children? No.

But there is a fourth possibility. Where would you as a church like to place them? (The audience will choose the greenhouse.)

(Note: complete the illustration by having the children place their own flower inside the greenhouse. The children may then exit.)

(Note: identify one of the women who brought a flower to the front of the auditorium earlier and ask her to retrieve that flower.)

"Mrs. _____, what kind of flower did you bring? It's a beautiful flower. This flower represents you. Where would you like to be placed?"

(Note: complete the illustration by placing her flower inside the greenhouse. She may then return to her seat.)

I have a question for everyone, "Do you think our greenhouse can help her grow? Do you think our greenhouse can help these children grow? Do you think our greenhouse can help all of us grow?"

It seems to me we have a big assignment in front of us!

There is one more idea I want you to see before we finish. It is a very important idea. It is in the first part of verse nine where the Apostle Paul writes, "We are God's coworkers." The King James Version says, "We are laborers together with God." The concept is that we are coworkers with God.

That brings us to a statement I want everyone to write down. It's item number thirteen on the study sheet. You'll then want to write it down in your Bible because this statement will become critically important in our future studies.

Here is the statement. (Note: put the statement on the screen.) "We cannot do it without God, and He has chosen not to do it without us!" In other words, it won't get done if we don't do our part, and that means EVERYONE doing his or her part.

Let me finish with this illustration.

(Note: call two new believers to the front. Point out that our assignment is to create a greenhouse environment where these new converts can grow and reach their full potential for Jesus Christ. But that won't happen unless specific things happen Sunday after Sunday! What are those specific things? We will begin discussing them in our next study.)

How much do you want a church where *people* can grow? That is a different question than asking, how much do you want your *church* to grow? In this new way of thinking, ***your goal is not one of growing a church but rather one of growing people!*** It is not a goal of growing a thing but of growing actual, living people like the person seated next to you as well as you personally.

How much do you want a church *where people can grow?*

2

GOD'S FIRST GREENHOUSE

A Place Called Eden

Preparation: a few volunteers, under the direction of the Flower Coordinator, have brought flowers to serve as exhibits in the greenhouse for today's message. This process is repeated throughout the messages in Section One. Share the name of each flower and place the flower in the greenhouse. Encourage more volunteers to provide flowers for future services.

During the 1980s my wife, Ruth Ellen, and I rented a two-story house that was located only thirty feet from the largest greenhouse complex in the Tri-State area. Both the house and the greenhouse complex were owned by the Weber family. No one (except us) treated the house as noteworthy, but the greenhouse complex was a sight to behold! The complex had been constructed in the 1920s; very little had changed over the next sixty years.

The complex consisted of five long greenhouses which were heated with steam from a coal-fired system. The family's website stated, "This plant covered 28,700 square feet and proved to be one of the most modern greenhouses in the state of Ohio."

During our years there, we observed people coming from more than a hundred miles away to view firsthand something that had become a historical wonder. Students from nearby Marshall University often came to study its construction and techniques.

This greenhouse was uniquely composed of glass panes—thousands of them—that were held firm in a wooden frame by nails. A sheet of plastic often covered the glass roof. It was very dangerous to climb on the greenhouse roof to replace broken glass. One could easily break through the surrounding glass and suffer a serious cut. Indeed, replacing the broken glass was an art in itself!

Sometimes a thunderstorm would play havoc with the greenhouse! A strong gust of wind would slip under a pane of glass, lift it up, and send it soaring through the air! It was no big deal if the pane landed in the distant field, but, far too often, the pane fell on another pane and shattered both panes! The resulting chaos sounded like shotguns at target practice. Bang! Bang! Bang!

I never worked a single day in those greenhouses, but I will never forget walking through them and feeling the humidity, watching the family care for the plants, looking overhead and seeing snow on the roof, realizing that nothing on the outside mattered to what was happening on the inside.

The greenhouse environment was of such high quality that I concluded a plant had no choice but to grow! If a plant somehow did not grow, well, that was an aberration, an anomaly, highly unusual!

It is important to recognize that the principles associated with the greenhouse complex carry over to the greenhouse we know as God's church.

Imagine a spiritual greenhouse where people can grow twelve months a year instead of merely growing during the growing season! Imagine a spiritual greenhouse where lives can be changed year-around! Where people can grow at a faster, more sustainable rate than can be achieved on their own outside the greenhouse!

The Apostle Paul provides the basis for this biblical teaching in 1 Corinthians 3:5-9. The Bible says:

> *"What then is Apollos? And what is Paul? They are servants through whom you believed, and each has the role the Lord has given. I planted, Apollos watered, but God gave the growth. So then neither the one who plants nor the one who waters is anything, but only God who gives the growth. Now the one planting and the one watering are one in purpose, and each will receive his own reward according to his own labor. For we are God's coworkers. You are God's field, God's building." (1 Corinthians 3:5-9, HCSB)*

Notice the many gardening references to planting (three times), watering (three times), growth (two times), plus the word field where all of this activity takes place. The word field suggests a cultivated field, a tillage, a garden, or my favorite word is the word greenhouse. It is in such a greenhouse environment that God gives the growth (the King James Version uses the word "increase").

It's fill-in-the-blank time. It is not stretching the point in the least to render verse nine like this, "You are God's farm, cultivated field, or garden." We could also translate the phrase like this, "You are God's greenhouse—the place where God grows people."

This concept is not limited to our text! It is expressed numerous times in the Old Testament. For example, the psalmist said, "You brought a vine out of Egypt; you drove out the nations and planted it. You cleared the ground for it; it took deep root and filled the land." (Psalm 80:8-9, ESV)

Isaiah said, "For the vineyard of the LORD of hosts is the house of Israel and the men of Judah His delightful plant." (Isaiah 5:7, NASB)

Jeremiah asked, "Is my heritage to me like a hyena's lair? Are the birds of prey against her all around? Go, assemble all the wild beasts;

bring them to devour. Many shepherds have destroyed my vineyard; they have trampled down my portion; they have made my pleasant portion a desolate wilderness." (Jeremiah 12:9-10, ESV)

We come to the New Testament, and we read Jesus' words in John chapter fifteen.

> *"I am the true vine, and My Father is the vineyard keeper. Every branch in Me that does not produce fruit He removes, and He prunes every branch that produces fruit so that it will produce more fruit. You are already clean because of the word I have spoken to you. Remain in Me, and I in you. Just as a branch is unable to produce fruit by itself unless it remains on the vine, so neither can you unless you remain in Me. I am the vine; you are the branches. The one who remains in Me and I in him produces much fruit because you can do nothing without Me." (John 15:1-5, HCSB)*

Ah, do you see it now? ***God specializes in growing!*** But God's specialty is not growing inanimate plants. Rather God's specialty is growing people! 1 Corinthians 3:9 states "We are God's coworkers" in this endeavor! The Bible portrays us as working alongside God in His greenhouse (garden or field).

Let's go on a very short rabbit trail! It is worth noting that our text is addressed to the most unlikely of all the churches! The First Baptist Church of Corinth! Every preacher knows this particular church's reputation. Indeed, it is the one church to which no pastor sends his résumé! It is similar to Nineveh in the story of Jonah. It is not recorded in Jonah chapter one, but one can easily assume Jonah muttering, "Lord, not Nineveh! They know how to skin a Jew down there! And I don't mean figuratively either!"

This greenhouse passage is not written to the very spiritual churches at Ephesus or Philippi. In our way of thinking, one would have expected Paul to write this passage to those churches, not to the carnal, fleshly church at Corinth!

After all, Corinth is known for every problem in the book! It may have even invented some new problems to be added in the next edition, too! It is not surprising that Paul expressed his frustration time and time again with the unspiritual state of the Corinthians.

But it is important to note *even that church* had the potential to be God's greenhouse in Corinth! Yes, perhaps it is time to remind ourselves that there is hope for all of our churches! What does the Bible say? "With God nothing is impossible!" (Luke 1:37) *Maybe it is time to look more at His abilities than our abilities!* We need to identify the One who is really in charge of the growing process.

Every series of messages needs a foundation; we began to lay that foundation in Chapter One. The leadership team presented what our church is expected to be in the overall plan of God, that is, a spiritual hospital for those who need to be uplifted and spiritually restored, a family for us to enjoy holy companionship, a witness to win others to Jesus, and so on.

One of our women told me that the last message came together for her when she saw the children place their flowers inside the greenhouse. She said, "I realized that plant was me! That suddenly made this study very personal."

Let's add a few points and fill in some gaps in our thinking.

The greenhouse includes all of our facilities from the front door to the back door including all of the classrooms, the gymnasium, the vans, etc. It is any and every place where God wants to grow people! In totality, it is our church experience.

The plant represents you. Likewise, the plant represents me. The Bible says, "*You* are God's greenhouse or garden or field." We are in this together!

God has a great desire, even an insatiable desire, for us to grow. We need a greenhouse environment for us to grow. That greenhouse environment is supposed to be a local church like our church.

Last, and most importantly, if the greenhouse is not healthy, the plants will not grow!

That brings us to the Key Question for this hour: ***What is it like to live and thrive in a greenhouse environment? Does the Bible give us any clues?***

The answer is yes because the Bible *begins* with God's first greenhouse. That's a fill-in-the-blank. The Bible *begins*, of course, with a garden—yes, a very special garden called Eden.

The book of Genesis teaches:

> *"[T]hen the LORD God formed the man of dust from the ground and breathed into his nostrils the breath of life, and the man became a living creature. And the LORD God planted a garden in Eden, in the east, and there he put the man whom he had formed. And out of the ground the LORD God made to spring up every tree that is pleasant to the sight and good for food. The tree of life was in the midst of the garden, and the tree of the knowledge of good and evil." (Genesis 2:7-9, ESV)*

How interesting! The Bible begins with a garden, has a garden named Gethsemane in the middle, and ultimately ends with a garden which is regarded as the paradise of God! The Bible teaches on its last page, "The tree of life was on both sides of the river, bearing twelve kinds of fruit, producing its fruit every month. The leaves of the tree are for healing the nations, and there will no longer be any curse." (Revelation 22:2, HCSB)

From the first page of Genesis to the last page of the Revelation, we read about good fruit and bad fruit, sowing the precious seed, and growing in grace! Yes, the Bible is a book full of gardens!

In many ways, the first garden—the Garden of Eden—provides a picture of what every local church should be. This is a fill-in-the-blank. You may not know this, but the name Eden means "*delight.*" In other words, it is a POSITIVE word! Would to God every church could be described as a "delight." A delight to the members, to the pastor, and especially to God! "A sweet-smelling aroma" like in the Old Testament sacrifices.

Look carefully at the wording *as well as the order* in our text. "The Lord God first planted a garden . . . and then, second, placed the man in the garden." This means the environment was crucial to the development of the man. Indeed, the environment was established before the placing of Adam!

That brings us to a very important fill-in-the-blank. Let these words sink in. *Our first goal is to create an environment where God can grow His children.*

It's time to step back and look for a moment at the bigger picture. This critical idea of environment falls into the category known as "church health." When I began my ministry in the 1970s, the emphasis was on "church growth." "How to Grow a Sunday School in 100 Easy Steps" and "How to Do A Bus Ministry" were emphasized. Some churches became very large by implementing those strategies. As time passed, though, the large church tended to become a smaller church, and, as a result, *the focus changed from quantity to quality.*

One comment I have never forgotten is in an email I received in the year 2000 from Executive Director Lloyd Hamblin of the West Virginia Baptist Convention. Lloyd was one of those people who was really good at seeing the forest and presenting his thoughts in an easy-to-understand fashion! Let me share the entire email with you. This is also a fill-in-the-blank.

"I recently returned from a conference led by Tom Bandy. He has written several books including Kicking Habits and Coaching Change. If you have not read these, I would recommend them to you as well as his website easumbandy.com. His main point is that the church must develop or re-develop the core process for making disciples. We have made many church members but not many disciples. Interesting stuff."

The underlined statement, "We have made many church members but not many disciples" describes the dilemma in many churches. Fast forward to today! We now find ourselves not only struggling with the issue of quantity but also with the issue of quality! We seem to be losing on both fronts at the same time!

"Quality" is a church health issue. God's Greenhouse is also a church health issue. In this chapter, we will look closely at the environment because the environment has much to do with church health!

Let's remember that God wanted Adam to achieve his full potential! Parents usually wish the same for their own children. Thus, they provide the right education, provide safeguards, regulate acquaintances, establish college savings, and on and on the list goes. Parents sacrifice immeasurably for their child to have the greatest possible chance to achieve his full potential!

The Garden of Eden was such a place. It was the best environment any earthling has ever experienced! We will never know how far Adam could have gone, what he could have achieved, if he had avoided his sin. For instance, would Adam have been the first space traveler and perhaps traveled to Mars or even beyond? Due to his sin and its resulting degradation, we will never know the depths of his God-given genius or abilities.

Let's do a Bible study and note some of the characteristics of God's first garden.

1. Abundant Fruit

First, the Garden contained abundant fruit. One should place extra emphasis on the word abundant! Genesis 2:9 says, "Out of the ground the Lord God caused to grow every tree that is pleasing to the sight and good for food; the tree of life also in the midst of the garden, and the tree of the knowledge of good and evil." (Genesis 2:9, NASB) There was no shortage of trees that bore good, healthy food in the Garden! This is supported by Genesis 1:29-30, also.

> "God also said, 'Look, I have given you every seed-bearing plant on the surface of the entire earth and every tree whose fruit contains seed. This food will be for you, for all the wildlife of the earth, for every bird of the sky, and for every creature that crawls on the earth—everything having

the breath of life in it. I have given every green plant for food.' And it was so." (Genesis 1:29-30, HCSB)

These trees were designed to be much more than self-serving. They were actually designed to add value to someone, namely Adam.

One immediately thinks of such "fruity" Bible passages as Proverbs 11:30. We can paraphrase it like this, "The fruit of the righteous is a tree of eternal, spiritual life, and he who is committed to winning souls is wise."

Let's add the words of the psalmist.

> *"How blessed is the man who does not walk in the counsel of the wicked, Nor stand in the path of sinners, Nor sit in the seat of scoffers! But his delight is in the law of the Lord, And in His law he meditates day and night. He will be like a tree firmly planted by streams of water, Which yields its fruit in its season And its leaf does not wither; And in whatever he does, he prospers." (Psalm 1:1-3, NASB)*

The abundant fruit of the Holy Spirit is mentioned in Galatians chapter five: "love, joy, peace, patient/long-suffering, gentleness/kindness, goodness, faithfulness, gentleness/meekness, and self-control." That is a good definition of walking in the Spirit in Galatians 5:25!

Jesus taught, "I am the vine; you are the branches. The one who remains in Me and I in him produces much fruit because you can do nothing without Me." (John 15:5, HCSB) At first glance, the kind of fruit in that John passage is not identified, but at second glance it is identified! "I in Him" means "Christ living out His life in me!" (Galatians 2:20) which is another way of saying that "whatever Jesus Himself would be doing on earth will now be done by me!" That's truly exceptional living!

Jesus said, "I have come that you might have life and have it more what? Abundantly!" The Garden of Eden pictures the "abundant life" of John 10:10.

2. Like Begets Like

The second truth taught in the Garden of Eden is that like begets like. "God said, 'Let the earth sprout vegetation, plants yielding seed, and fruit trees on the earth bearing fruit after their kind with seed in them;' and it was so." (Genesis 1:11, NASB)

"After their kind" is God's universal pattern for all of creation. The old sayings, "what goes around also comes around" and "he who forgets history is doomed to repeat history" are both true because of the principle that like begets like. It is our nature to keep reverting back to the same pattern! In this case, fruit-bearing trees and bushes produced more fruit-bearing trees and bushes!

This principle is true in our churches, too. Almost without fail, *a church reproduces the kind of people it already has!* If the people are interested in soul-winning, then those people tend to instill that same belief in others! If they are deep Bible thinkers, then future deep Bible thinkers will be rewarded, and future shallow Bible readers will struggle. If the church is really good in prayer, then prayer warriors will likely arise within that church! Those prayer warriors will experience the results of Jeremiah 31:3 which says, "Call to me and I will answer you, and will tell you great and hidden things that you have not known." (Jeremiah 31:3, ESV)

Of course, the reverse is also true! *If the people are uninterested, the assembly line will produce uninterested whatever-you-want-to-call-them, but they aren't disciples.*

It is wise for the church to periodically make an internal inspection and ask, "What kind of people are we right now?" That question should be answered before we try to mold someone else. We might like the results of our internal evaluation; then again, we may not, but at least we have identified areas that need work!

3. Every Need Supplied

Third, God supplied everything necessary for His greenhouse in the Garden of Eden. Every need was supplied!

In a similar manner, Paul wrote to the Philippians, "But my God shall supply all your need according to his riches in glory by Christ Jesus. Now unto God and our Father be glory for ever and ever. Amen." (Philippians 4:19-20, KJV)

We see a wonderful picture of that Bible teaching in the Garden of Eden. There was no shortage of any necessity in the first garden! The air quality was excellent for both human and plant. The ground produced abundant fruit. The companionship between man and woman was splendid. The temperature setting was acceptable! The water was drinkable! God Himself met their spiritual needs by often coming down to visit! "And He walks with me and talks with me" was more than a song to Adam and Eve!

The above description sounds like a greenhouse environment to me!

What does a rose need to fulfill its purpose? Its needs are many! Those needs will not be met at the top of snow-covered Mount Everest or in the lowest, hottest part of Death Valley.

The greenhouse, though, can overcome all of those limitations. The controlled environment inside the greenhouse provides the plant with access to everything it needs to grow to its full potential.

History records that church life was different in the 1800s than it is today. Those days preceded television, couch potatoes, cell phones, and modern travel! The church of the 1800s was the center of home life and community life. Most community activities passed in some way through the church or were hosted by the church. As time passed, though, we forfeited that aspect of church life to the schools or community organizations.

I believe we need to seriously consider making the church more like a Garden of Eden, a place where the total needs of our people are met.

There is nothing on the face of God's earth which provides a better environment for a family than God's church. Nothing anywhere!

One such area for me personally is the need for fellowship. If you are reading this material, you are probably as busy as I am and you will understand the next statement. *We need time when we don't have to be the pastor or teacher or deacon* but a time when we can come, fellowship, unwind, be ourselves, talk about frivolous, even idiotic things, and in so doing have our other needs met (including our social needs). Ministry can be overwhelming at times. I need a greenhouse for me. How about you?

4. State of Innocence

The first two people had the advantage of being created beings. Adam came from the dust of the ground, and Eve came from the side of Adam. More importantly, Bible scholars believe they were created in a state of innocence. That description means they differed significantly from everyone else because Romans 5:19 teaches, "by or through Adam's sin the rest of us became sinners."

It is not the purpose of this study to be a theological study, but this is what happened to us in a nutshell. Adam's sin changed him *in his core being* from a state of innocence (not yet knowing wrong) to one of being contaminated or diseased by sin. Theologians often describe the sinful condition in terms of being under the dominion of sin, but I prefer the concept of being contaminated or diseased by sin. As a result, sin infects man's thought process and therefore his conclusions, and his diseased conclusions lead to a diseased lifestyle.

Unfortunately, all of us are now born into this diseased condition. Such a condition limits man in many ways and prevents man from being able to know God. This condition can only be corrected by a sinner acknowledging his sinful condition and receiving Jesus Christ as his personal Lord and Savior.

Robert Lowry wrote, "What can wash away my sin? Nothing but the blood of Jesus." Coming to the cross and receiving Jesus as the One and Only Savior results in a sinner being born again with a new spiritual nature that allows him to know God and experience God in his life.

This diseased condition, though, did not happen until *after* Genesis chapter two. Our sinful disposition was not part of God's original design!

God's Greenhouse was a place of complete innocence. Adam could be himself in Eden. It was a relaxing place to live. No one had any reason to point a finger at Adam in an accusing way. No one specialized in looking for faults in others. No one exercised by jumping to conclusions! The word "criticism" was not yet a part of anyone's vocabulary. The environment was so much different than our pick-'em-apart world.

In their innocence, Adam and Eve were constantly edifying one another! Edifying includes the concept of building up, not tearing down. I don't know about you, but I respond very well to encouragement. I don't respond well to discouraging comments, especially after I have given something my best effort.

Churches tend to develop a negative culture that results in a thumbs-down verdict toward any new ideas. One of my pastorates had gone twenty years since successfully implementing a new idea of any significance. The negative culture quickly drained the life from any new idea and discouraged anyone from reaching for the stars. I remember presenting a certificate called "A License to Dream Again" to everyone in my Saturday morning leadership class. I urged them to dream again!

How different was the Garden of Eden! The Garden of Eden demonstrates how different a greenhouse environment can be. *In its totality, the greenhouse is a complete support system for the plants!*

Our text states that we are coworkers with God in His greenhouse. "State of Innocence" means we don't discourage God from doing what He wants to do *even if it is new to us!* Such discouragement happens far too often and is described as "grieving or hindering the Holy Spirit" in Ephesians 4:30. Likewise, "State of Innocence" means we don't discourage our fellow coworkers from doing what God has laid upon their hearts even if it is new to us!

What did Gamaliel say to the critics surrounding him? Acts 5:39 quotes Gamaliel saying, "If their purpose or activity is of human origin, it will fail. But if their activity is motivated by God, you will not be able to stop these men; you will only find yourselves fighting against God."

God provides dreamers to every church such as Joseph of the Old Testament. We might call them visionaries although that word may be a stretch. But they are people who will challenge the rest of us to move outside our comfort zone. And we must concede that every church needs to get out of its comfort zone!

Let me hasten to add a State of Innocence means more than just vision. *It also means that people feel comfortable stepping into the water and getting involved.* A State of Criticism drives people away from making such an effort, but a State of Innocence convinces people to try, and some will try for the first time.

How would you describe your own church in this regard? I hope I don't have to apologize for asking!

5. Authentic Companionship

It was the season of spring. A man went to his supervisor in the front office. He said, "Boss, we're doing some spring-cleaning at home tomorrow. My wife needs me to help with moving stuff in the attic and the garage."

The boss became upset and said, "What do you mean asking me a stupid question like that? We're short-handed. I can't give you the day off."

The man said, "Thanks, boss. I knew I could count on you!"

Let me ask a serious question: who are you able to really, I mean really, count on? Question number two, how many people can you name?

Back in 2003, I was watching the war coverage of the second Iraq war when something jumped out at me. The media was interviewing some of our veterans who had been taken prisoner during our previous wars.

The interviewer asked, "What was the worst part of being a prisoner of war?" I thought the number one answer would be the torture endured by some of them, but it was not.

Do you know what the number one answer was? It was the isolation they went through. Some of them were placed in solitary confinement. During that suffering, they were totally alone against the enemy. Sometimes the worst enemy of all was their own mind! They did not have any friends for a support system! To many of those POWs, the isolation was even worse than the torture!

Do you know what that teaches us? That teaches us that man is not meant to be isolated or alone, but rather man is meant to be surrounded by companions or friends.

As for me, there is no doubt one of my greatest needs is the need for authentic companionship—for other companions to join me in my ship.

The church of God is able to meet that need because, as we learned in Chapter One, the church is also a family. The people in God's family are described as brothers and sisters, not tyrant and slave, or employer and employee, but brother and sister. Not as close as husband and wife but really, really close!

Adam and Eve experienced such a life in the Garden before their sin in chapter three. Adam learned in the first part of chapter two that no animal could meet his need for companionship. That included the dog, cat, lion, elephant, squirrel, and you name it! (Which, of course, he did!) But Eve was a living, human being and she did indeed meet his need for companionship!

It has been said by many, "If all my friends were to jump off a bridge, I wouldn't jump with them. I'd be at the bottom to catch them when they reach the bottom."

How different was an acquaintance of mine from years ago! We'll call him Zack. One day I asked Zack (Zack was around eighty years of age) why his life had been a mess for so long. Zack honestly said, "I was married eleven times by the age of thirty-eight. Twice I remarried the same woman, so I was actually married to only nine different women."

He went on to say, "I was a drunk and valium addict. What kind of women do you find in bars? That's what I married."

I have now pastored for approximately thirty-five years. I have had all kinds of church members, but I would put *all* of my female church members against *any* of his wives and wager *any* of my female church members would have improved his life.

Church people aren't perfect, and no, I don't care very much for the line "just forgiven." Those words seem like too much of a cop-out to me. But church people know God and possess a different value system than the bar people.

I'd much rather take my chance with a companion who's a sister in Christ than a companion who's a barhopper!

David and Jonathan had an authentic companionship kind of relationship. Paul and Silas were a special duo in the New Testament. Jesus had His inner circle of Peter, James, and John. Billy Graham had his Cliff Barrows and George Beverly Shea. I have had my Carl Riggle, Paul Edwards, Raymond May, and so many others. Many marriages are blessed in that same manner. Such companions make life bearable and enjoyable!

6. Absent Devil

(Note: if you are presenting this material to the church it would be good to let them conduct their own Bible study at this time. Divide the audience into three sections. The left section is to examine Genesis 2:1-8 and count the references to the devil. The center section is to examine 2:9-16 and count the references to the devil. The right section is to examine the remaining verses in chapter two and count the references to the devil.)

How many did you count? The answer, of course, is zero in each section of scripture. The devil is not present until chapter three.

Imagine living in paradise for heaven knows how long and not being harassed by the devil or his people or his standards or his temptations!

Someone may be thinking, "But, Pastor Tom, you can't control anything nowadays." Oh, but the Bible disagrees. The Apostle Paul wrote,

> *"Don't give the Devil an opportunity. The thief must no longer steal. Instead, he must do honest work with his own hands, so that he has something to share with anyone in need. No foul language is to come from your mouth, but only what is good for building up someone in need, so that it gives grace to those who hear. And don't grieve God's Holy Spirit. You were sealed by Him for the day of redemption. All bitterness, anger and wrath, shouting and slander must be removed from you, along with all malice. And be kind and compassionate to one another, forgiving one another, just as God also forgave you in Christ." (Ephesians 4:27-30, HCSB)*

The devil has a deep hatred for the blood-bought church of God. He knows how to hinder our growth and hinder an Eden environment!

Matthew chapter thirteen talks about the devil arriving mere seconds after the sermon and snatching the message away from the hearer! Other passages talk about him sowing discord among the brothers and sisters. For instance, Paul begged two women named Euodia and Syntyche to end their bickering and to "let this attitude be in you which was also in Jesus Christ."

A church which is at war with itself is of little value to the Lord, but a church which is at war with the devil for the souls of men, the welfare of our homes, and proclaiming the truth is of great value to our Lord.

7. Christian Home

A Christian home is a thing of immense beauty in the eyes of God, the church, and the community. It involves much more than a family attending church. It involves more than having members who know Jesus Christ as their personal Lord and Savior. It is actually a home where God is an active part and a welcomed member.

The Garden of Eden could also be called the Garden of God. It was God's Garden, a part of His creation and designed for His glory. God graciously chose to share His garden with His creation. And, most importantly, it was the place where God chose to share Himself with Adam and Eve.

Genesis 1:28 reveals God talked with Adam and Eve. I personally believe it was an audible, face-to-face conversation! Genesis 2:21 teaches that God performed the first surgery on His patient, Adam. Genesis 3:8 pictures God walking casually (apparently in a human body known as a theophany) through the Garden as if it was an everyday occurrence, and perhaps it was!

Adam and Eve were not afraid of God's presence until *after* they sinned. The Bible gives the indication that they were instead accustomed to God's visible presence before the day of their sin. That means they had the greatest privilege of all time to enjoy a Christian home composed of all three of them: Adam, Eve *and* God. Sadly, Adam and Eve ruined all of us when they chose to sin against God in chapter three.

But suppose they had not sinned. Do you remember that their son Cain murdered his own brother Abel? Wonder how different Cain's life would have been if Adam and Eve had chosen to walk with God forever instead of walk with the devil? Taking a walk on the wild side cost them, along with their offspring for thousands of years to come, everything of spiritual value.

But the Christian home was a reality for them in chapter two. The original garden promoted the Christian home and the feeling of togetherness. Likewise, our own church greenhouse can promote the building of Christian homes throughout our church family.

Were you raised in church? I was raised in church on Sunday morning, Sunday night, Wednesday night, the monthly Saturday business meeting, the two-and-three-week revivals, plus the occasional Women's

Missionary service. I profited immensely from being around my church family in those many services.

Indeed, my church buddies became my closest friends! They became even closer than my schoolmates or relatives. Perhaps that was because my church provided a wholesome environment for me. I enjoyed being at church! I enjoyed seeing my church buddies!

My church served as my Garden of Eden experience. I truly wish I could recreate that experience for everyone everywhere.

8. Meeting God

Let's briefly elaborate on a point started, but not fully developed, in the "Christian Home" section. We're still in chapter two. Look in your King James Version at the first four words of verses seven, eight, fifteen, sixteen, eighteen and twenty-one. Notice that all of those verses begin in the same identical manner. "And the Lord God" did this or did that.

Chapter two is a chapter where Adam and Eve are able to meet with God. It was so much more than meeting with God in spirit! They had the awesome opportunity to be in God's physical presence, perhaps to even have a meal with Him.

Wonder what God talked about? It could have been any subject from biology to zoology to the origin of the universe to raising a future child.

The garden was holy ground set apart as the one place where ordinary people could meet the extraordinary God!

God visited there! Maybe He even stayed overnight! What a thought!

I remember the story of the little boy who attended church for the first time. He listened in awe to the pastor and got confused. On the way home he asked, "Does the pastor come down from heaven every Sunday or does he live here?"

A true greenhouse experience is one where the Master Gardener is present! Jesus promised, "If two of you (who needs three?) are gathered in My name, I will be among you." (Matthew 18:20) "I will never leave you nor forsake you." (Hebrews 13:5) "I will be with you forever, even unto the end of the age." (Matthew 28:20)

God's presence makes the greenhouse the most unique place on this planet! The greenhouse becomes its own Garden of Eden. It becomes a place where people can meet God, respond to the call of God, enjoy serving God, and corporately worship the one true God!

Praise the Lord, God can do a work among us because He is here!

9. Warning Signs

A greenhouse is a place for growing! But if one does the wrong thing, the plant growth may be thwarted. The same is true in practically every area of life. The electrician must know what not to do just as much as what to do. A healthy respect of electricity is a rule of life for him! A truck driver must know the rules of the road, or he becomes a danger to everyone.

God posted one enormous warning sign in the Garden of Eden. The sign said, "You are not to eat, even nibble, from the tree of the knowledge of good and evil." I do not know if God put flashing lights on the sign, but His warning was crystal clear. Adam and Eve, though, chose to disobey the warning, and the resulting chaos is still with us to this day.

The Ten Commandments were given by God in Exodus chapter twenty. The King James Version says very forcefully, "Thou shalt not" and then mentions a number of items we are not to do. Each of those verses is a warning sign to "stay away from this dangerous place or be ready to face the consequences!"

One day a nanny placed a little boy in his upstairs crib for his after-noon nap. The mother was occupying herself downstairs with a magazine. The little boy began crying. The mother yelled upstairs to the nanny, "What is wrong?" The nanny said, "He wants something that isn't good for him." The mother said, "Well, give it to him anyway." The nanny said, "If you say so." A few moments later the boy screamed much louder than before. The mother asked, "What is the matter now?" The nanny replied, "You told me to give him what he wanted and what he wanted was a wasp!"

Warning signs serve to keep us out of trouble. God's Garden included warning signs. God's Greenhouse in our church must also include warning signs. Unfortunately, I have learned that we adults need warning signs just as much as our children. (The book of Proverbs contains many warning signs.)

Thank God, we can know the way not to go as well as the way to go! And who helps me with that? It is the faithful teaching I receive in God's Greenhouse at _____ Church!

10. Tree of Life

One of Hollywood's war actors faced the prospect of death by telling his fellow soldiers, "A man can't live forever." Well, I won't ever say those words because I want to live forever. The movie character viewed life as a temporary existence which is extinguished in much the same way as one extinguishes a candle.

The Bible, though, indicates that this current life is temporary only in the sense that it precedes an even longer, forever life called eternity. Jesus taught in Mark chapter nine that Gehenna (also known as hell or the final resting place described as the lake of fire) is the place reserved for the damned where "their worm dieth not and the fire is never quenched." (KJV) Matthew chapter twenty-five closes with the words that the damned "shall go away into everlasting punishment." The total annihilation of the damned is an attractive teaching to some, but such teaching is not found in the Bible. Indeed, the Bible teaches just the opposite!

But the Bible also teaches there is a place of eternal blessedness for the born-again, blood-bought ones in the family of God! The closing verse in Matthew chapter twenty-five also includes the words, "but the righteous or justified shall go the way of everlasting life." The Bible describes such people as the "saved," because they have been saved or rescued or delivered from the hell to come!

The tree of life was in the Garden of Eden. Its purpose has been debated for centuries. Such a debate is beyond the scope of this discussion. But what we can safely deduce is that it was a tree of life and not death! Also, it apparently had the ability to sustain life beyond its normalcy. We deduce that from Genesis 3:22 where God said, "We must keep Adam from eating of the tree of life and living forever *in his fallen condition*." (Italics are mine.)

How many characteristics did we list on our study sheet? Ten. In these same ten ways, God's Greenhouse *in our church* can be a reproduction of God's Garden in the book of Genesis. It cannot be stressed too much that God's Greenhouse is *all about life*. It is about living in contrast to dying. It is about growing in contrast to decaying. It is about becoming more in contrast to becoming less.

Is there a tree of life in God's Greenhouse? Yes! God's Greenhouse at _____ Church has the wonderful privilege to tell people about it! We have the best news the world has ever known, and it is available for all in our own greenhouse!

> *On a hill far away, stood an old rugged Cross*
> *The emblem of suff'ring and shame*
> *And I love that old Cross where the dearest and best*
> *For a world of lost sinners was slain.*
>
> *To the old rugged Cross, I will ever be true*
> *Its shame and reproach gladly bear*
> *Then He'll call me some day to my home far away*
> *Where his glory forever I'll share.*
>
> *So I'll cherish the old rugged Cross*
> *Till my trophies at last I lay down*
> *I will cling to the old rugged Cross*
> *And exchange it some day for a crown.*
>
> *George Bennard*

3

CHARACTERISTICS OF A SPIRITUAL GREENHOUSE

Understanding the Environment

Preparation: the skits will require many people. Also, you will need a flower which has been sheltered inside a closet for two weeks.

(Chapter Three provides a general overview of the many characteristics that are associated with a physical greenhouse. As you might suspect, those characteristics also carry over to our spiritual greenhouse. The material in Chapter Three will be a refresher course for the serious Bible student, but it will be very educational for those lacking in Bible knowledge. It will also provide an opportunity for you to discuss certain issues which may be pertinent to your own situation.)

Sometimes the hare wins the race, and sometimes the tortoise wins the race. This course is laid out, so both win the race. We don't want anyone to lose, but for everyone to gain a thorough understanding of what needs to be done to grow our plants/people.

This material is laid out in lesson fashion as I delivered it to my congregation. It is considerably longer than can be covered in one session. Think of this material in terms of a guide to which you can adjust for your own particular situation. Dr. B. R. Lakin of Cadle Tabernacle fame would often say, "My sermons are like trains. If someone wants to shout and testify in the middle of my sermon, I'll just stop, kick out a few boxcars and then resume when they're finished." He did that once for my shouting grandma! I have chosen to provide all of my material in the hope you will find a way to make it work for you!

Appendix #5 "Handout for Chapter Three" is to be used in conjunction with this material. I suggest you keep it alongside you as you read this material. Let's begin!

Let's continue our study, *God's Greenhouse: How to Grow People God's Way.* Our text is found in 1 Corinthians chapter three. The Holman Christian Standard Bible translates this passage as follows:

> *"What then is Apollos? And what is Paul? They are servants through whom you believed, and each has the role the Lord has given. I planted, Apollos watered, but God gave the growth. So then neither the one who plants nor the one who waters is anything, but only God who gives the growth. Now the one planting and the one watering are one in purpose, and each will receive his own reward according to his own labor. For we are God's coworkers. You are God's field, God's building." (1 Corinthians 3:5-9)*

Notice the many references to sowing, watering, and God giving the increase.

All of us are acquainted with the gardening concept. We know about preparing the soil, maybe even replacing some of the soil with better soil, then comes the planting, watering, weeding, and finally enjoying the results of our effort when the flower blooms.

Some of us have green thumbs that can grow anything, but some of us are apparently missing our thumbs because we cannot grow anything! I am just wondering: how many of you have green thumbs? On the other hand, how many of you are missing your thumbs? I think the "no thumbs" people outnumber the "green thumbs" people!

I want you to pay particular attention also to the last part of the process—to what happens *after* you have done your part! Notice the Bible says God *does not* give the increase until *after* Paul plants and Apollos waters.

We will cover this thought in depth at a later time, but at this time I want to plant the idea in your mind that God's greenhouse is not an accident. *It does not happen unless we do our part to make it happen.*

Verse nine could be rendered, *"You are God's greenhouse."*

Fill in the first bullet on your study sheet with the name of our church and then complete this phrase, "You are God's greenhouse."

We can also fill in the second bullet on our study sheet. "Our church is the place where God grows people."

But let me emphasize that none of this is possible unless you first have a greenhouse environment where God is free to work in the hearts of His people. It is then that you can experience what we call a true and lasting revival!

Our display for this message includes two basic items:

The greenhouse represents all of our facilities from the front door to the back door including all of the classrooms, the gymnasium, the vans, etc. It is any place where God wants to grow people!

The plant represents people like you and me. The Bible emphasizes, *"You* are God's greenhouse or garden or field where people grow unto the Lord." All of us are in this together!

We have some beautiful plants for today's greenhouse. (Note: some women previously volunteered to bring flowers for today's service that will fit inside the greenhouse. The pastor should recognize each flower by saying, "This flower is from co-worker #1 and is an insert plant name." Repeat the same process for the remaining flowers. Use this as an opportunity to reinforce the concept of being a co-worker. Last, encourage more volunteers to see the Flower Coordinator.)

You grow beautiful plants at your home, but what do we grow in this church? What are we to grow in our own greenhouse?

Let me show you what we are to grow!

(Note: bring in the Children's Church or another children's class at this time. Pose the following questions to the audience. How many of you want to see these children stay at the same age that they are now? How many of you want to see these children stay at the same height? Or maintain the same knowledge? The truth is we want them to do what? To grow physically, mentally, emotionally, and keep growing all the days of their life! We as a church should dedicate ourselves to helping them grow spiritually!)

Is there anyone else in this building that still needs to grow as a Christian?

(Note: eight people were selected before the service for this exhibit. These eight people will now move to the front. Four will stand on the left, and four will stand on the right.)

We now have two groups of people at the front. A few moments ago, you agreed as a church that we want to see these children grow and keep growing all the days of their life. I then asked, "Is there anyone else in this building that still needs to grow as a Christian?" These eight people, who happen to be much older than children, came forward and acknowledged that they also still need to grow.

Now here is the point, and it is the third bullet on your study sheet: *Each one of these people is a plant for us to grow in God's greenhouse at _____ Church.*

I am just curious. Who will admit to being the youngest in this group? How old are you? Who is the oldest in this group? I won't ask your age! But the point is that you still need to grow.

Thank you for coming forward and being part of our program. You may now return to your seats.

Here is another fill-in-the-blank. Look at the fourth bullet on your study sheet. Our first goal is to create an environment where God can grow His children.

Some churches totally miss what you just wrote down. I think of one brother whose church philosophy could be summed up in the words,

"We've opened the door and rung the church bell,
If they won't come, they can go to a flaming hell!"

Look again at what we just wrote. Our first goal is to create an environment where God can grow His children. It is very important you understand what this means. So listen closely. *We are not here for an hour and fifteen minutes to give us something to do on Sunday morning, but we are here to grow a seed to full maturity in Jesus Christ!* In other words, we are here for a very specific purpose, and that purpose is growing people to be like Jesus.

Jesus taught a parable that ties directly into this point. That parable is found in Luke chapter fourteen. Let me read you the part that ties in with our study. Jesus said, "A man who was apparently a rather wealthy man prepared an enormous banquet and invited many, many guests. This man then sent his servant to personally invite the guests, and the servant told each of them, 'Come because everything for this banquet is now ready.'" The key phrase is, "Everything for this banquet is now ready!"

Can you imagine all of those guests arriving only to find a barren table? An empty table? And yet that happens all across America every Sunday morning because the people come to many churches only to find that everything is not ready! The preparations have not been made!

So, let me say this again! We are not here for an hour and fifteen minutes to give us something to do on Sunday morning, but we are here to grow a seed to full maturity in Jesus Christ! In other words, we are here for a very specific purpose, and that purpose is growing people to be like Jesus.

There are two questions on your study sheet that we need to answer. It is best if you answer these questions honestly. That means you may want to think for a time before you answer, and that is okay. But you do need to answer these questions sometime today. So here goes.

Circle the answer to the following two questions:

Am I growing as a Christian? Yes   No

Am I helping anyone to grow as a Christian? Yes   No

God expects us not only to grow but also to help others grow, and that is what this greenhouse environment is all about!

Let's ask the question, "What can we learn from a common, ordinary greenhouse?" The answer is a lot more than you might think! As a matter of fact, the answers will fill the rest of your study sheet. We will look in detail at each one of these answers.

For many of you, this will be a once-in-a-lifetime study, so I encourage you to listen closely and take more notes than appear on your study sheet.

What can we learn from a common, ordinary greenhouse?

1. Single Owner

Let's focus our attention first on what I call the Single Owner (the single proprietor) of this greenhouse. If you open the yellow pages in the telephone book, you will find a list of greenhouses with the owner's name. I have already mentioned that in our earlier years we rented a house from the Weber family. The Weber family operated the largest greenhouse within a hundred-mile radius. It was known both far and wide as Webers Greenhouse. That greenhouse belonged to the Weber family; it was operated daily by two brothers named Leo Weber and Ray Weber.

The first question which must be answered is, who owns this spiritual greenhouse called _____ Church? Is it owned by the pastor? Is it owned by the deacons? How about the trustees since they are responsible for the property? Or how about the membership?

Now listen and don't miss what I am about to say! The number one reason some churches fail as a greenhouse is because they have never figured out who the sole owner is supposed to be!

There are two passages in the Bible which establish who owns this church body along with its property. The first passage is Matthew 16:18. Jesus said (and He said it with so much authority that all translations phrase it the same way), "Upon this Rock I will build— does anyone know the next part? My church!"

Do you know the meaning of the word "my?" All you must do is ask a two-year-old child. What does that child say? "My, my, my—it's mine! Give it to me! It's mine!"

The word "my" carries with it the idea of ownership. The person who says "my" is saying the object belongs to me. The object does not belong to you but to me and me alone. The reason this idea is important is because Jesus said, "I will build My church."

This creates a problem because there is another word you and I often use when we talk about this church. That word is only three letters in length, but it has a much different meaning. Would anyone like to guess those three letters? They are the three letters o-u-r. I want you to know there is a big difference between Jesus saying, "My" and you and I saying, "Our."

Jesus said, "Upon this rock, I will build My church. That means it is not your church. It is not even *our* church. It is Jesus's church."

In other words, _____ Church is supposed to belong solely to God! To be honest, we should never think in terms of this church being *our* church because *the only way it can ever truly become our church is if we steal it from Him!*

61

It is one thing to invite someone to "come to my church," and we use the word "my" to distinguish this church from some other church. But it is an entirely different thing when we actually *behave* like the church is "my" church and "I want my way" or "you better do it my way."

I once knew a very wealthy couple who committed a grave sin. The wife told the leadership team, "If you elect that man as pastor, we won't give you our money, and we give a lot of money to this church. As a matter of fact, we're probably your biggest donors!" One of the church leaders called me sixty minutes later to tell me about her threat. Interestingly, the church ignored the threat and elected the pastor anyway.

A few weeks passed. The husband and wife decided to go away on a vacation. One day the wife experienced some indigestion. The husband went to a pharmacy to buy some medicine. He returned to the room and found his wife lying on the floor between the two beds. She was already dead. Nothing could be done for her.

The same church leader called me later that evening and told me the story. He said, "I heard about her death, and my very first thought was her threat to our church."

Never forget: the church belongs to Jesus and to Him alone.

The second passage of scripture is Ephesians 2:20-22. It says, "built on the foundation of the apostles and prophets, with Christ Jesus Himself as the cornerstone. The whole building, being put together by Him, grows into a holy sanctuary in the Lord. You also are being built together for God's dwelling in the Spirit." (Ephesians 2:20-22, HCSB)

The last verse mentions that we have become God's dwelling place. The King James Version likes the phrase, "habitation of God." That's a very fitting term! The sense is that God wants to live in His people both individually and corporately! We know from many scriptures that God lives in our hearts through the Holy Spirit (Romans 8:9). One of the greatest wonders of the universe is how Someone as big as God the Creator can live in something as small as my heart! But He does! That means we as individuals have become God's little temples.

But there's more! Ephesians chapter two says that *all of us little temples then come together in this holy place and become one large temple!* We are a unified temple in which God Himself dwells!

God Himself is making a home right here in this fellowship! It is not a case of God dwelling physically in this building like He did in the Old Testament temple. But it is a case of God dwelling spiritually in the building of our hearts.

That means God is *at home* in this greenhouse we call _____ Church. God is busy at this very moment growing people in this greenhouse!

Now listen closely. The only person who has the right to say, *"I want"* at this church is Almighty God Himself because it is His church and His church alone! He bought it for Himself with the blood of the cross. No one else can buy the church except him! *We might steal the church from Him, but we do not have the resources to buy it from Him!* He owns the church because He bought the church! He can keep the doors open, or He can close the doors!

That leads me to say this: if the church is a true church, then the church belongs to Him and Him alone! It does not belong to the pastor nor to the board nor to a deacon nor to a committee nor to a Sunday School class nor to any small group!

That is why He has given us the manual which often contains the phrase, "Thus saith the Lord!" It cannot be stated enough that His manual is not "A" manual, but it is "THE" manual. He has left us with one and only one manual to direct His church, and that manual, of course, is the inspired, inerrant Word of God known as the Bible.

Mark Stump preached it like this, *"If Jesus Christ is Lord of this church, then that settles all of the issues in this church!"* Someone became upset when he said it! But what he said was very, very true! "If Jesus Christ is Lord of this church, then that settles all of the issues in this church!"

The church is not free to determine its own course of action even though we often proclaim our belief in the autonomy of the local church.

The church belongs to God! If the church is to be successful, it must adhere to God's manual. Otherwise, the church is denying God's right of ownership!

God's manual is a light to guide us in this world of religious darkness. The manual tells us what to do, and, quite honestly, there is no doubt about our mission!

Every church would do itself a lot of good if it focused on accomplishing the Great Commission in its community. (The Great Commission is found in Matthew 28:18-20, Mark 16:15, Luke 24:46-49, John 20:21-22, and Acts 1:8.)

Let me paraphrase the Matthew passage and relate it to the five widely accepted purposes of God's church. "All authority to rule absolutely in heaven and earth has been given to me (*worship Him as Lord of all*). Therefore, as you are going daily into the world, make disciples (*evangelism or winning them to Jesus*) of all nations, baptizing them (*bringing them into the fellowship*) in the name of the Father and of the Son and of the Holy Spirit, and teaching (*discipleship or learning how to follow Jesus*) them to obey (*ministry through living out the will of God*) everything I have commanded you. And surely, I am with you always, to the very end of the age."

I will insist to my dying day that a commitment to the Great Commission will keep a church focused on *what God has promised to bless*! God, in turn, will bless His church because God believes in the Great Commission even more than our most dedicated believer!

Mark my words: when we run the show, we mess things up! I say this to our shame, but did you ever get into anything as a church or as a believer then wished you had waited on God?

Let me take it one step further and give you something you have likely never considered before.

(Note: someone was previously selected to get seed for 1,000 tomatoes. That person is now called to the front with the seed. The person explains what he brought and gives the seed to the pastor.)

I chose this type of seed because the Webers grew tomato plants from the seed. They then sold thousands of plants to people like you and me.

(Note: read the instructions on the packet or from another source. The instructions will indicate the seed is planted in a greenhouse environment perhaps six weeks before being transplanted outside to the garden. The planting depth and spacing width should also be noted. The instructions might also discuss the best temperature for the seed.)

Do you know what I think? I think that sounds like a lot of preparation to me. It reminds me of the banquet where the servant said, "Come to our banquet because everything is now ready."

I ask you, "Will just any greenhouse work for this seed?" No. My friend just brought me seed for hundreds of tomatoes. He wants me to grow his tomatoes and have them ready when it is time to plant them in his field. He wants to make certain these seeds are planted at the right time—for example, not in October, but rather about six weeks before he will plant them in his field. Furthermore, he wants to know if I will water his seed with the right amount of water, if I will nurture the seed with a warm environment, etc. Does that make sense?

Suppose he concludes that I cannot be trusted to grow his plants. What do you think he will do? He will take his seed to another greenhouse!

Here is the point: you won't trust your seed to a greenhouse you cannot trust!

You may not know this, but God is the One with the tomato seed. The seed represents His children.

Now listen closely! *When God finds a church that is growing healthy Christians, God sends that church plenty of seed to work with.*

The opposite is equally true. After all, why would God send good seed to a bad greenhouse, that is, to a bad church, knowing the seed would be poorly invested? Surely God wants to get a good return on His investment (Matthew 25:21). Jesus even discussed getting a hundredfold return on His investment in Matthew chapter thirteen! That's like investing in Apple at its very beginning!

That leads me to ask, if you were God would you trust us with the good seed? Is the banquet table truly prepared?

2. Size

Let's turn our attention next to the size or scope of the greenhouse. One of the most impressive things about the Webers complex was its size. It consisted of five greenhouses measuring 28,700 square feet. That was very impressive to this novice!

Its size allowed Leo and Ray to grow a vast number of plants. Some plants were for the florist shops in the area. Other plants such as tomatoes were for the farmers. And some plants were unique to the owners themselves.

Consider for a moment the size—not the number of the people but the overall size of the ministry—of God's Greenhouse in your own church. Acts 2:41-47 says,

> *So those who accepted his message were baptized, and that day about 3,000 people were added to them. And they devoted themselves to the apostles' teaching, to the fellowship, to the breaking of bread, and to the prayers. Then fear came over everyone, and many wonders and signs were being performed through the apostles. Now all the believers were together and held all things in common. They sold their possessions and property and distributed the proceeds to all, as anyone had a need. Every day they devoted themselves to meeting together in the temple complex, and broke bread from house to house. They ate their food with a joyful and humble attitude, praising God and having favor with all the people. And every day the Lord added to them those who were being saved. (Acts 2:41-47, HCSB)*

The size of the early church's ministry began with "the apostles' teaching, fellowship, the breaking of bread, and prayers." That was plenty, but the church went even further. We read about their spiritual power, their financial gifts, along with more and more people getting saved.

Someone said, "The church at Jerusalem was a live church!" and, yes, it was! It seemed that whatever they tried just happened to also work! Whatever they threw at the wall just happened to stick! Whatever darts they threw just happened to hit the bull's-eye! The joy of the Lord permeated the entire ministry in a way few churches ever experience.

It seems obvious that every activity of the Jerusalem greenhouse was blessed by God because *God was in the middle of everything* including their fellowship meals. Somehow everyone was going in the same direction! The entire church was God-serving instead of self-serving. And it showed throughout the community! Luke even adds the idea that the church experienced favor with the entire city! That feat is not easily accomplished.

It is not easy to reproduce such an effort in our churches. I recall a television interview from thirty years ago with the president of defense contractor Loral Corporation. Loral was well known as being a very efficient operation. The interviewer asked, "Do you believe your business operates at 80% efficiency?" The president laughed and said, "How I wish! That would be a marked improvement!" Even well-run businesses have difficulty reproducing the Acts chapter two greenhouse environment.

What do we have in our own greenhouse that can make a positive contribution for Jesus? It is time to make a list of everything that happens inside our greenhouse, so everything can now be challenged to bring itself into captivity for the cause of Jesus Christ. (Note: this exercise would be a good brainstorming effort if this material is being taught in a small class)

For example, the greenhouse includes *every ministry* of our church including the children's program, Sunday School, basketball program, music, committees, pastoral care, senior adults, small groups, finances, business meetings, Vacation Bible School, ushers, and the church office! You can probably mention areas I forgot!

In other words, we have a lot of things happening inside God's greenhouse, and sometimes it is easy to leave God out of what we are doing.

That leads me to the second fill-in-the-blank for number 2 on your study sheet. We need to consciously and prayerfully make God the most important part of the process. The Jerusalem church allowed God to be in the *middle* of every single ministry!

Being in the middle means God is holding the first part to the last part. In other words, if you take out the middle, the ministry falls apart! It does not matter how good the first part is or the last part is. Neither part can work without God in the middle!

Guess what? This is not easy to accomplish. It's much harder to do than to say. It's a lot easier to know it's true than to make it true.

It takes a conscious effort on the part of every one of us to make sure that everything we do has God in the middle of it! We need to be constantly reminded—that means over and over again—that if God is not in the middle of it, then we need to stop what we are doing.

Jesus taught us in John chapter fifteen, "You can accomplish nothing without Me. But if you are in communion with Me—abiding in Me— you will produce much fruit." The reason that is so is that Jesus is in the middle and His power is flowing like electricity through the first part and the last part. The ministry is energized with Jesus because Jesus is in the ministry!

One of the hardest lessons I have learned—perhaps partially learned is a better way to say this—is it is not enough for an idea to be a good idea. (We pastors keep folder upon folder of good ideas that either we or someone else has developed. Many of those ideas will go with us to the grave without ever being tried.) The most important ingredient in implementing new ministries or new ideas is waiting on God and making certain that God is in the middle of it.

Experience is a great teacher. Experience teaches that if God is in the middle of it, it will be done at the right *time* and with the right *people* and in the right *way*!

We have many programs and committees in our church that need to be surrendered to God. I'd like to do something unusual, but I believe it needs to be done in front of everyone in this building. I'd like for two or three people from the following groups to come forward and make a line across the front row facing me.

Evangelistic committee
Trustees
Music committee
Deacons
Sunday School teachers
AWANA children's ministry
Women's Missionary Union
Board of Christian Education
Activity Committee
Senior Adult Ministry
Finance Committee
Ushers
Youth Committee

I believe God would like for you to begin your next occasion together by discussing three questions.

Is Jesus in the middle of this ministry? That's a good question.

Will our ministry help create a greenhouse environment so that people can grow in our church?

Will God want to invest more seed in our greenhouse and grow even more people in the future?

(Note: Have prayer for them then dismiss them back to their seats.)

3. Security

The third characteristic of a spiritual greenhouse is the greenhouse provides security for the plants to grow.

How many of you have read the Charlie Brown comic strip called *Peanuts*? One of the most famous Charlie Brown characters is his buddy named Linus.

Linus is known for two things. Number one, he sucks his thumb. Number two, he carries his what? His security blanket. Why does he carry his security blanket? Is it because he needs a blanket? No. It is because he needs security.

I remember one of our daughters sucking her thumb when she was little! She would hold a security towel (not a blanket) and untangle the threads with one hand while she sucked the thumb on her other hand. Thread after thread disappeared until there was only one thread left. One!

Let me ask you a question: how much security is in a single thread? None in the real world but *everything in the mind*.

One of our most basic needs is the need for security, for feeling safe, for protection!

I want you to know that God's Greenhouse can help you with your need for security. 1 Corinthians 12:12 says, "For even as the body is one and yet has many members, and all the members of the body, though they are many, are one body, so also is Christ." (1 Corinthians 12:12, NASB) We read a few verses further:

> *"[A]and those members of the body which we deem less honorable, on these we bestow more abundant honor, and our less presentable members become much more presentable, whereas our more presentable members have no need of it. But God has so composed the body, giving more abundant honor to that member which lacked, so that there may be no division in the body, but that the members may have the same care for one another." (1 Corinthians 12:23-25, NASB)*

What a passage of scripture! It finishes with the members having the same care for one another. In other words, this church ought to be your security blanket—something you can hold to when the going gets tough!

Imagine the care which a plant receives in a greenhouse. It does not matter if the plant has money or no money, a good personality or no personality, beauty or no beauty, relatives in the greenhouse or no relatives, a position as a deacon or an usher, can sing in the choir or can't even sing in the shower.

The plant still gets love, care, and protection at every stage of its development because *the gardener is dedicated to helping that individual plant grow*!

In the very same way, this church ought to be a place of protection for each and every one of us! It is a place where you can come when the devil is after you, when the world is falling apart, when there are problems at home, when the factory is shutting down—a place where people will still love you and pray with you and encourage you and build you up! And all of that can indeed happen because you are one of us!

This means we need to be conscious of the needs of the people around us! We can't just come and sit and shut everyone out, but we have to come wanting to be a blessing to our brothers and sisters!

I'll never forget Sister Thelma. My wife Ruth Ellen was a young mother at that time. She had gone through a horrible week. You young mothers know what that's like, don't you? It came time for church on Wednesday night. It was a struggle for my wife to just get to church, let alone feel like worshipping and listening to a Bible lesson. And it showed on her face, too.

The church did not have very much aisle space. There were only about two feet between the pew and the wall. Sister Thelma was so large that she really struggled to make it down the wall aisle to her seat. But that was where she had always sat, and that was where she would sit until the day she died.

When the service was finished, she would always reverse her steps and slip out the back. I always thought she had to hold her breath to squeeze that far!

But when this particular service was finished, Thelma squeezed her way down the wall aisle in the opposite direction . . . to Ruth Ellen's pew. She put her arms around Ruth Ellen in a big hug, smiled, said a few comforting words, and then left. She didn't do it for anyone else that night—just for Ruth Ellen.

That happened in 1983. I have never forgotten Ruth Ellen telling me about that hug.

Do you know what needs to happen Sunday after Sunday in God's greenhouse at _____ Church? We need a lot of Thelmas to do what Thelma did.

I would like for us to be known as the church where you never forget the hugs and the kind words and the friendly handshake and the pleasant smile and the security you feel when you come to this greenhouse because it is here at God's greenhouse that the "members have the same care one for another."

4. Stability

That brings us to stability! The concept of stability is one of consistency. Heaven knows, along with every earthling, that a greenhouse must have stability in a wide variety of areas for a plant to grow!

Let me go back to Webers Greenhouse again. That complex consisted of five glass greenhouses. Each greenhouse measured a little more than one hundred feet long and fifty feet wide. That was a lot of space!

Yet, even so, they managed to maintain a stable temperature in January or August. The greenhouse was heated in January by steam from an old-fashioned boiler; the cold pipes would pop like shotgun blasts as hot steam rushed through them. It was loud! By contrast, the greenhouse was cooled in August with huge fans pulling in air from outside. It constantly amazed me that such an old facility could maintain a stable growing environment regardless of the season.

The plants were given a stable temperature, a stable water supply, and steady plant food if that became necessary.

Leo and Ray taught me that plants do not adjust well to sharp fluctuations in temperature or water supply! Thus, one of them worked every day of the week to make certain the environment was a *stable* environment for the plants.

The same stability needs to take place in God's greenhouse at this church, too!

The Bible talks about the importance of stability in Ephesians 4:11-15.

> *And He personally gave some to be apostles, some prophets, some evangelists, some pastors and teachers, for the training of the saints in the work of ministry, to build up the body of Christ, until we all reach unity in the faith and in the knowledge of God's Son, growing into a mature man with a stature measured by Christ's fullness. Then we will no longer be little children, tossed by the waves and blown around by every wind of teaching, by human cunning with cleverness in the techniques of deceit. But speaking the truth in love, let us grow in every way into Him who is the head—Christ. From Him the whole body, fitted and knit together by every supporting ligament, promotes the growth of the body for building up itself in love by the proper working of each individual part. (Ephesians 4:11-15, HCSB)*

Notice the process of growing in verse fifteen follows the creation of stability in verse fourteen. You can't "grow in every way" in verse fifteen if you are being "tossed by the waves and blown around" in verse fourteen.

Psalm 1 talks about the man who has found stability in the Lord! "How happy is the man who does not follow the advice of the wicked or take the path of sinners or join a group of mockers! Instead, his delight is in the LORD's instruction, and he meditates on it day and night. He is like a tree planted beside streams of water that bears its fruit in season and whose leaf does not wither. Whatever he does prospers." (Psalm 1:1-3, HCSB)

All greenhouses, including the spiritual greenhouse, need stability!

It is important for you to think through what I am now about to say. Churches do not have a growing environment *when they have continual change*—for example, when they're continually changing their church staff whether it be the pastor or music director or teachers or some department director.

Or continually changing their music style, so one week it's southern gospel, the next week it's traditional, the next week it's praise and worship, and the fourth week it's all choir music!

Or continually changing their philosophy from this year's "it's a senior adult ministry emphasis" to next year's "it's a children's ministry emphasis."

The Bible says in 1 Corinthians chapter fourteen, "God is not the author of confusion" but rather He is a God of stability!

Think about this! God gave us the completed Bible around the year A.D. 100. *Can you imagine how confused we would be if God was changing the Bible as fast as we change policies and people in our churches?* We wouldn't stand a chance!

But that is not the way God operates. God's Word is the same today that it was in A.D. 100.

God gave the Mosaic Law to Israel in 1500 B.C. That law did not change (pass away) for the next 1,500 years. Then along came Jesus Christ who established a new age which we often describe as the Age of Grace. That age has now lasted 2,000 years. Someday God will begin a new age which we premillennialists call the Millennial Kingdom, and that age will last 1,000 years. Then will come the New Heaven and the New Earth, and thank God, that age will never end, and we shall be forevermore with the Lord. I can live with that final plan, how about you?

In other words, *God stays with His plan for a very long time, and He expects us to get with His plan for a very long time*. The issue is not one of personalities—the issue is, do we want to rise above petty personalities, above petty personal likes and dislikes and get with His plan?

I recall having a conversation with the director of the Pastoral Care Ministry in one of our area hospitals. This director was one of the smartest men in understanding the human psyche that I have ever known. At one time his father had pastored one of the largest churches in our area. This director knew churches and their mood swings quite well.

We talked about a church whose pastor had recently left for greener pastures. It was not an amicable parting, but it was not a church-splitting parting either.

I said, "You know that church quite well. What kind of pastor will they select next?" He quickly answered, "The exact opposite of what they just had." And they did!

I have experienced his words in my own ministry. I have always been known as a Great Commission pastor. My philosophy is, "Let's evangelize our community, get them saved and then taught!" After doing that in one church for six years, I was replaced by a pastor who specialized in counseling! The church made a 180-degree turn and tried to become something else. The shift, though, did not work. The fact is that church needed to stay with God's two-thousand-year-old program of the Great Commission, or it was going to close its doors! And, sure enough, it did indeed close its doors one decade later after a horrible church-closing split!

What did my friend say? "The exact opposite of what they just had."

Is that stability? No, it is not.

Most churches have the tendency to replace the pastor with someone totally different, but the issue is still the same: *Will the church get with God's plan? God's plan has not changed for two thousand years!*

Too many churches replace the leadership team (including the deacons) and get totally new faces. We blame people who should not be blamed because the issue is still the same. Will the church get with God's plan?

Research shows that churches need consistent leadership (that's called stability) to have a growing environment because a consistent leadership team means you have a consistent, established way of doing things! Remember: a few newcomers can more easily transition to a new system than *everyone* transitioning to a new leader's system!

In my early years, I pastored a small church that was recovering from a near-fatal church fight. A wonderful lady attended our church for a few months. One day I told her, "It's about time you joined our church." She said something I never forgot. She said she liked me a lot, but she would not join our church because, in her own words, "they don't keep a pastor very long and I want stability! I don't want to go through pastor after pastor!" Needless to say, she didn't join our church.

By contrast, a wonderful man of God named Mel Efaw pastored Grace Gospel Church in our town for over forty years! He had the same music director and visitation director for much of that same time. Amazing! As a result, when you attended Grace Gospel, you knew what you were going to get!

How many of you can remember a man named Moses? Moses provided forty years of stability for Israel! Imagine Israel's condition if they had gone through ten pastors or ten deacon chairmen in those forty years. They would have been totally dysfunctional!

How about Joshua? Twenty-five years as a leader.

How about King David? Forty years as a king! Do you see a pattern in God's method? An outsider from another country would pass through Israel and ask, "Who is your king?" The answer would be, "King David." The outsider would say, "Well, I know how things must be because you have the same king you did the last time I passed through. You must still be following the same God and obeying the same ten commandments." He could say that because there was stability!

In *The Purpose Driven Church*, Rick Warren said, "A long pastorate does not guarantee a church will grow, but changing pastors every few years guarantees a church won't grow."

The evidence to support that statement is all around us!

Can you imagine what the kids would be like if they got a new daddy every two or three years? And yet many churches are doing just exactly that and then wondering what is wrong!

Someone said to me, "What our church needs is change." I said, "No, what our church needs is stability—to get back to having church and doing what God called us to do!" *Our problem is not that we need more change but that we have changed too much and too often!*

We need stability in our church staff, stability in our organization, stability in our goals, stability in our processes, stability in our constitution, stability in the youth program and the Sunday School and how we approach problems and the kind of literature we use and the programs that we follow and on and on the list goes.

We need people to look past people until they see the purpose for why this church exists, and then commit themselves to work with each other to become the greenhouse that every one of us needs!

Alas, you cannot grow people if those same people are being continually tossed to and fro.

5. Site

Let's say it's January in Ohio. If you want to grow petunias or roses or whatever, you must have a greenhouse—a physical location where that growing can take place. The Bible plainly reveals the location of God's Greenhouse. 1 Thessalonians 1:1, 8 says, "From Paul, Silas and Timothy, To the local church (assembly) of the Thessalonians . . . the Lord's message has been loudly proclaimed! In Macedonia and Achaia and even beyond your home area your faith in God is well known."

What the church in Thessalonica meant to its community can now be replicated by our own church in this community!

It cannot be emphasized enough that the art of growing people requires, even demands, the greenhouse ministry of a local church. *Nothing else can substitute for the local church.* I do not mean to minimize the help associated with a television church, radio ministry, or an internet ministry, but those helps are a poor substitute for everything that happens in a local church.

It is sad to say, but there is another world outside the walls of our church. I wish sometimes I did not have to go outside our building and enter that world. That world is cold, harsh, sometimes hostile, and extremely difficult. Our present world resembles Antarctica to a child of God, and, unfortunately, it is like Antarctica twelve months a year!

Our world is similar to the month of January in the Ohio Valley. There is no life, the trees are barren, and there is nothing pleasant for the soul. It is cold!

But God has given me a site or a place where I can escape that world, a place where I can grow even though the entire world is in the grips of a very cold January, and that site is a greenhouse like _____ Church where God can feed my soul, and I can keep on growing in Him!

Look with me at Hebrews 10:23–25. "Let us hold fast the confession of our hope without wavering, for he who promised is faithful. And let us consider how to stir up one another to love and good works, not neglecting to meet together, as is the habit of some, but encouraging one another, and all the more as you see the Day drawing near." (Hebrews 10:23-25, ESV)

Those verses explain what God's church can do for me! First, verse twenty-three reminds me that I am not alone in this struggle against this anti-God world. It says, "Let us!" "Us" is plural. That means we are in this together. Singing "Onward, Christian soldiers (plural), marching as to war!" is a lot better than singing, "Onward, Christian soldier (singular), marching on to war!" Being in church reminds me that there are others who believe what I believe!

Second, verse twenty-four says I am loved inside these walls. I worked nineteen years at an electric utility and found there was very little true love in our workforce. Our relationship was not based on love but on a paycheck. However, my need is much greater than a paycheck. I need to be loved! I want you to know the world may not love me, but I am loved by many in the church of God!

Third, verse twenty-five says there is also encouragement in this sacred place. It says, "encouraging one another." The verb encourage is a present tense verb in the Greek text. That means this encouragement happens over and over again! If I stumble—maybe I should change that to *when* I stumble—I have some brother who will reach out his hand and help me get back on my feet!

No television ministry can do all of that! One of our homebound members said, "I need someone I can touch. I can't touch a television ministry, but I can touch the people who visit me from my church."

That's another reason why everyone ought to have a local church membership—why they ought to devote themselves to their local church because that's where God does His very best work!

Someone has said that claiming to be a Christian without being an active church member is like:

A student who will not go school.
A soldier who will not join the army.
A citizen who does not pay taxes or vote.
A salesman with no customers.
An explorer with no base camp.
A seaman on a ship without a crew.
A businessman on a deserted island.
An author without readers.
A tuba player without an orchestra.
A parent without a family.
A football player without a team.
A politician who is a hermit.
A scientist who does not share his findings.
A bee without a hive.

There is no better place to grow in Christ than the local church. I read of a group discussion among some church members. One said, "I can't remember the content of any sermon in the past ten years, and I've heard them all!" Another person added, "What's the use of going to church if we can't remember what we've heard! Maybe we can use our time better in another way!" Then a lady put everything in perspective by saying, "I have eaten 30,000 meals, and I can't remember them. But I know this. If I had not eaten those meals, I would be dead today!"

I say amen to that line of reasoning!

There is an idea that you can just go anywhere and drift here and there and grow in Christ. Well, the Greek language has a word for that idea. The word is "baloney!" The truth is you are a human being who is made like every other human being. That means you need roots if you're going to grow! You have to get rooted somewhere! And stay there!

That means you need to make a commitment to a local Bible-believing church where you can grow with people who believe the Bible and are committed to the work of God!

The fact is we are trying to be that kind of local church! God has placed us in this city so we can personally touch this city for the glory of God!

Never forget: We are the site where God wants to make this happen—we who make up _____ Church!

6. Seasonality

"To everything there is a season." Thus, begins Ecclesiastes chapter three.

You may never have considered this concept, but some plants are seasonal even in a greenhouse. In other words, there are special projects for special times of the year! For example, the Webers grew poinsettias for the Christmas season, lilies for Easter, plus geraniums and petunias and tomatoes for spring. As master gardeners, they were sensitive to the seasonal demand.

One of the most important passages about sowing and reap is found in John chapter four. Let me paraphrase that passage for you.

> *Jesus said to His apostles, "My purpose is to do the will of him that sent me and to finish his work. Do not imagine there are four months until the harvest. Look, I am already saying to you, Lift up your eyes, and look upon the fields because the fields are already white and ready for harvest. The one who reaps is receiving wages for his work. He is gathering fruit for life eternal and the world to come. Listen! The one who sows and the one who reaps will rejoice together. This will prove the old saying, One sows and another reaps. I have sent you to reap in some cases where you have done no work until now. Other men did all the preparatory work and you have merely entered into their labors." (John 4:34-38)*

This passage coincides with Paul's discussion in 1 Corinthians chapter three about planting, watering, and reaping.

Other passages teach that there are times to march around Jericho, but there are also times to wait on God to part the Red Sea.

Even the birth of our Lord took place at a certain season! The Bible says, "But when the fulness of the appointed time arrived, God sent forth His Son. " (Galatians 4:4) Although Israel had prayed hundreds of years for the Messiah, God waited on His own time! Jesus finally came . . . but He only came once!

These events proved to be times when the ordinary day-by-day greenhouse process was *supplemented* with an additional project. This is still true today. God occasionally supplements our growing process by giving us an additional assignment or project. We as a church need to be sensitive to the way God moves.

This next statement is very important. Our church should maintain an environment where *God can do anything He wishes at any point in time!* This statement goes back to the words in point 1: God is the only One who has the right to say, "I want" in our church. We need to realize there are certain special projects—certain special ministries—which God may emphasize from time to time.

Let us never forget the Holy Spirit has ways to reach people that we have never tried before!

It is critically important we keep an open mind about the possibilities of serving a God of infinite resources. We need to be sensitive to the Holy Spirit and get it done when He wants it done!

It is also important to remember that God's time is always the right time even if it does not appear to be the right time. Ecclesiastes 11:4 can be paraphrased, "If you as a farmer wait for optimum conditions, you will never get anything done." Fanny Crosby's "Victory Through Grace" includes the words, "Not to the strong is the battle, Not to the swift is the race, Yet to the true and the faithful Vict'ry is promised through grace." Isaiah 55:9 teaches that God's ways are much higher than man's ways, so we need flexibility to move when God moves!

Let me mention two examples. Perhaps one or both will speak to you at some point in your future ministry.

I grew up in an era of revivals which lasted three, and even four, weeks. I recall one of the best revivals I ever saw! Someone was saved in our Sunday night service. The pastor, who happened to be my father, shared with the church that the leadership had been praying about revival. They felt like they ought to begin a revival (series of services) that very night. "We have no time to advertise. We do not know when it will end. The preacher has not even been contacted. But we believe this is what God wants us to do." The church unanimously agreed. The meeting lasted two weeks, and a number of souls were wonderfully saved! That meeting made a big impression on me about the importance of keeping a tender heart toward the Holy Spirit!

The second example comes from Dutch Brammer. Dutch was a full-time farmer and part-time pastor. He married my parents and became my first pastor. He didn't graduate from high school, may not have even made it to high school, but he was a wise man in the ways of God. He said something that every young church leader needs to write down and never forget. Regarding the issue of seasonality, he taught my father, "Sometimes you mark time waiting on God to do a work." Does that seem reasonable? Not to an impatient pastor like me but it does make sense to a farmer. He knows there is a time to plow, plant, water, and reap! Then you do other farm work *and* wait until the next cycle appears on the calendar!

Be sensitive to what God wants to do and when God wants it done.

7. Simplicity

One of the most remarkable items about Webers Greenhouse was its simplicity in design, organization, and process. It was built before anyone conceived of a modernized facility run by a computer. It was built by people without college degrees. It did not have layers of management figuring out what to do! Yet it stood the test of time for seventy years. Always doing what it was designed to do. Always adjusting smoothly to the changing demands of its clientele.

The K.I.S.S. formula is one of my most basic formulas for life. That formula stands for "Keep It Simple, Stupid." Based on the condition of our modern world (including our churches), it seems obvious that Stupid is alive and well on Planet Earth.

The Bible's equivalent formula is found in 1 Corinthians 14:40, "All things in God's church should be done decently and in an orderly manner."

God's work should not be complicated! The Great Commandment (Matthew 22:36-40) focuses on loving people. Is that complicated? No. The Great Commission (Matthew 28:18-20) focuses on discipling people from the stage of conversion to the stage of fruitful ministry. Is that complicated? No. Indeed, that may actually seem too simple, but that is what God expects of His church. Why then do we allow other items to drain our resources?

Gary Arrington, a good pastor friend of mine, was often approached about new ideas. He had a canned response which was also a biblical response. He would say, "Will this bring glory to Jesus? If yes, we'll do it! If no, we have other more important things to do!" In that manner, Gary kept the people focused on the higher priority items!

Far too often churches complicate things with unnecessary rules and policies! I think some folk lay awake at night deliberately thinking of new rules to further strangle the church's ministry! Unfortunately, I recall one pastorate where even I did not know all the rules or policies! No one else did either! Yikes! How do we allow such things to happen?

Isn't loving God and loving each other a much better alternative?

I take comfort in reading the book of Acts and realizing the early church reached 5,000 before its members recognized the need for deacons. I do not mean to minimize the deacon office, but there is an important lesson here. The early church did not establish such an office in its infancy because *people naturally responded to the needs*. Their means of naturally caring for one another, as in the case of selling property, is a testimony of how they were motivated by meeting the needs of others.

Let me pose a somewhat silly example, but there is some underlying truth in this example. We recognize there is nothing wrong with an order for the worship service. Every church has an order regardless of whether the Sunday bulletin includes it. But the early church prospered without a bulletin telling them when to stand or when to sit. The Apostle Paul wrote in 2 Corinthians 3:17, "Wherever the Holy Spirit is, there you will also find a spirit of liberty or freedom."

Have you ever experienced the philosophy in the next statement? "We have a free night this week on the church calendar so let's call a meeting!"

The old joke is still true! A lady said she would like to join the local church, but she wasn't physically up to the challenge. She said there were too many meetings and functions to attend!

Too many churches are too busy with frivolous "stuff" that won't make any difference in eternity.

One business executive called a meeting of his staff. The staff arrived and found no chairs. The executive explained, "No chairs means you'll only talk about something that needs to be discussed!" Smart thinking!

Simplicity is an art. Sometimes I think it must be a science, too! It is hard to train ourselves to keep it simple, stupid!

Have you ever attended a revival tent meeting? You should! Those meetings can be very refreshing because of their simplicity. There isn't time to put together a big organization. We just do what has to be done and often do it on the fly. Sometimes we even use a hat to collect the offering! And it works!

There is so much that *needs* to be done. Things like preparing a Bible lesson for Sunday or contacting our new attendees or sharing Jesus with the community or how about this oft-neglected item called prayer!

I urge you to do your best *not* to complicate the ministry in your own church. Try to keep everyone informed, be open and transparent with all the people, create an environment of trust, emphasize yielding to the leadership of the Holy Spirit, and don't ridicule failure but view failure as an opportunity for personal growth!

Remember: "When the Holy Spirit is welcome, you will also find a spirit of liberty or freedom."

8. See-Through

This is a great teaching moment for all of us about something we cannot afford to forget! Consider these three questions.

"Will all of you look at our greenhouse and tell me what you see inside the greenhouse?" (The audience's answer: "A flower.")

"Where are you in relation to the greenhouse?" (The audience's answer: "On the outside of the greenhouse.")

"Why are you able to see the plant?" (The audience's answer: "Because of the clear plastic. We can see through the plastic covering.")

This is very important. Do you know people on the outside of the greenhouse can see what is happening on the inside of the greenhouse?

Not only that, but do you also know that people on the outside of the church can see what is happening on the inside of the church?

One of the most important characteristics of a greenhouse is its transparency—that you can be on the outside but still see what is on the inside! The Apostle Paul described the Corinthians (2 Corinthians 3:2) as an *open* letter which had been permanently imprinted upon Paul's heart—but it was a letter so transparent that it could be read by everyone. In other words, "the world is reading you Corinthians as if the world is reading an open letter which has been published in the newspaper!"

We often forget that the church is just as transparent as this greenhouse. *That means there are no secrets that stay secret for long.* That includes good secrets as well as bad secrets, good news as well as bad news, good decisions as well as bad decisions, agreements as well as disagreements!

I recall one time being surprised by how fast good news moved throughout the church membership. I had visited a homebound brother at ten o'clock in the evening. Everyone knew about the visit by noon the next day! I mentioned it to one of the deacons. He laughed—he actually laughed at my surprise—and said, "Good news travels fast in this church, but bad news travels even faster!"

It is as if everything done in and by the church is being posted on the internet!

During World War II, our military personnel were often warned, "Loose lips sink ships." That warning was a recognition of a basic weakness within humanity: the weakness of a desire to talk and share what we know!

I was raised in an environment where the church conducted its business meeting on Saturday night. You may be surprised to know that visitors (including spouses who were not church members) were not allowed to attend the business meeting. I recall one such meeting where an outside building consultant was allowed to speak at the beginning of our meeting about some construction issues. He was then asked to leave before the church began its deliberations. The issue was deemed one of *secrecy*, the utmost secrecy. The policy was patterned after the secrecy associated with the Masonic Lodge because many of the church members were Masons. The church wished to keep the public from knowing its business.

Of course, that philosophy did not work very well. Quite often, the very people who made the decisions were the ones spilling the beans to the community! It turned out Washington D.C. was not the only place where there were leaks!

None of my pastorates followed this practice. Furthermore, I suspect your church does not exclude visitors from its deliberations. (On the contrary, I recommend *publishing* the minutes and making them available to anyone who desires! That includes the financial statements, too.)

Transparency is all about building trust. It is hard to trust if things are done in secret. It is hard to trust a government or a management or a community organization or a church if things are done in secret. Transparency is associated with the words, "I have nothing to hide." It is all about openness!

How does this issue affect us? First and foremost, let's think about the very important issue of our church's reputation. This may surprise you, but every person has a reputation. Furthermore, every church has a reputation! Someone said, "I don't care what my own reputation is." I said, "I do. I don't want my family to have to apologize for me when I'm dead."

The reputation of this church is important to this pastor and it ought to be important to you, too. Why? If this community hears a lot of bad stuff about our church, they will never come to our church! We will forfeit the opportunity to minister to them! We may try to minister, but they will say, "Oh, you go to thaaaat church. Sorry."

I recall pastoring one church which had experienced a series of horrible splits. Sixty people left in one business meeting. Interestingly, the remaining people still couldn't get along with one another! The church had a beautiful sign in the front yard that included the words, "Friendly Church."

I mentioned to the chairman of the deacons that they ought to remove those words from that sign. He said, "Oh no, we're a friendly church! Why should we remove it?" I answered, "Because the community knows you're not a friendly church."

Rest assured, the community does indeed know what kind of church we are! Are we self-centered or community-centered? Are we a closed society or an open society? Is "friendliness" just a slogan or really true? Is the Bible followed or not followed? Are people more important than rules?

Let's make this personal. This community knows all about us! One way this community knows about us is because people listen to how we talk about our church. For example, do we talk well about the church, or do we talk bad about the church? Do we like the pastor or not like the pastor? How well do we talk about the Sunday School or children's program or youth program or music program or senior adult program? *After all, would you visit a church if you only heard bad news about it?*

You may not be aware of this, but you are actually a walking billboard in this community! It doesn't matter where you go! The people are reading your attitudes about this church.

We can take out a full-page advertisement in the newspaper fifty-two weeks a year, but the impact of that advertisement will be less than the impact of the advertisers seated in front of me at this very moment!

It's time to answer a very big question: how do you talk about your church? How well do you represent your church when you're outside these walls?

May I remind you of Matthew 5:14, "Ye are the light of the world; a city that is set on a hill cannot be hid. Let your light so shine before men that men may see your good works and glorify your Father who is in heaven."

Everything in our church should be a light to this community—no fussing, no fighting, no criticism, nothing which causes the name of Jesus to be ridiculed. We need to conduct ourselves as if Jesus Himself is here because He is here! Jesus taught us in Matthew 18:20, "When two or three come together in My name to lift Me up, My presence will be in their presence."

A newspaper editor published some news on a business that greatly bothered the business owner. The businessman called the editor and complained. The editor answered, "If you don't want it printed, then don't let it happen."

Let me offer a word of advice to all of us who love this church so very much: *If we don't want it talked about in our community, then don't let it happen!*

I like the story of the people who moved to St. Louis so many years ago. They wanted to go to church on Sunday morning. They stopped a policeman and asked him if he would recommend a church. The policeman pointed them to a church a few miles away.

They asked the policeman why he recommended that particular church. The policeman said, "I am not a religious man. There are several other churches between here and there, but I recommended that church because those people always leave their service with a smile on their face. They are the happiest people I have ever seen. If I was going to choose a church for myself that would be the one."

That sounds like something people ought to say about us!

9. Sunlight

A master gardener was asked to speak to a garden club. He began his speech with these words, "Gardening begins with the sun."

I have mentioned before that Webers Greenhouse was made of glass—thousands of panes of glass. The walls and the roof were the same—glass everywhere! That glass meant the greenhouse was transparent. The greenhouse had electrical lighting for certain special needs, but do you know where it received the vast majority of light to grow the plants? From the sun!

We were taught in school that plants obtain their energy from light through a process called photosynthesis. If there is no light, the plant will not be able to grow. The plant requires light and the best light, of course, is God's sunlight!

The parallel truth is that our own greenhouse at _____ Church needs sunlight to grow people.

Where do we get our sunlight to grow mature Christians?

You already know the answer if you were taught the children's song, "This Little Light of Mine." Jesus said in John 8:12, "I am the light of the world. If you follow Me, you will not walk in darkness but shall be blessed with the light of eternal life."

We have a bad habit of minimizing Jesus! We forget that the light of life, Jesus Himself, wants to shine down upon this congregation! We forget that Jesus wants to fill you with His power, His energy, His love, and His priorities and to gradually change you into His own image so that when people see you, they are seeing Him!

Do you want to grow a church of beautiful people? Then turn Jesus loose in this church. How can we do that? We can do that by turning Jesus loose in our own lives seven days a week!

But Jesus can't shine inside these walls on Sunday unless He shines in your life the other six days!

The Bible says Jesus rose from the dead on the first day of the week. One of the best statements about that day is found in John 20:20. "Then were the disciples glad when they saw the Lord!" What a difference it makes when Jesus is shining in the hearts of His people! (By the way, "Jesus shining" is a great way to define the Beatitudes in Matthew chapter five.)

But there is something which can cut off that sunshine from heaven, and it happens in many churches Sunday after Sunday. Let me show you what the cutting off is like.

We have a plant inside the greenhouse. We already know that the plant needs light. Let's imagine that something comes between the light outside the greenhouse and the plant inside.

(Note: Cover the greenhouse with a large non-transparent sheet.)

We now have a big problem! The sunlight has now been cut off from getting inside the greenhouse, from getting to the plant.

The Bible describes this action in Isaiah 59:1-2. Let me say it my own way. "We know the Lord's arm is not too short to save, aren't you thankful for that? We also know the Lord's ear is not hard of hearing like some of us, but He can hear us from anywhere we call." Long distance is no problem to God. But there is a problem, and that problem is covered in verse two. "Your iniquities—another word for iniquities is the word sin or acts of disobedience against God—have caused a separation from your God. You're not as close as you used to be, and your sins have caused God to hide his face from you, so He will no longer hear your prayers."

Let me show you what happens.

(Note: A volunteer bought some plants two months ago and kept those plants in total darkness in a closet for those two months. Those plants have not grown because they have been deprived of sunlight. Show those plants at this time to the congregation. Discuss the importance of sunlight to the plant and the importance of Jesus in growing people! If the sunlight does not shine into the greenhouse, the plants can never grow! Sin will block the sunlight from entering our greenhouse. Sin keeps the sunshine from shining on the seed.)

Elisha Hoffman asked, "Is thy heart right with God, Washed in the crimson flood, Cleansed and made holy, humble and lowly, Right in the sight of God?"

Did you bring any sunshine with you today?

10. Stock

We come to the last item on our study sheet. Let's talk about the stock we intend to have in our greenhouse. Sometimes we go shopping, and we ask, "Do you have any of this product in stock?" The clerk might say, "We don't have any today, but we have a shipment coming in tomorrow." Or the clerk might say, "We never have any of that product in stock."

There is a big difference between those two answers. One store will get my business in the future; the other store won't see me again.

So, what do we carry in stock at our church? There are three passages of scripture that help us to answer that question.

1 Corinthians 3:1-3 says,

> *"Brothers and sisters, I cannot write to you as church members under the control of the Holy Spirit but rather as people who are under the control of the world—indeed, as mere infants in Christ. I must resort to giving you milk rather than solid food because you are not yet mature enough for solid food. You should be ready, but you're not! You are still too worldly. There is jealousy and squabbling among you; doesn't that prove you are still worldly?"*

1 Peter 2:1-2 teaches, "Discard immediately all of the following: malice, deceit, hypocrisy, jealousy, and slanderous speech. In a way similar to newborn infants you should seek intensely the pure spiritual milk, so that you may grow."

Ephesians 4:11-13 says,

> *"And he gave the apostles, the prophets, the evangelists, the shepherds, and teachers, to equip the saints for the work of ministry, for building up the body of Christ, until we all attain to the unity of the faith and of the knowledge of the Son of God, to mature manhood." (Ephesians 4:11-13, ESV)*

This brings us to another fill-in-the-blank in our study sheet. Based on those three texts, what kind of plants do we as a church grow? Here is the answer. Our greenhouse is for large plants called grown-ups and small plants called children.

God's church isn't just for the apostles and the older saints. It is also for the children because Jesus had a philosophy which said, "Allow the little children to come unto Me."

In other words, God's Greenhouse is for everyone from the cradle to the grave, and 100% of us are somewhere in between those two ages.

I grew up in a church where we had only one annual event for the children. Once a year we would go to an amusement park called Camden Park. You can think of Camden Park as a miniaturized King's Island or Cedar Point or one of the other big amusement parks. We were limited to only one event per year!

My father told the story of being the revival speaker in an area church. One night a church member came to him and said, "Starting a youth program is the worst thing you can do for your church." So sad! Perhaps Dad should have said, "I have heard starting an adult program is even worse than that!" Yes, that church needed revival!

Let me pose a question to you. What age group do you want to have in this church? Then again, what age group don't you want to have in this church? We might say, "None," but what does the evidence show? We have already answered both questions.

(Note: The following questions should be explored in a Saturday leadership seminar. List the existing growth processes in each category!)

Do we want children? If, yes where is the proof? What is our process to help them grow?

Do we want young adults? If yes, where is the proof? What is our process to help them grow?

Do we want retirees? If yes, where is the proof? What is our process to help them grow?

Do we want people who are not white? If yes, where is the proof? What is our process to help them grow?

Do we want young parents? If yes, where is the proof? What is our process to help them grow?

Do we want to grow new converts from the new birth to the maturity of ministry? If yes, where is the proof? What is our process to help them grow?

Do we want to minister to the down-and-out or the up-and-in or both? Do we have any processes already established to help them grow? You may not know this, but the up-and-in put on their pants one leg at a time just like the down-and-out.

What stock do we really want to grow in our church? And what stock don't we really want? Our actions speak louder than our words.

God has a lot of seed in this city which needs a greenhouse.

I wonder: does God trust us enough to invest that seed here at _____ Church?

4

THE PNEUMA IN THE
GREENHOUSE

Holy Spirit, You Are Welcome Here!

We have a new handout for this study. The first paragraph is a review of our previous studies. Let's fill in number one and then get deep into today's study as quickly as we can.

It says, "Our central text for this series is 1 Corinthians 3:9, *"you (speaking of us at* _____*Church) are God's farm/cultivated field/ garden."* We could also translate this phrase, *"you are God's* greenhouse.*"*

Fill in number two. "Our church is the place where God grows people."

Let me remind you that none of this is possible unless you first have a condition we call a greenhouse environment—an environment where God is free to work in the hearts of His people.

Today's message focuses on the next key ingredient we need for plants, that is, people to grow!

I want you to think with me about the moon. How many of you have ever been to the moon? How many of you have seen close-up pictures of the moon? I want you to describe the moon for me. (Note: The congregation's answers will likely be similar to "barren, a place where nothing grows.") What are some of the items on Planet Earth which are missing on the moon? (Note: The desired answer is "air.")

It's remarkable to think that you cannot have a hot air balloon on the moon because there's no air to make hot.

Someone said, "But what about the flag planted by the astronauts? The flag is straight out and stiff rather than hanging down. The only way it can be straight out and stiff is if it's held up by some air."

That is usually true, but there is something you may not know. The astronauts planted a flag that included a metal "curtain rod." The rod was sewn into the top seam of the flag. The flag has the appearance of waving in the wind, but it's actually held in place by the metal curtain rod. The only time the flag moves is when something or someone touches it and makes it move.

I'll say it again: there is no air on the moon. As a result, something else is missing from the moon. Life is missing from the moon.

That brings us to a very basic lesson about our greenhouse. It is number three on your handout.

Plants need air to grow. If we were to create a vacuum inside our greenhouse, these plants would die. We could surround them with plenty of plant food and even good singing and good preaching, but they would still die. The reality is no plant can grow without air.

Let's think about us. If we create a vacuum inside this entire auditorium, from door to door, every one of us will die physically.

There has to be air for there to be life!

But what does the air do? The air surrounds the entire plant. The air is not just in one tiny area, but it is spread throughout the entire greenhouse. We know that living plants take in air which includes a mixture of gases like oxygen, nitrogen, and carbon dioxide. The plant then uses the oxygen and stored sugars to make carbon dioxide. And presto! You end up with a beautiful plant because the air allows the plant to grow.

Now here is where this discussion gets really interesting.

Where does the church get the air that allows people to be born again and then to grow? You have probably figured out that God, the Master Gardener, has something to do with it!

Let's look at number four on our study sheet. All of us have heard of a pneumatic tool, a tool which operates by air pressure. (Note: Ask the audience to provide examples of pneumatic tools.)

It continues with the words, "The word pneumatic comes from the Greek word *pneuma* which means 'air' or 'spirit.' It is also the same Greek word for the Holy Spirit or Holy Ghost (*pneuma*). In other words, the Holy Spirit is the air in God's Greenhouse! Without Him there is no life!"

Let's look at two verses in the Word of God. 1 Corinthians 3:16 says, "Don't you know that you, meaning all of us (the Greek word is plural meaning all of us combined rather than us as individuals), are the one temple of God and this temple called _____ Church is indwelt by God's Holy Spirit?"

That means God Himself is here with us today; God is doing a work today. That means right now at this very moment.

It is like what happened at the dedication of Solomon's temple in the Old Testament. The story is recorded in 2 Chronicles chapter five! The physical temple had been built; the ark of the Lord (the same one that Indiana Jones was looking for) was brought into the temple. The Bible says the priests sacrificed so many sheep and cattle that no one could count that high. The orchestra was playing music with every instrument known to Israel. The choir was singing a song similar to the "Hallelujah Chorus."

All of that was very impressive, but it was still missing one very important thing! That thing was the most important item of all! The event was missing the "Air of God" or the "Presence of God" or the "Holy Spirit of God."

Consider this: If there is no air, all of the other activities are in vain!

But then came the Air of God! The shekinah glory cloud representing God's presence descended from heaven and entered the temple! The cloud was so overwhelming the priests could no longer perform their priestly work! Yes, the glory cloud of the Lord filled the temple!

Likewise, we can say something similar on this very day! We can now say, "You whom we call _____ Church are the New Testament temple of God where God does His business!"

The second verse is Ephesians 2:22. This verse is also about us as a local church that belongs to God. In verse twenty-one, Paul talks about all born-again people everywhere being (not *becoming* because this temple already exists) one temple in the Lord, but in verse twenty-two, Paul brings that truth down to the local church level. Paul talks about God's work here in this place, in this greenhouse we call _____ Church.

Verse twenty-two says, and this is my own version, "in Christ, the Anointed One, you in _____ Church are being molded together to become a permanent dwelling place in which God Himself lives by or through His Holy Spirit."

You and me, molded together, built together. Peter says we're not only the walls, but we're also the priests doing the work inside the walls. All of that is good, but the most important part is that God has given us His own Air—His own Holy Spirit!

The book of Zechariah teaches us that God's work is not done by human might, by human power, nor by human reasoning—in other words, God's work is not done by any human ability but solely by the Holy Spirit of God!

D. L. Moody used to say, "There is not a better evangelist in the world than the Holy Spirit." How much we need Him to do what only He can do!

You can mark this down in your notes: Without the Holy Spirit nothing can be done, but with the Holy Spirit everything can be done!

Remember this about Solomon's temple: The musicians were great, the sacrifices were great, the ark of the covenant was great, the building itself was one for the ages, but none of that could provide the air that was needed! *None of that was a substitute for the presence of God and what God can do!*

It is sad to say, but there are churches all over the Tri-State where it will be hard to preach today! There are churches where it will be hard to teach the Bible or even smile when you sing! Or pray a public prayer!

It is as if the church is in a straitjacket! I know the experience because I have been in such places! It was not only hard to preach in those places, but it was even hard to pray! Dr. B. R. Lakin said the ushers in those churches needed to be careful coming down the aisle—they might slip on the ice!

Do you know what is missing from those churches? It is the presence of the Holy Spirit. 2 Corinthians 3:17 teaches, "in any place where you find the Spirit of the Lord you will also find liberty in that place." The reverse is also true—where there is no liberty or freedom there is no Spirit!

And where there is no Spirit, there is no air in the greenhouse for the plants to grow!

Now listen, the most important item which distinguishes our church from so many dead churches is that the Holy Spirit is still here! *We actually want the Holy Spirit to be here!*

Think of it like this. Between the city of Boston and the state of Virginia, there are several houses which have a sign in the front yard. The sign says, "George Washington slept here." The first president of the United States slept here! I submit that we need a sign in the front yard of our church which says something far more important than that. We need a sign which says, "The Holy Spirit lives here."

Let me ask you a question. Which sign would you rather have on your property? "George Washington slept here" or "The Holy Spirit lives here"?

That brings us to how we can make sure the Holy Spirit is present in every church service, every Sunday School class, every meeting, every fellowship, and every activity!

It's fill-in-the-blank time for the section titled, "How to have the Holy Spirit present in a church service." These are simple steps, but I have found the simple steps are the most crucial steps of all!

First, ask the Holy Spirit to come with you to church. The most important person in the church service is not the pastor or the music director or even you, but He is the Holy Spirit!

Pay close attention to the next statement. Step #1 won't happen unless you spend time with the Holy Spirit *before* the service! One lesson we need to emphasize over and over again is that a good church service, a good class meeting or even a good committee meeting has to begin at home! The Bible says in the book of Proverbs chapter eight and verse seventeen, "those who seek Me early shall find Me." *What you do before coming to church is very important because that is the time when the Holy Spirit prepares your heart!*

There is a big difference between those people who come to church ready to enjoy church and those people who come because it is time for church. The difference shows in our faces, in the way we sing, in how well we pay attention, and in our overall enthusiasm for doing the work of God.

How much time did you spend this morning preparing your heart for today's service? Did you bring the Holy Spirit with you? Or did you just hope He would be here when you arrived? We must first ask the Holy Spirit to come with us to church.

The second fill-in-the-blank is to ask the Holy Spirit to bless someone through you! Write down "bless someone." It might be the person on the front row or the person on the back row. It might be someone you know very well or someone you hardly know.

Do you know you can be a blessing to someone in today's service? When I was a boy, we would often sing Ira B. Wilson's song, "Make Me a Blessing to Someone Today!" That song was written in the form of a prayer to God. It is a prayer to do what? "Dear God, make me a blessing to someone today!"

This song is based upon two truths. First, even I can be a blessing! I'm not to come here just to be a sponge and absorb everything I can, but I am also here to contribute and make today's service a blessing for you. Second, this means there are people here today who need blessed. I am just curious—how many people need blessed when they come to our church? We are a church of needy people, and we need the people around us.

That means we should come through our doors intending to be a blessing! In so doing, you will already be focused on the service!

Third, ask the Holy Spirit to remind you that He is a real person with real feelings. We too often forget the Holy Spirit is not an "it" like the Force in Star Wars, but the Holy Spirit is actually a "He." The Greek manuscript often uses the masculine gender, thereby indicating He is a real person!

It is true the King James Version occasionally uses "it" (see Romans 8:16 for an example) rather than "He." That is usually an accurate translation due to the rules associated with translating the Greek language. It is accurate because the Greek word *pneuma* is actually neuter—not masculine or feminine but neuter. Therefore, the associated pronoun has to be neuter to be grammatically correct.

However, and what I am about to say is true in that great passage in John chapters fourteen through sixteen, the Bible writer uses the *masculine* gender when he writes about the Holy Spirit in any other way.

For example, the Bible says in the book of John chapter sixteen, "It is necessary for you believers that I, Jesus, go back to heaven. If I do not go away, the Comforter who is the Holy Spirit will not come to you. But if I go away, I will send HIM (masculine gender) to you, and when HE (masculine gender) comes, HE (masculine gender) will convince the world it is sinning against God. HE (masculine gender) will come as the Spirit of truth, and HE (masculine gender) will guide you into all truth."

Rest assured, God the Holy Spirit is just as much a real, living personality as God the Father or God the Son. *That means the Holy Spirit has feelings just like Jesus has feelings!*

Have you ever had your feelings hurt? Was it fun or was it a real downer? How many of your friends enjoy having their feelings hurt? How many people schedule a "Come over and hurt my feelings" party? Probably none.

Let's take it one step further. Suppose someone hurt your feelings as you walked in the door this morning just as the church service began.

Would you feel like participating in today's service? It probably would ruin the entire service for you.

Do you know the Holy Spirit is the same way? Ephesians 4:30 says, "Stop grieving the Holy Spirit. Stop hurting the Holy Spirit. Stop insulting the Holy Spirit." The Greek construction of that verse indicates that the grieving was already happening as a daily routine, but the grieving needed to stop! The literal translation is, "Stop doing what you are doing and what you are doing is grieving or hurting or insulting the Holy Spirit."

The idea of grieving someone means that someone has feelings. In Ephesians 4:30 that someone is God the Holy Spirit.

I sometimes think His feelings are more sensitive than ours because His feelings are holy feelings. By contrast, our feelings have been hardened by sin. His feelings, though, are still soft because God is love, mercy, and grace all wrapped up in one person.

Do you know you can chase away the Holy Spirit from a church service? The Holy Spirit wants to be here, most of you want Him to be here, but someone can actually grieve the Holy Spirit and chase Him away from our church service.

Think with me about how we can disturb the Holy Spirit and even chase Him away. Here are four simple ways.

The first way is being irreverent—for example, talking in church and disturbing the people around you. Sometimes we talk so loudly we drown out the Holy Spirit. We draw the people's attention away from the Holy Spirit, and that is a big no-no. The Holy Spirit is trying to speak to them, but we're telling Him to get lost. My wife constantly reminds me that my whispering carries farther than my normal speaking voice. Some of us aren't blessed when it comes to being able to whisper.

How many of you have been bothered in church by people talking when they should not be talking? How many of you would like to be honest and say, "I've done it!" How many of you would like to apologize to the people around you? The old saying is so true, "Confession is good for the soul, but it's sure hard on the reputation."

The second way is not greeting one another with genuineness. In the days of the early church, the apostles urged the church members to greet one another with a holy kiss. In that day, a kiss on the cheek was an accepted way for men to greet men and women to greet women. That was the way of welcoming everyone to the church service. Notice it was also designed to be a "holy" kiss with the idea of genuineness or no hypocrisy. There was to be no shaking of hands and saying, "Good to see you," then moving on and saying, "I wish the old bat had stayed home today."

A "holy kiss" means I place value on seeing my brother or sister in Christ. I learned a long time ago that if Jesus could love me when I was unlovable, then He can help me love others who are sometimes unlovable.

The third way is by not having a submissive attitude. The Apostle Paul said one of the evidences of being filled with the Holy Spirit is "submitting yourselves one to another in the fear or reverence of God." (Ephesians 5:21)

Remember this: The only person in this church who has the right to use the two words, 'I want' is who? God because it is His church!

One of the hardest lessons we Christians have to learn is that everyone can't get their way at church. This may surprise you, but even pastors don't get their way on everything!

The worst thing which can happen in a church is when two hardhead-ed Christians bang heads and neither one is willing to submit to the other.

Do you know why so many churches split? It is because someone in-sisted on having his way!

I'll let you in on a little secret. The issue in most church fights isn't about the Bible. It isn't doctrinal! It may have been a silly issue like what songbook to buy (yes, it actually happened), which side the piano should be on (yes, it actually happened), or choosing new choir robes or even if we're going to allow choir robes (yes, both actually happened). I could mention so many arguments (I should not leave out the color of the carpet or who should be the new custodian), but when it came down to the end, the issue was all about power! Which party will rule?

This story may make you laugh when I tell you the name of the church. I recall preaching in a church named Harmony, but its real name was Dis-Harmony. The church had once been a good church with around seventy-five people in attendance, but then the fighting began. The peo-ple had been fighting for decades. Neither side would give in to the other side on anything.

They called me to preach one Sunday night. The service was as dead as a doornail. The best part about the service was when it was over. One side sat on the left; the other side sat on the right. I could tell which side had invited me because the right side amened my sermon, but the left side did not amen anything I said. If I had said, "Say amen if you're glad to be saved," the left side would not have amened.

Many years passed. They asked me to come back and preach. We went back on a Sunday night. There were twelve people present includ-ing the five in our own family. The amazing thing was they still hadn't learned to submit to one another. But the name on the door still said Harmony.

Let me mention a fourth way that can happen in those churches which end their service with a time of invitation. Some churches have gone away from the invitation, but it is my practice to end all of my Sunday morning services with an invitation.

You may not know this, but the invitation is the most sacred time of the entire church service. Everything in our service is pointed like an arrow to getting people to respond to God's call during the invitation. The music is directed to the human heart. The sermon is directed to the human heart. Then we come to the invitation, and we urge the human heart to surrender to the call of God.

Our normal practice is to stand and sing a gospel song. Please think through with me what we are doing at this time of the service.

Christians are praying for souls to be saved.

The preacher is urging people to come to Jesus.

People are singing, "If you are tired of the load of your sin, Let Jesus come into your heart."

One other thing is happening, and that one thing is the most important thing of all: The Holy Spirit is knocking on the door to someone's heart.

You can feel the Holy Spirit moving through the congregation. He is finding someone who needs the Lord!

Hey, the invitation becomes the highest peak in the entire service because the invitation is when you have to do something with what God has laid upon your heart.

But sometimes Christians forget what is happening. I have actually seen Christians use that time as "let's put on our coats so we can be the first out the door." They're announcing to everyone, "Your salvation isn't worth me staying here five more minutes. Your going to hell isn't as important as something else I have to do." In so doing, they slap the Holy Spirit in the face and say to Him, "Holy Spirit, Your work of dealing with people isn't important to me either."

And the Holy Spirit is grieved. His feelings are hurt because we're not on the same side that He is. The Holy Spirit then stops working in the hearts of the people. As a result, the man who might have gotten

saved doesn't get saved, and that backslider who might have gotten revived doesn't get revived!

May I ask you a very serious question? How much is a soul worth? Is
a soul worth five more minutes of your time?

I hope you think seriously about how we can hinder the Holy Spirit's
work in our church. *I pray you will dedicate yourself to making sure you
are not a problem for the Holy Spirit.*

Let's go back to our study sheet and the section titled "How to have
the Holy Spirit present in our church services."

Number four - ask the Holy Spirit to show you the good in your
brothers and sisters. (Note: Pick out a man of good reputation and ask
the congregation if _____ has some good points. Then ask his wife,
"Does he have any not-so-good points?" Everyone does! Which do you
think the devil wants us to think about?)

Do you think God wants us to focus on just the negative?

I once pastored a man who was like the Energizer Bunny. Let's call
him Bill. Bill was always going! He loved to get involved in things. He
would pester people to death about getting things done. There is usually
someone in every church who thinks the world will come to an end if
everything doesn't get done today and he was that person!

Bill would draw up plans for a new gym and get bids on it. He wanted a new shed roof for the vans and got bids on it, too. He did those
things even if we didn't have the money to pay for it!

Bill had more ideas than anyone I've ever seen. He would continually
pester me in a friendly way with those ideas. He was truly one of a kind.

My work schedule then changed, and I had to resign that ministry.
My friend, though, was not done with me! He sent me snail mail every
two weeks to keep me up to date with the church and community. He
even wrote a letter to the President of the Southern Baptist Convention.
President Paige Patterson was so kind that he took the time to respond
with a personal letter.

I loved Bill and Bill loved me. Like I say, he was one of a kind.

Well, we were invited back to the church for their 50th anniversary service. It came time for people to get up and talk about what their church meant to them. They knew that Bill wanted to go first, so they let him get up and talk.

Bill talked for fifteen minutes about the history of the church. The people fidgeted the entire time. Bill knew everything you could imagine about that church, and he told everything he knew! He finally sat down, then someone else stood up and said something about the church.

Then it came time for me to speak. I said, "Every pastor ought to be blessed with a Bill." Mouths dropped open! Then I said, "Because there are very few people who have as much pride in their church or take their church as seriously as Bill." When I finished my talk, those same mouths were now closed, and the people said, "Amen." Like I said earlier, he was truly one of a kind, and in a good sort of way. I will always miss him.

The Bible says, "By this action, all men will know that you are my disciples if you have love one for another." (John 13:35)

I'd like you to search your mind for a Christian that is hard to love. It might be a member of our church or someone at work or a neighbor. Then write down something that is good about that person—something you can thank God for. I say again, something in that person's life you can thank God for!

Do you know what? You have some really good brothers and sisters in this church! They are not perfect! No, not a single one of them! We know many of their faults, but they're still fairly good! Take a moment to thank God for them!

That brings us to number five on our study sheet. "Ask Him to speak to your heart in every service." Don't be like the Christian who went home and said, "I wish so-and-so had been there to hear that sermon. The pastor was preaching right at him."

"Ask God to speak to *your* heart in every service." A woman once went to her pastor and said, "I don't get anything out of your sermons." He said, "Did you bring anything to catch it in so you could take it home with you?" The best way to take the service home with you is to take it home in your heart.

"Ask Him to speak to your heart in every service." Personalize the service before the first song is sung, and you will be surprised at what might happen!

Far too many Christians go to church simply to occupy an hour of their day. They have no objective when they come. They contribute nothing while they are there. Unfortunately, they then leave with nothing to show they were even here.

But that was not so with King David in the Old Testament! David said in the 122nd Psalm,

> *I was glad when they said unto me, let us go up into the house of the Lord. One item have I desired of the Lord, that will I seek after: that I may dwell in the house of the Lord all the days of my life to behold the beauty of the Lord and to inquire in His temple. When Thou, Lord, said, 'Seek ye my face,' my heart said unto thee, 'Thy face, Lord, will I seek. Teach me Thy way, O Lord, and lead me in a plain path' . . . Wait on the Lord, be of good courage, and He shall strengthen thine heart. Wait, I say, on the Lord.*

Sometimes we forget that God is interested in talking not only to the person sitting next to us ("Now, Lord, You be sure to talk to that sinner next to me"), but He is also interested in talking to you.

Do you know that God wants to have a personal relationship with you? As a matter of fact, God is going to let you live with Him in heaven! We will someday live in the Father's house; that is another way of saying "God Himself shall be with us." We will live with the Father! That describes how much He wants to have a personal relationship with me. And with you, too!

We should come to church with the idea of developing further our personal relationship with Him.

Let's add some items to our study sheet. First, ask the Holy Spirit to speak to your heart through the singing. The singing touches our hearts and reminds us of how great God is, what he has done for us, plus what He is going to do for us! Teach yourself to pay attention to the words! I mean every word! Through the years I have noticed you can always tell if the people have their minds on the song by whether they sing with a smile. Unfortunately, some people look so sad they must be singing about hell!

Second, ask the Holy Spirit to speak to your heart through the praying. I enjoy hearing people pray and get hold of God! I don't like a formal prayer, but I do like a heart prayer—a prayer from the heart! Sometimes they remind me to pray about things I have forgotten!

Third, ask the Holy Spirit to speak to your heart through the older saints in the church. I remember one day driving past Charlie Dial's house. Charlie had been the music director for many years, but age had forced him to resign. I looked at his house and said, "I will miss that man when he's gone. His prayers and his life are a great blessing to me!" Charlie was as genuine as they come!

Our younger folk should never ever forget the gray-haired people or the no-haired people! Their journey will soon be your journey! They have already walked where you will someday walk! They have already fought the battles that you will someday fight! And please notice that they have survived! Let them teach you what they have learned by personal experience.

Fourth, ask the Holy Spirit to speak to your heart through the preaching from the Word of God. We live in an age which minimizes the work of preaching, but the Bible says it is by the foolishness of preaching that God still does His business. God has chosen the delivery method of preaching to do His work! And it still works!

I have heard all kinds of preaching in my life. I have heard great speakers like Lee Roberson, W. A. Criswell, B. R. Lakin, Hyman Appelman, and Adrian Rogers. I've even heard the old-time country preachers who would hack when they preached! Some preachers used outlines, whereas others didn't even know what an outline was! Their strategy was, "I am a letter preacher. I let 'er fly!"

The styles were different, and the methods of delivery were different! But I have learned through the years that I can be blessed by any style of preaching if I am right with God!

Whatever you do, don't turn off the preacher if his style rubs you the wrong way! Just pretend you're in Africa and he's the only preacher within a hundred miles! Then you'll listen as if your life depended upon it!

Fifth, ask the Holy Spirit to speak to your heart through the invitation. During one revival crusade, I asked the people to pray one particular prayer over and over again. It was the prayer, "Lord, give me a tender heart. Lord, give me tenderness toward the Holy Spirit!" Tenderness toward God's call upon your life! Tenderness toward someone in need! Ah, if you can sing an invitation hymn like "I Surrender All" without it touching your heart, all I can say is something must be wrong with you! How much we need a tender heart!

Now, what about you? Did you come today with the idea of making this particular service count not only for you but also for the rest of us? Or did you just show up with no particular agenda in mind?

I will never forget what happened one Sunday morning in the first church I pastored. I was directing the choir. We were singing some of our favorite songs such as "He Hides Me Behind the Cross." The people in the choir got happy and were singing with really big smiles! The Holy Spirit was all over the place!

There are three verses in that particular song. We enjoyed the song so much that we sang the last verse twice. (You can repeat verses in small churches!)

We then moved on to another song. Everyone was so happy! Then something bad happened. As we sang verse two, it was as if the doors and windows had opened and the Holy Spirit had run for the hills of West Virginia!

I didn't know what had happened. I was facing the choir at the time. I knew nothing had happened in the choir to change the mood, but it was obvious to me (and to others) that something bad had happened. The service died in that micro-second of time.

We sang another song, but the Holy Spirit did not return in that service. He was gone! I mean, totally gone!

I was so confused. I turned around toward the congregation. The only difference in the congregation was that a woman had entered the building during that one song!

I tried preaching then finally quit. The old preacher often said, "If you're still pumping sand after ten minutes, just quit trying!" It was no use!

When the service was over, I called the deacons to the front. I asked, "What happened to this service?" One deacon said, "Pastor, I don't know, but it happened when so-and-so came in the door. I felt the Holy Spirit leave, too."

The second deacon said, "I know what happened. That woman is our neighbor. This morning she and her son got into a fight. She grounded him. She said he couldn't come to Sunday School. Well, he sneaked out the back door and came to our house without telling us what had happened. He hitched a ride to Sunday School with my wife. His mother is now mad at my wife. My wife, though, didn't know what was happening until just a few minutes ago. His mother is now mad at all of us. That is why the Holy Spirit left the service today."

Have you ever heard a story like that? I have heard similar stories over the years. *It cannot be emphasized too much that the Holy Spirit has feelings, and He wants to feel welcome in our services.*

Let me ask you a question. Based on you alone in today's service, does the Holy Spirit feel welcome in this church service? Did you willingly receive from Him, or did you willfully refuse and reject Him? Did you say, "Holy Spirit, come and sit with me today," or did you say, "Not today . . . got other things on my mind."

Suppose we have someone here today who has never been saved and who will never be in church again for the rest of his life. That person needs Jesus. Could that person count on you to help him get to Jesus?

We are going to finish this service in a very unusual way. Please listen closely.

(Note: Have a large chair carried from the back of the church to the front of the church. Place the chair on the congregation's floor level directly in front of the pulpit.)

Who would you like to join us in this church service? I recommend God the Holy Spirit. I want to personally welcome God the Holy Spirit into this church service, and into every church service from this day forward. This chair is where the Holy Spirit can sit during our service.

Would you like to also invite the Holy Spirit to come and live here with us? If the answer is yes, I want you to slip out of your seat, to come and kneel around this chair and personally invite the Holy Spirit to come here and live with us.

Holy Spirit, you are welcome here!

5

WARNING SIGNS!

Can A Local Church Lose God's Presence?

Preparation: Prep some actors and gather the specified tools.

I hope all of you have the privilege to someday attend a pastor ordination service. The ordination usually begins with a very stressful event for the candidate called catechizing. The goal is to determine if the candidate is doctrinally qualified to be a pastor. After the questioning, the ordaining council (usually consisting of pastors from nearby churches) votes to approve or disapprove the candidate. If the answer is "we approve," the service moves on to the instruction phase. Pastors issue instructions, also known as charges, to the candidate and the church. The service normally concludes with a ceremony called the laying on of hands (a fancy way of saying all the preachers gather around the candidate and pray for his future ministry).

My own ordination began early on a Saturday morning and finished late in the afternoon. That day remains one of the happiest days of my life.

I recall attending a pastor ordination service for a young man who began his own ministry under me. The service was in its opening stage. The council was asking questions. Some of the questions were hard, but some were very easy.

One of the easy questions was, "Do you believe God will never leave you nor forsake you?" The answer, of course was, "I believe God will always be with me until the end of the world."

The same person then asked a question which ought to scare every pastor, every deacon, every teacher, and every church member half to death. He asked, *"But can God remove His presence from a local church?"*

Do you know what happened? It became very quiet.

We are going to answer that very question from the Word of God.

Can God remove His presence from _____ Church, from our own church?

Our text is found in two places. First, let's look at Matthew 21:18-20. This story is about Jesus. The Bible says, "In the morning, as he was returning to the city, he became hungry. And seeing a fig tree by the wayside, he went to it and found nothing on it but only leaves. And he said to it, 'May no fruit ever come from you again!' And the fig tree withered at once. When the disciples saw it, they marveled, saying, 'How did the fig tree wither at once?'" (Matthew 21:18-20, ESV) Keep this thought in your mind: Jesus condemned a once prosperous fig tree, and the fig tree withered away!

The second text is Revelation 2:1-5.

> *"To the angel of the church in Ephesus write: The One who holds the seven stars in His right hand, the One who walks among the seven golden lampstands, says this: 'I know your deeds and your toil and perseverance, and that you cannot tolerate evil men, and you put to the test those*

> *who call themselves apostles, and they are not, and you found them to be false; and you have perseverance and have endured for My name's sake, and have not grown weary. But I have this against you, that you have left your first love. Therefore remember from where you have fallen, and repent and do the deeds you did at first; or else I am coming to you and will remove your lampstand out of its place—unless you repent." (Revelation 2:1-5, NASB)*

This is a hard question, but it is a question which must be asked. Can God remove His presence from _____ Church, from our own church?

Verse five warns that the lampstand representing God's presence is *not* a permanent thing for any church. It *can be* removed. Let this warning sink in! The lampstand of God's presence is not a permanent thing for any church. It can be removed.

This letter was written to the church in the city of Ephesus. Forty years earlier the Apostle Paul wrote a letter to this same church called Ephesians. Those six chapters form one of the most glorious books in the entire Bible. Paul made it plain that everyone in that region should visit the church of Ephesus at least once in their lifetime! It was a very special place in much the same way as Spurgeon's Tabernacle!

Listen to what Paul wrote. "God has made you spiritually alive who were once dead in your sins!" "For by grace you have been saved and are still saved through faith!" "Unto Jesus Christ be glory in the church forever and ever, world without end!" "One Lord, one faith, one baptism!" And on and on the golden nuggets go.

It was the golden age for that church! The Church of Ephesus probably even wrote manuals on how to do church. It was a truly awesome church!

But then something changed, and Jesus wrote a much different letter forty years later. Jesus warned that He might remove the lampstand of God's presence from the same church which had once been a model church for everyone to study.

Two thousand years have now passed. No one in today's world talks about the modern, thriving church of Ephesus. No one!

Evidently, the church of Ephesus ignored the warning of Jesus. Sometime later God followed through with His warning. God pulled the plug on the church at Ephesus. *The church at Ephesus lost the presence of God!* It was not long until the church, which had once been something special, became the church which was now nothing.

How could such a thing happen to a once-thriving church? *Why did God's Greenhouse fail? Where did it go so badly wrong?*

Now pay attention. It is because of one basic reason, and this is a fill-in-the-blank. *The church of Ephesus was no longer a healthy church for God to grow people!*

Let's read of another church which was very similar to the church of Ephesus. This church was located in the city of Laodicea.

> *"'I know your works: you are neither cold nor hot. Would that you were either cold or hot! So because you are lukewarm, and neither hot nor cold, I will spit you out of my mouth. For you say, I am rich, I have prospered, and I need nothing, not realizing that you are wretched, pitiable, poor, blind, and naked. I counsel you to buy from me gold refined by fire, so that you may be rich, and white garments so that you may clothe yourself and the shame of your nakedness may not be seen, and salve to anoint your eyes, so that you may see." (Revelation 3:15-18, ESV)*

The church at Laodicea was another church which had everything going for it, but it was no longer a healthy church for God to grow people. This church was very similar to the fig tree in our first text. The tree existed, but it did not produce fruit. Therefore, Jesus pronounced a curse upon the tree. The fig tree immediately withered away and died. It was a miracle of the worst kind!

Fast forward to the 21st century! We can no longer attend the great Bible-believing church at Ephesus. We can no longer attend the prosperous church at Laodicea. We can no longer attend some churches in our own day which were once-thriving churches. Why? Sometimes the simplest answer is the best answer: those churches evolved from healthy churches to unhealthy churches! They were no longer healthy churches where God could grow people!

We look around us in this church, and we say, "That could never happen to us. We have a pastor who gives us the Word of God. We have a good Sunday School and worship attendance. Our choir's latest musical program was as good as any choir in town! We have a wonderful children's program and a good senior adult program, too! Surely the same thing could never happen to us."

But we can walk one block away from this church and see an empty church building where those people probably said the same words. We can see empty church buildings throughout this city, and in the neighboring countryside where churches used to exist, people used to get saved and baptized and grow, but something went very badly wrong, and those churches dwindled away.

Now pay attention! I know this series on the greenhouse seems very simple, perhaps even elementary, but in reality, it focuses on the most important issue in our church—in any church—and that is the issue of a healthy greenhouse.

If you want your children to achieve their potential, they will need a healthy, wholesome home environment. If you want a good effort from your employees, you must have a healthy, wholesome work environment where people have a desire to work. Likewise, if you want people to attend your church (and we do), you must have a healthy, wholesome environment where God can minister to your needs.

Rick Warren has written extensively on this very issue. In *The Purpose Driven Church*, he writes, "The key issue for churches in the 21st century will be church health, not church growth. Focusing on growth alone misses the point. When congregations are healthy, they grow the way God intends. Healthy churches don't need gimmicks to grow—they grow naturally."

The sad truth is that many more of our churches will close their doors in the upcoming decade if Jesus does not return first. During the 1950s, 1960s, 1970s, and 1980s the church was in a favorable environment for growth. The demographics were in our favor! The population was increasing! Living standards were improving! Wage growth was significant for most families!

But during that same time well over half of the Protestant churches either experienced a decrease in worship attendance, merged with another church or disbanded and closed their doors. Not just half but well over half! What makes it even worse is that this decline occurred *before* the Baby Boomers became senior adults!

In other words, the problem existed even when we did not realize it existed! The growth in the so-called "mega-churches" masked the problem that was happening in so many other churches.

Is there a process which will keep this sad ending from happening to us? The answer is yes. It is very important we learn from the mistakes of others, so we do not repeat those same mistakes ourselves. George Santayana gave us some very wise words when he said, "Those who cannot remember the past are condemned to repeat it."

What can we learn from the mistakes of other churches in this city?

What causes a greenhouse to fail?

1. Wrong Attitude by the Workers

Webers Greenhouse was the largest greenhouse for a hundred miles in any direction. People would travel a great distance to tour that greenhouse. I even remember an occasion when one group hosted its annual meeting inside those facilities. The complex met many, many needs.

But the greenhouse no longer exists. It was razed to the ground a few years ago. What happened? Two men (Leo and Ray) operated the greenhouse for their entire adult life. Their youthful years became middle-age years and their middle-age years became senior-adult years, and quite honestly, their get up and go got up and went. Declining health forced both men to give up a work they enjoyed with all their heart!

The family reviewed its options and found it had no attractive options. Most importantly, no one in the family wanted to assume the responsibility of maintaining the operation! Then one day the greenhouse quietly closed. Sometime later it was demolished, and the property was sold. Even our rental house was demolished! The property became a trailer park!

There is a parallel truth that relates to churches like our own. Let me share how it works in a church.

We say, "Yes, I believe in the children's program, but don't ask me to get involved. I believe in the outreach program and seeing people saved, but don't ask me to get involved. I fully support the Sunday School, but don't expect me to be here. I believe we need a midweek service, but don't look for me!"

There is an old saying which all of us need to heed: "A church like ours is made up of people just like me." What kind of church would we have if everyone was exactly like you?

The point is you are the greenhouse! Each and every one of you! So, get involved!

2. Wrong Ingredients Are Used

Let's assume our greenhouse wants to grow one thousand petunias. Suppose we feed pizza every day to our petunias! How much will our petunias grow? Suppose we substitute Pepsi for water. Let's throw in some spaghetti, too! What would then happen? The answer is not much would happen!

Think back to our goal as a greenhouse. Is our goal one of growing people physically or spiritually? If we wish to grow people physically, we will need plenty of fruit, vegetables, meat, milk, water and throw in some ice cream, too!

On the other hand, if the goal is to grow people spiritually, we will need spiritual ingredients!

1 Peter 2:1 teaches we are to be like, "newborn infants who have just been born again into the family of God; as newborn infants, we are to thirst for the spiritual milk of God's Word so that we can start growing toward adulthood." The newborn stage, of course, will be followed by a later stage when we can start on the meat or the deeper teachings of the Word of God!

Let's be sure we can agree on this issue. Jesus prayed to God the Father in John chapter seventeen. He prayed, "Father, sanctify these apostles through the truth. Let them experience transforming truth! Your Word—the written Word of God—is truth!"

Let me do this very simply and make sure you get it. I need milk—where do I get milk? I get milk from the Word of God. Second, I need meat. Where do I get meat? I get meat from the Word of God. Third, I need truth. Where do I get truth? I get truth from the Word of God.

Those three statements are very significant. One of the temptations for the modern church is to become more entertainment-oriented and less Bible-oriented.

Pastor Mark Stump blessed us as our revival evangelist. Mark pastors one of the largest churches in West Virginia, yet he preaches some of the longest sermons you will hear anywhere. He is definitely not an entertainment preacher! If you like the Bible, you will enjoy Mark! If you don't like the Bible, you probably won't attend more than one time! Mark discussed this very issue at great length in one sermon. He pointed out that too many people attend church to be entertained, not to grow! He was right!

Jesus faced a similar problem when He fed the 5,000! John chapter six begins with Jesus feeding the 5,000, but it ends with the 5,000 leaving! Jesus then asked the remaining twelve, "Are you also leaving Me?" (We should note that one of the remaining twelve would eventually leave. At that time Jesus identified Judas as a *diabolos* or devil. Perhaps

Judas was looking for political or financial gain rather than spiritual gain. We'll leave that subject for another day.)

It is critically important we understand what God *did not* promise to bless and what God *did* promise to bless. For example, God did not promise to bless entertainment! But God did promise to bless His Word! Isaiah 55:11 teaches, "My Word that I proclaim shall not return to Me empty, but it will accomplish whatever My goal is!"

The Bible also adds in 1 Corinthians 1:21, "It pleased God by the foolish or moronic technique of preaching to save those who believe." Verse eighteen adds, "through preaching God demonstrates His power to those of us who are saved!" Mark 9:29 says, "This kind of demon is very powerful and can be exorcised only by prayer." (The KJV includes the phrase "and fasting.") One final, powerful scripture: "Jesus said, 'When I am lifted up, I will draw all men to Me.'" (John 12:32)

What stands out in all of those verses? It is the absolute certainty of success in the way that God defines success! "*Knowing* that your labor is not in vain *in the Lord!*" (1 Corinthians 15:58) Praise the Lord for such a certainty!

Interestingly, failure is not caused by competition such as Sunday night television or family outings, etc. Leo's plants grew the same regardless of how those worldly activities played out. The plants grew because Leo and Ray were committed to the greenhouse process. They allowed nature to grow the plants regardless of the competition!

"When we stay with God, God will stay with us. The competition will be God's problem to solve—not our problem to solve."

The evangelist D. L. Moody often said, "The world has yet to see what God can do with a man who is wholly yielded to Him." We can paraphrase those words to read, "The world has yet to see what God can do with a church which is totally yielded to Him."

Rest assured, God is not worried about the competition! I submit to you that worrying about the competition is worrying about the wrong thing!

The biblical answer for competition is found in Acts 17:6. "The rebellious crowd criticized Paul and his companions by telling the city council, 'These men have turned the world upside down and are now doing the same in our own community.'" My goodness! Such great results even though Paul was faced with the competition of demon-possessed sorcerers! Try topping that level of competition! Thank God, we're just dealing with the competition of things like television!

Our attention should not be on the competition but upon building the best greenhouse we can build. Yes, God will then be free to do His work in His way for His glory!

3. Wrong Tools Are Used

There are some tools which are appropriate for a greenhouse. There are other tools which are inappropriate. For example, Leo and Ray never used a bulldozer to take care of the weeds. They never used dynamite to get rid of a pebble.

Unfortunately, the devil has many free tools which he has made available to our church. These tools will destroy our plants.

(Note: The youth will bring in the tools mentioned below. The youth will read a script associated with each tool. It's okay to have two or more youth carrying the same tool. The participation of all is important.)

- *"Digging Up the Past Tool"*—a shovel. Script: I have the "Digging Up the Past Tool." My tool enables me to dig up the past. I know what everyone did ten years ago in this church. My calling in life is to make sure we never forget what happened or forgive what happened. My favorite words are, "Do you remember when so-and-so did that? How can we ever trust that person again? Don't you think it's time that person apologized for what he did? Yes, I LOOOOOOOOOVE to dig up the past!"

122

- *"Criticism Tool"*—a hedge trimmer. Script: I have the "Criticism Tool." My tool enables me to cut people down. I can critique your performance and show you where you have room for improvement. I want you to know that's especially true for all of you who are listening to me today! If you people were really smart, you would ask me to run this church! My advice to all of you is this: To avoid hearing my criticism simply say nothing, do nothing, and be nothing. If you do that, you won't have to listen to me!

- *"Gossip Tool"*—a seed spreader. Script: My tool is one of the most valuable tools. It is the "Gossip Tool." This tool enables me to tell everyone what is happening down at the church and I do mean everyone. The church bulletin doesn't always tell the whole story. You see, I want everyone to know all of the really juicy stuff. The more my tool is quoted and used, the more I am believed. My victims cannot protect themselves against me because I have no name, no face, and tracking me down is impossible. Praise the devil, once I touch a reputation that reputation is never the same. My tool is a really good one. I'll even loan it to you after church. It is the Gossip Tool.

- *"Clock Watching Tool"*—an alarm clock. (Arrange for the alarm clock to ring during the presentation.) Script: The "Clock Watching Tool" is available for $19.99 plus $20.00 for shipping and handling. My tool allows me to keep everything on schedule. I know whether the church service is on time, or if it is going too slow. It never goes too fast, so we don't have to worry about that being a problem. I know the right length of time to spend on the prayer list, the right amount of time for the offering prayer, and even how long it takes to sing all four verses of "The Old Rugged Cross." I have insisted for years we need to place a clock on the pulpit so everyone will stay on schedule. How about someone giving the preacher a five-minute warning when it is time to go home? Well, my time is up, and I hope the next person stays on time, too!

- *"You Didn't Do It My Way Tool"*—double ended wrench. Script: "I am the "You Didn't Do It My Way Tool," and I don't really care how the Clock Watching Tool said to do it. I am happy to say my tool is the busiest tool in this church. This tool is great because there are two ends to my tool, but for some reason, the church people are always using the wrong end! It never fails! No one does it the way I would do it! The deacons don't do it my way. The trustees sure don't do it my way. The Sunday School—I've given up on the Sunday School. And the offerings—we can't even take up the offerings the right way. What my church needs to do is put me in charge for a few weeks and then we'd all be happy because I know all of you would LOOOOOOOOOOOOOOOVE to do it my way."

- *"Discouragement Tool"*—rake. Script: Hear ye! Hear ye! Any of you can use my "Discouragement Tool." I hear the church leaders talking about doing this or doing that. I'm here to tell you it can't be done. No, it can't be done. Did you hear me? It just can't be done. You see, we've never done it that way before. Besides, it will cost too much money to do it, plus no one here knows how to organize it! Then again, we don't have the right-sized facilities. As a matter of fact, we probably would need a government permit to even begin. Plus, if it worked, we'd probably need to expand the auditorium to take in all the newcomers, and you know how newcomers are—they just bring problems, and if there's one thing we don't need, it is more problems. I think we ought to just leave things the way they are. AMEN!

(Note: The youth leave to applause.)

Let this pastor add one more. Sometimes we very selfishly use the wrong tool of our own people. I knew of one young man who announced his calling to the ministry. He had a special ability, but the church stood in his way. The church discouraged him from pursuing his dream of going away to school to study for the ministry. Do you know why? The church did not want to lose a good worker even if he was moving on to a better work! It was one of the most selfish things I have ever seen in a church! That church had lost sight of its purpose! *Its purpose was to grow people rather than having people grow the church!*

One truth should stand out in this study: If we take care of growing people, God will take care of growing His church.

4. Wrong Goal Is Pursued

Let's go back to Revelation chapter three and verse seventeen. Look with me at what the church of Laodicea pursued. Verse seventeen says this church pursued material wealth. The verse seems to indicate the church accomplished that goal because the church saw itself as needing nothing more.

Let me share with you the words of an unknown preacher. I have his quote, but I do not have his name. He wrote,

I would warn you about the peril of a lesser goal. Often what was merely meant to be the means becomes the end, and we arrive at our little goals and have no ambition to reach the main objective.

I asked a preacher, 'How are you getting along?'

He said, 'We are living in idolatry—just sitting around admiring our new church. We have arrived; we have it made—no more worlds to conquer.'

What ought to be a milestone has become a millstone. We have run out of goals."

I am afraid too many churches are now skipping the planting process. They are limiting their ministry to growing the seed they, or others, have already planted. This is especially true of a satisfied church. The thinking is, "Everyone in my family is saved. Why should I care about another family?" Or "I educated my children in the children's program. Why should I do the same for someone else's children?"

Why should I? Who cares? Well, I know of one Person who cares! The Bible says, "For God so loved the **whole** world!" The whole world is more than my own little world or your own little world. The last time I checked, it is a world of more than *seven billion people*. If I love like God, I will now love seven billion people. That's seven billion more than my own family.

Jesus said, "Lift up your eyes and look upon the fields at how much still remains to be harvested." It is not a time to retire, but it is a time to reap.

God wants fruit! Proverbs 11:30 reminds us that "he who wins souls is wise." John 15:16 says, "I chose you to go forth and produce lasting fruit!"

Maybe we can summarize it like this. It's the last fill-in-the-blank. Our task is, *"To develop an environment where God can plant His seed and bring that seed to full maturity in Jesus Christ."* The church of Ephesus forgot that. The church of Laodicea forgot that. Will we also forget that?

One of my greatest blessings was to be a member of Highland Park Baptist Church in Chattanooga, Tennessee, in the late 1970s. The church had 50,000 members at the time. It averaged more than 10,000 in Sunday School including its seventy branch churches, two City Missions and afternoon Sunday School. It was believed to be the second highest average attendance in the United States at that time. The church even owned a free summer camp for children, especially the less fortunate children of downtown Chattanooga. It was an incredible ministry to be around.

The front wall of the auditorium (over the choir) posted the motto of the church (also known as "The Church of The Green Light"). The lower part of the wall included a map of the world. The upper part of the wall included the words of Mark 16:15, "Go ye into all the world and preach the gospel to every creature." More than fifty percent of the offerings went to mission work of some kind!

There was nothing more to add to that church's motto! The main thing is to *keep* the main thing as the main thing. I have never known a church to lose its spiritual health *if* that church was deeply committed to the Great Commission! Never! That kind of church is doing what God most wants done! That's the kind of church where God wants to grow people to be His kind of people!

But I have known too many churches which tried to find success in bypassing the Great Commission. If someone approached the altar, they had to be careful not to slip on the ice in the aisle!

Highland Park Baptist Church accomplished the Great Commission goal for more than four decades. That greenhouse changed so many lives including my own. But, unfortunately, life happens, and there was a generational change. And then there was another generational change. The focus changed, too. I am sure there were a myriad of reasons why the focus changed. The church's decline came quickly. The property was sold, and the few remaining members relocated to another location.

If such a decline could happen to Highland Park Baptist Church as well as the First Baptist Church of both Ephesus and Laodicea, it can also happen to us. *And it will happen to us if we fail to do what God has called us to do.*

The story of Westminster Cathedral in London, England, is worth repeating. Everyone has heard of that prestigious church. One day an old woman visited the cathedral. The guide showed her where all the famous people were buried—people like Oliver Cromwell, Isaac Newton, Charles Dickens, David Livingstone, and Lord Alfred Tennyson. The guide bragged about the building's architecture and its history.

Finally, this old woman stopped him and asked, "Sonny, has anyone been saved around here lately?"

The most important thing to God was the one thing that no longer counted to man.

Can a local church lose God's presence? Yes, it can.

The big question is: Will you let it happen to us?

6

KEY INGREDIENTS TO A SUCCESSFUL GREENHOUSE ENVIRONMENT

How Important Is 'Us'?

Preparation: a flip chart, four packages of seed. Prep some actors.

A man saw a worker pushing a wheelbarrow over a rough piece of ground. This worker was hot, dirty, and tired. It was plain to everyone that he had worked hard that day.

The man asked the worker what he was doing. The worker replied, "I am making a garden." The naïve onlooker said in surprise, "But I thought gardens just grew on their own."

I wonder, how many of you believe gardens grow on their own without any help from anyone? How many of you believe Christians grow on their own without any help from anyone? How many of you believe churches grow on their own without any help from anyone? How many of you believe the choir sings well on its own without any help from anyone? How many of you believe the offering gets received on its own without any help from anyone? How many of you believe communion gets prepared and served on its own without any help from anyone? How many of you believe the AWANA children get here on their own without any help from anyone?

The answer, of course, is none of you. Not one of those items can happen on its own.

That leads me to the question, What makes those items happen? Those items happen because of a very simple lesson that we sometimes forget.

Let's read our text again and fill in the first blank on our study sheet. We haven't read the entire text for a few sessions, so it would be good to read all of it again and get it in our minds.

For the sake of simplicity, let's read from the Holman Christian Standard Bible. The text is 1 Corinthians 3:1-10.

> *Brothers, I was not able to speak to you as spiritual people but as people of the flesh, as babies in Christ. I gave you milk to drink, not solid food because you were not yet ready for it. In fact, you are still not ready because you are still fleshly. For since there is envy and strife among you, are you not fleshly and living like unbelievers? For whenever someone says, "I'm with Paul," and another, "I'm with Apollos," are you not unspiritual people? What then is Apollos? And what is Paul? They are servants through whom you believed, and each has the role the Lord has given. I planted, Apollos watered, but God gave the growth. So then neither the one who plants nor the one who waters is anything, but only God who gives the growth. Now the one planting and the one watering are one in purpose, and each will receive his own reward according to his own labor. For we are God's coworkers. You are God's field, God's building. According to God's grace that was given to me, I have laid a foundation as a skilled master builder, and another builds on it. But each one must be careful how he builds on it. (1 Corinthians 3:1-10, HCSB)*

The concept is very simple. Everything you see around you including the building, the carpet, the windows along with the people are God's plowed field. This whole thing we call a church experience is a place where plants are grown. It is a place just like the miniature greenhouse which is in front of us. Our church is a greenhouse designed to grow plants, and the plants represent people like you and me!

What does our greenhouse need to grow you and me to maturity?

Let's fill in the first blank on today's study sheet. Verse nine says, "We are God's coworkers." The King James Version says, "laborers together with God." In other words, we are working directly alongside God in the very same work!

That leads us to another fill-in-the-blank. "The work cannot be done without God, but He has decided not to do it without us!"

Let's talk about the last word you wrote down: the little two-letter word "us." What kind of people does "US" have to be for God to do His work? Does "us" have to be college graduates because if that's the requirement some of you would now be able to leave. Does "us" have to be wealthy people because if that's the requirement some of you would now be able to leave. Does "us" have to be good singers or good teachers or good administrators because if that's the requirement some of you would now be able to leave. Does "us" have to be great with children or great with senior adults or great in visiting the sick because if that's the requirement some of you would now be able to leave.

What kind of people does "US" have to be for God to do His work?

Look again at verse seven at how the Bible answers that question. It reads like this: "neither is the one who plants anything (that means it does not depend upon whether we have great abilities or no abilities), neither is the one who waters anything either!" Once again, it does not depend upon whether we have great abilities or no abilities because in the end who is it that gives the increase? It is God! That means God can use every single one of us as His co-worker!

Ask yourself, "Have I been born again? Am I saved by the blood of the crucified Son of God?" If the answer is yes, then you are qualified to be one of God's coworkers! Laborers together with Almighty God Himself!

Let me share something with you which is very important. Sometimes we get the idea that the church can't get along without us! We have this idea, "I'm so important, and if you don't believe it then let me tell you how important I am. I'm the best singer in the choir . . . the best deacon . . . the best teacher . . . the best giver . . . the best administrator . . . the best worker because I'm involved in everything . . . if I leave everything will fall apart!"

So that person leaves for whatever reason, and do you know what happens? It happens over and over again, doesn't it? That person leaves, and the church *doesn't* fall apart. Instead, sinners still get saved, the Bible still gets preached, Christians still get blessed, the Sunday School and children's program keep plugging along.

Time passes. Those people then start pouting because no one begged them to come back. No one went to them on bended knees and said, "Please, come back." Those people then become the most miserable Christians you have ever seen!

I am not trying to minimize what you personally are doing in this church but what I am saying is this: whatever you do, don't ever get impressed with your ability because your ability is still nothing to God! Just when you think you can't be replaced, God will raise up someone to replace you! After all, it's His church, and He has more available resources than just you!

Remember this (by the way this is another fill-in-the-blank): We don't come here to be the *boss* but we come here to *serve,* and it is a wonderful privilege to serve Jesus at _____ Church! AMEN!

So what kind of people does "US" have to be for God to do His work?

Fill in the blank on item C. Here is the answer: "US" is not based upon our ability but upon our availability.

Therefore, are you—not the person sitting next to you but are you—available to help build "God's Greenhouse, an environment where God can plant His seed and bring that seed to full maturity in Jesus Christ"?

If the answer is yes—if you are making yourself available—let's look at four key ingredients to us having a successful greenhouse at

---

1. Defined Goal

We know what our broad goal is because it is a clearly defined goal. We will narrow this broad goal as we progress through the God's Greenhouse study, but our first emphasis must be the broad goal. If we don't succeed at the broad goal, we'll never succeed at the narrower goal of making the greenhouse experience very personal to each one of us.

Here is our broad goal: we want to create an environment where God can plant His seed and bring that seed to full maturity in Jesus Christ. Let me show you what it means to have a defined goal.

(Note: Display a flip chart next to the pulpit. The chart has a giant bull's-eye drawn on it. Ask two teenagers to stand at a distance of three feet from the chart. Give them a marker. Ask the congregation to identify their goal. The goal is to put a mark inside the bull's-eye. Ask the teens to close their eyes, count to ten very quickly, step forward and touch the marker to the chart. The teens will hopefully put a mark inside the bull's-eye.)

(Note: Ask an adult to do the same. This adult has previously been clued in as to what will soon happen. His distance is also three feet from the chart. Give him a marker. Ask the congregation to identify his goal. The goal is to put a mark inside the bull's-eye. Ask the adult to close his eyes, count to ten very slowly *to compensate for his age*, step forward and touch the marker to the chart. As he counts, *turn the flip chart around* so there is no bull's-eye for him to touch. His mark is obviously *outside* the bull's-eye.)

(Note: The pastor then asks the congregation if the adult hit the bull's-eye. The answer is no. Then comes the punch line! The adult disagrees with our conclusion and states, "Yes, I did because I always set my goals *after* I finish the work. That way I always hit my goal.")

(The adult proceeds to draw a bull's-eye plus other circles around his mark. The pastor then makes the point that you can always hit your goal, if you set your goal after the work is done. But did the adult hit the goal which we established in the beginning? No.)

Now here is why that is so important. Millions of church people will be in church today who have no idea what their goal is. They will sing, listen to the sermon, give their offering, then go home. Suppose someone asks them, "Did you accomplish your goal today?" They will probably answer, "What goal are you talking about?"

They are like the woman who was talking to another woman as they were leaving church. She said, "Did you see the hat Mrs. So-and-So had on today?" "No." "Did you see the yellow dress that So-and-So had on today?" "No." "Did you see the new hairdo of So-and-So?" "No." "Well, it didn't do you any good to go to church today, did it?"

The truth is if you aim at nothing, you will also hit nothing. That is tragic! If you set your goals *after* you finish, you will *always* hit your goals. That is equally tragic!

What then is the scriptural basis for our goal? It is Matthew 28:19-20. Remember: This passage affects every ministry we undertake. The passage says, "Go therefore and make disciples of all nations, baptizing them in the name of the Father and of the Son and of the Holy Spirit, teaching them to observe all that I have commanded you. And behold, I am with you always, to the end of the age." (Matthew 28:19-20, ESV)

This passage contains two basic stages. The first stage is getting people saved! The word "saved" has the idea of being rescued. That's why we sing, "Rescue the perishing, care for the dying, snatch them in pity from sin and the grave!" The whole world is going to hell. That's a staggering thought. The Bible even goes so far as to say that hell has enlarged itself. That means hell has grown bigger than its original design in order to handle the growing number of people! Most people in this community are blind to the truth. We want to snatch them out of the fire!

Do you believe people can get saved because you pray for them? Isn't it a thrill when you pray for someone and that someone gets saved?

Don't raise your hands, but think about your prayer time. Can you give me the names of three people on your prayer list for salvation? I am not asking for twenty or ten or even five but just three. Three people who can count on you to pray for their salvation!

You say, "Pastor, I cannot think of ten or five or even three. I can tell you about people who are sick because we publish their names in the bulletin, but I cannot tell you about people who are lost."

Let me give you a suggestion. One church had a TEN MOST WANTED LIST. They published the list weekly! What an idea for a church or small group! The church then prayed for those ten names. Some people prayed for the list once a week, some people prayed for the list two or three times a week, and some people prayed for the list seven times a week. As a result, some unsaved people were mentioned in prayer at least fifty times in seven days! Imagine the consequences! If those ten people don't get saved, they'll become so miserable that they'll wish they had gotten saved!

If you have never been saved, I want you to know one of our reasons for existing is to help you get saved!

The second stage of ministry in the Matthew passage is help people grow and eventually grow up to look like Jesus! Jesus said we are to teach you the Bible so you can obey everything Jesus has commanded you!

The Apostle Paul said it like this, "Now that you've gotten saved let this attitude be in you which was also in Christ Jesus so I may present every single one of you to God as a mature, grown-up Christian—a Christian who is able to handle anything the devil throws against him because he is mature in the faith."

Fill in the blank. The only thing which is more beautiful than a flower is a mature, Spirit-filled Christian who looks just like Jesus.

Keep writing! The only way this goal can be achieved is to win them one by one and then to grow them one by one! Do you think this is a good way to express our goal?

But if you don't aim at that goal in the church service, you're not going to hit that goal! If you don't aim at that goal in the youth program, you're not going to hit that goal! If you don't aim at that goal in the Sunday School class—hey, you can be the best teacher the world has ever known, but if you don't aim at that goal, you're not going to hit that goal!

The same truth applies to the children's program, the senior adult program, the music program, the prayer groups, including all of our outreach programs!

Let me throw something in for free! Do you ever think about how a normal church service is structured? Every church follows the same basic pattern. It begins with what? Singing, followed by what? Preaching, and the service ends with an invitation.

How many services begin with the invitation followed by the preaching then the singing? Why not?

(Note: Flip to a plain sheet on the flip chart and draw an arrowhead. The arrowhead is wide at the bottom but comes to a point at the top.)

Every church service is like an arrowhead because every service is pointed toward a goal.

(Note: Write the word "singing" at the broadest part of the arrowhead. Review today's bulletin for the song selection.)

This morning we began by singing, "I Remember the Day." That was a hymn about our salvation! The second song was an old favorite about salvation written by William Newell, "At Calvary." The third song was, "All Because Of God's Amazing Grace." Then came the fourth song, "Let the Lower Lights Be Burning." That hymn was about our responsibility to others. I am just wondering, did that song challenge you?

The singing is normally followed by the sermon. The sermon is usually focused on a particular theme. The pastor's message may be focused on evangelism or maybe on encouragement. The sermon may be designed to challenge you or maybe to educate you. The sermon continues to move the service to its conclusion.

Then we come to what we call the invitation. Why do we call it the invitation? It is a very sacred time when *we invite everyone to do what God wants us to do!*

Did God somehow touch your heart in the service? If yes, then it is time to make a commitment to what God wants you to do! You can make that commitment in your seat or by coming forward for prayer.

You see, the singing is not an end in itself, but often we act like it is. The preaching is not an end in itself, but often we preachers act like it is. All of the prayers, testimonies and greeting are not an end in themselves. Even the invitation is not an end in itself, but rather it is a time to get people to do what God wants them to do!

We can walk away today saying, "That was the prettiest singing I ever heard or the best sermon I ever heard or what a Sunday School lesson that was!"

All of that is nice, but what is really nice is being able to say, "I did what God wanted me to do with that service. I allowed God to draw me closer to Him in that service so that I know Him better! I know even better what He wants me to do! I feel His touch upon my life, and I love Him more now than I did yesterday!"

Do you know that God wants to do something in your heart today? He wants to draw you closer to Him!

This may sound crude, but the church service is like a big fish hook with the juiciest worm you have ever seen! You're the fish! Our goal is to get you to go after the worm and get hooked for Jesus!

The choir has sung, and you have gotten a taste for how juicy Jesus is. The special music told you how juicy Jesus is. Someone testified about how juicy Jesus is. The preacher told you how juicy Jesus is. Now comes the invitation, and you want more of Jesus than you have ever had before!

When you sing "I Surrender All," you now mean "I Surrender All." When you sing, "Have Thine Own Way, Lord," you now mean "Have

Thine Own Way." You now agree with the words, "Were the whole realm of nature mine, that were a present far too small, love so amazing, so divine, demands my soul, my life, my all."

You're like the Apostle Paul crying out, "That I may know Him!" Why? Because there is no one quite like Jesus, that's why!"

Luther B. Bridgers wrote the words,

> *"Jesus, Jesus, Jesus,*
> *Sweetest name I know,*
> *Fills my every longing,*
> *Keeps me singing as I go."*

Paul wrote, "Our goal is that we may present every man as a mature man in Christ Jesus—nothing lacking but rather mature in love, joy, peace, long-suffering, gentleness, goodness, faith, meekness and self-control!"

It happened in a church service in New York City. A man walked to the pulpit and said, "The time has come to dismiss the service, but before we do, I want to introduce a very famous preacher who is visiting with us tonight. His name is Gypsy Smith. Brother Smith, will you come and speak to us?"

The great preacher moved quietly to the pulpit. Everyone wondered what the great preacher would say. Without a word he lifted his hands toward heaven, and he began to sing, "Where He leads me, I will follow! I'll go with Him, with Him all the way!"

When he finished singing, the place was so quiet you could have heard a pin drop. He then looked at the people and said, "When we give Jesus the privilege of leading our lives every day that we live, life will then become beautiful."

What does God want you to do with today's service?

2. Directions Are Followed

If we want God to give the increase, we must do the planting and watering God's way! Have you ever put something together then checked the instructions to see what went wrong? Some of you women think that's the way a man is automatically wired, and I won't disagree with that!

Is there anyone here who would consider himself to be a master gardener?

(Note: Before the service choose a very unlikely prospect as a master gardener! That person raises his hand and says, "Pastor, I am so good I could even write books about gardening." Of course, the church knows otherwise! The pastor responds, "I have some seed I need planted. Would you like to plant this seed for me?" The person takes four seed packages and places a package under the front pew pad, one in the window sill, one in someone's shirt pocket, and one in a lady's purse. He is then seated.)

How many of you have faith those seeds will grow?

(Note: Read the instructions on the seed package. The instructions state how deep one is to bury the seed, etc. If you want to grow the seed, then you had better follow the instructions.)

The Bible is our instruction manual! 2 Timothy 3:16-17 says, "All scripture is God-breathed or inspired by God Himself. That means all scripture is therefore profitable for doctrinal teaching, for convicting you when you are wrong, for correction and getting you back to doing what is right, and all of that leads to training in the ways of righteousness so you can become complete or mature in the Christian faith."

The lesson is clear! When you get away from the Bible, you will not accomplish God's goal for our church!

For example, the Southern Baptist Convention wandered away from strong Bible teachings in the early 1900s. As a result, the churches experienced lower baptisms, lower attendance, and less Bible beliefs. The people became more involved in social issues than soul issues! Quite honestly, the convention lost its way. Many Bible-believing churches left the convention. Those churches added fuel to the independent Baptist movement which became a very important movement in much of the twentieth century.

Then along came Southern Baptist leaders like W. A. Criswell, Charles Stanley, Adrian Rogers, and others. They organized the Bible believers and restored the Bible to its rightful place. The Convention went back to doing the Great Commission. Doubts about inspiration were replaced with certainties about, "Thus saith the Lord." Some denominational leaders were let go and rightly so!

This started a mini-revival throughout the convention. A renewed emphasis upon the importance of missions, both at home and abroad, helped drive the success of the convention because the people went back to doing it God's way!

Fill in the blank. There is no substitute for doing it God's way. No substitute at all!

You may say, "But the Bible will offend someone!" That is true! Please remember, though, that person's problem will not be with us but with God! The Bible even admits the preaching of the cross is offensive to those who love their sin!

But that is not my problem. That is not your problem either. Our job is to follow God's directions so that God can give the increase!

3. Dealing with Big Life Issues

The third key ingredient we must keep constantly in front of us is that we are dealing with big life issues.

Let me ask you four very important questions. Question number one, where do you work? (Note: Get three people to mention the place of their employment.) Question number two, what do you deal with at that business? (Note: Get answers from two people.) Question number three, do you take your work seriously? Raise your hand if the answer is yes.

Last question, is there anything you do at work which is as important as dealing with a human life?

Let me ask the fourth question again. Is there anything you do at work which is as important as dealing with a human life? For most of us, the answer is no.

Let's imagine you are talking about the ballgame when one of your coworkers has a heart attack. Do you ignore the heart attack and keep talking about the ballgame? No! You call 9-1-1! You find someone who knows CPR! You make the person comfortable! That person gets all of your attention!

Why? It is because there is nothing at work which is more valuable than a human life!

Likewise, there is nothing more valuable on this property than the souls of men, women, boys, and girls. Jesus asked the question, "What does it profit a man if he gains the whole world and loses his very own soul? What will a man give in exchange for his soul?" (Matthew 16:26)

Matthew 25:46 says, "Those who do not believe in Jesus as Lord and Savior will go away into everlasting, unending punishment, but the righteous will go into everlasting, unending life."

Fill in the blank. The reality is that everyone we touch will live forever. I want you to know that forever is a very long time.

So often people just come to church and never think about what is happening—that we are dealing with life and all the issues associated with life.

Look at the person sitting next to you and say the word "hello." Keep looking at that person and understand one more item. That person may never sit there again. This may be the last time you ever see that person. Wonder what we need to tell that person today?

Maybe we need to talk to that person about the weather. How about college football, or the situation in the Middle East, or electing the next president?

Somehow those issues don't feel like big life issues. That person needs something for the soul because we are not dealing with their big toe, their bad eyesight, or their weak knees! We are here to deal with their life and with their soul!

You can look this direction now!

Many times, we are like the gardener who throws a bad plant into the trash can. He does not cry about that plant because he knows there will be another plant.

But that is not what a nurse does!

I remember a male nurse who was with us in the Intensive Care Unit for one week before my grandmother passed away. That nurse got very close to us—perhaps even too close. When grandma died, that nurse cried with my mother because it was the loss of a life that was very dear to us. Then the nurse said, "You go call your father. I'll take away all the tubes and the equipment. I want her to look as nice as possible for when your daddy comes in."

How much that nurse cared because he remembered that he was dealing with life!

You may be a child or an adult. The truth is you only get one chance to live your life. If you blow it, there is no way you can go back and live it again.

An adult once came to me and said, "I have ruined my life. I could have had such a beautiful life, but I ruined it by making so many careless mistakes."

Remember: The enemy of every life is the devil, the hope of every life is Jesus Christ, and we are the only ones who can share that hope with others!

Let us never forget we are here to deal with life—with making every life count for the glory of God!

4. Determined Staff

Our pastor, Dr. Lee Roberson, often repeated the old saying, "Everything rises and falls on leadership." I am a big believer in that statement.

That statement applies to everyone who describes himself or herself as a leader. It includes the pastor, the deacons, the trustees, the Sunday School staff, the AWANA staff along with all of us who have a role in making this greenhouse what God wants it to be.

Ephesians 4:12 states our church has been blessed with many different capabilities for the training of the saints to do the work of God's ministry!

I have mentioned before that Webers Greenhouse was eventually demolished because there was no determined spirit to keep it operating. No one stepped forward to assume the responsibility of maintaining that operation!

Everyone needs to listen closely to my next statement. ***You must believe in what you are doing!*** 100%! Even 1000% if that was possible!

Trials will come, shakeouts will come, feelings will be hurt! You will persevere only if you truly believe in what you are doing!

I like reading about the determination of the saints of God! Paul testified, "I am pressing on toward the mark!" He was more determined than me! Once he was stoned for preaching the gospel, but immediately afterward he rose up and went on and preached again!

Peter and the apostles were beaten for preaching about Jesus then walked away rejoicing that they were counted worthy to suffer for His name!

Shadrach, Meshach, Abednego, and Daniel refused to eat forbidden fruit from the king's table! They refused to bow before the king's statue! Their determination is a testimony to one and all!

Never forget that you are never alone in your effort for Jesus.

I read about a preacher who was afraid to go and deal with a problem. A veteran preacher said, "Would you be afraid if you knew Jesus was praying for you in the next room?" "No." "Well, He is praying for you in heaven, and that is as close as the next room." Remember that you are never alone in your effort for Jesus!

That is why Paul could say, "I can do all things through Christ who strengthens me!"

You say, "Pastor, I put so much time into my ministry, but so few people seem to care."

My friend, a long time ago I learned the secret to overcome that particular problem. I learned this lesson: Don't do it for the church because many in the church will never truly appreciate the effort. Instead, do it for Him! Lay your best effort on the altar for him!

Your effort may not be the best effort of all time, but if it is *your* best effort it will be blessed by God! Amen!

SECTION TWO: IMPLEMENTING GOD'S GREENHOUSE

7

A KINDER, GENTLER CHURCH

Is There a Barnabas Here?

Preparation: Prepare two people for the miserly Christian skit.

The year was 1988. The presidency of Ronald Reagan was coming to an end. The Democrats had nominated Michael Dukakis, governor of Massachusetts, as their presidential candidate. The Republicans had nominated Vice President George H. W. Bush as their candidate. When the Democrats finished their convention, Michael Dukakis surged ahead in the polls by about twenty percentage points. But in the end, George Bush won that election and became President of the United States of America.

In those days, I followed the world of politics with great interest. I watched all of the speeches from both sides, listened to the news reports, and read everything that the *USA Today* newspaper printed. I was really interested in politics at that point in my life.

Do you know what has stayed in my mind the longest about the 1988 campaign? It was not the final results. It was not the candidates' views on the economy, the Soviet Union, taxes, the defense budget, welfare, or Social Security. It was not even how I myself voted, but it was one statement which George H. W. Bush made in his acceptance speech at the Republican National Convention.

George Bush made a statement which has stood the test of time! He said, "I want a kinder, gentler nation." This man was so important that he was always surrounded by the Secret Service! Everyone was saying to him, "Yes, sir," and "No, sir," but even so, George Bush was still very cognizant of the overall temperament of America. He turned this slogan into one of his campaign goals: "I want a kinder, gentler nation."

He was referring to a nation with fewer murders, less drug abuse, less domestic violence, less child abuse, less parental neglect, less discrimination, less racism, less selfishness and on and on the list goes.

I realize there is much cynicism in our country regarding politics, but please allow the statement to sink into your heart. "I want a kinder, gentler nation."

Do you know what Jesus would probably say to His church today? I do not believe the message would be different for the Baptists, Presbyterians, Methodists, or whatever you happen to be. I believe He would say something like this, "I want a kinder, gentler church."

Jesus would like a church with less criticism and more encouragement, less gossip and more praying, less jealousy and more brotherly love, less caring for ourselves inside the walls and more caring for others outside the walls. A kinder, gentler church!

How many of you would like that to happen in our church? It begins with each one of us making a commitment that this is what I myself *am going to be!*

What exactly does this commitment involve? How do we get to a kinder, gentler church?

We have been studying for some time on the subject *God's Greenhouse: How to Grow People God's Way*. This study consists of two parts. The first part focused on the overall, general construction required to create a greenhouse environment or a greenhouse atmosphere. "Conceptualizing the Greenhouse" is a good title for the first part. The first part is now finished.

The second part is more specific; like an arrow, it goes directly to your heart and my heart. It is a goal worthy of our attention! How best can I say it? During the early days of this study, God laid a goal upon my heart. The goal was short and to the point. The goal was also achievable. It was only ten words in length, but those ten words were very powerful to me. God said, "I want you to focus the people's attention on this goal. Furthermore, I want you to do a series of messages on these ten words and allow Me time to develop this attitude in the hearts of My people."

I answered, "It's Your church, Lord. I'll do my best."

Here is what God laid upon my heart.

(Note: Display the goal on the screen or through some other visual.)

The goal is, *"Helping Believers Grow Together in Him Through Love and Forgiveness."* Would you repeat it with me? *"Helping Believers Grow Together in Him Through Love and Forgiveness."* Ten words, and all ten words including even "and" have a lot of meaning. You'll notice the word "and" is even important because it joins love to forgiveness. It's a lot easier to forgive if you first love the person you're supposed to forgive.

Let's read it together one more time, *"Helping Believers Grow Together in Him Through Love and Forgiveness."*

Would you agree those ten words are good for your marriage, your children, your class, your committee, your ministry, as well as the entire church?

Practicing those ten words will make the greenhouse a very special greenhouse where every plant is given the care it needs to become the plant it can be!

In this message, I want to introduce you to a man who practiced this goal in his everyday life. That means he accomplished this goal on Sunday, Monday, Tuesday, and the rest of the week. *As a result, this man made everyone better than they would otherwise be.*

Who was this man? Let's read his story in Acts 11:20-24.

> *But there were some of them, men of Cyprus and Cyrene, who on coming to Antioch spoke to the Hellenists also, preaching the Lord Jesus. And the hand of the Lord was with them, and a great number who believed turned to the Lord. The report of this came to the ears of the church in Jerusalem, and they sent Barnabas to Antioch. When he came and saw the grace of God, he was glad, and he exhorted them all to remain faithful to the Lord with steadfast purpose for he was a good man, full of the Holy Spirit and of faith. And a great many people were added to the Lord. (Acts 11:20-24, ESV)*

The key words are, "Barnabas exhorted, or encouraged, them all." In other words, you could not be around this man without becoming better than you already were! The result is in verse twenty-four; it is the good news that, "many people were added to the Lord."

Let me pose a question to you: What would you most like to be known for? Speaking for myself I would like to be known as a Barnabas—someone who always encourages people, someone who makes the day better for everyone he meets.

Verse twenty-four provides us with some very important details about this man. These are fill-in-the-blanks on your study sheet. First, he was a good (Greek *agathos*) man which seems to imply he was also a righteous man. He not only talked about religion, but he practiced his religion, too! There was no hypocrisy in this man. In the computer software days of the 1980s, he would have been known as WYSIWYG (What You See Is What You Get).

Second, he was full of the Holy Spirit or controlled by the Holy Spirit. The song "Have Thine Own Way, Lord" was more than a song to him! Barnabas was totally surrendered to his Lord!

Third, he was described as full of faith. The opposite of full of faith is full of doubt and uncertainty. Barnabas lived so close to God that he trusted God with every detail of his life. He was faithful or full of faith!

This man was totally surrendered to the presence of God in his life! As a result, he was totally committed to *helping believers grow together in Him through love and forgiveness!*

Next, look with me at the example of this man and how God blessed his efforts and his life.

1. A Giving Christian

One day a church member went to his pastor and said, "I am leaving the church. All I ever hear in this church is give, give, give!" The pastor said, "Thank you. That is the best definition of Christianity I have ever heard!"

The very first time we read about Barnabas is when he was giving to the needs of others. Imagine that! The very first item we learn about Barnabas is that there was not a selfish bone in his body.

The Bible says in Acts 4:32-37,

> *Now the large group of those who believed were of one heart and mind, and no one said that any of his possessions was his own, but instead they held everything in common. And the apostles were giving testimony with great power to the resurrection of the Lord Jesus, and great grace was on all of them. For there was not a needy person among them because all those who owned lands or houses sold them, brought the proceeds of the things that were sold, and laid them at the apostles' feet. This was then distributed for each person's basic needs Joseph, a Levite and a Cypriot by birth, the one the apostles called Barnabas, which is translated Son of Encouragement, sold a field he owned, brought the money, and laid it at the apostles' feet. (Acts 4:32-37, HCSB)*

This is the very first time we hear about Barnabas. It occurs in the context of one of the hardest areas for most Christians. That area concerns our innate selfishness! Deep down in our heart something keeps reminding us of the philosophy, "Get all you can, can all you get, then sit on the can!"

They tell the story about the stingiest man in town getting baptized in a creek. Just before being immersed, the candidate reached into his pocket and took out his billfold. He gave it to a nearby friend on the creek bank. Someone in the crowd knew this stingy man quite well. He yelled, "Pastor, his billfold needs to be baptized, too!"

If it is important to baptize one's billfold, we can readily conclude that Barnabas's billfold had been properly baptized! Apparently, his land, stocks, bonds, and business had been properly baptized, too! We can deduce from his generous gift that everything in his life had been dedicated to the work of God!

Barnabas was one of those people who would see a need then respond to that need. Verse thirty-seven says Barnabas saw a need then sold a parcel of land to meet the need.

Unfortunately, the story does not end there. The incident in chapter four leads directly into chapter five. Chapter five introduces us to a husband and wife named Ananias and Sapphira. The two of them were very impressed by the action of men like Barnabas! They decided to imitate the action with one major difference. They sold some land then pretended to give the *entire proceeds* to meet the needs of others. In other words, they gave their money for show! They pretended to be a Barnabas!

They were like the man who squeezes the ink out of his dollar bill before placing it in the offering plate! He even breaks out in a sweat every time the offering plate comes around!

Let me show you what he is like, and tell me if he is ever like you.

(Note: Before the service, select an individual to act as a miserly Christian. Ask the individual to come forward along with an usher. The usher brings the offering plate. The individual vocally reviews the different bills in his billfold then selects the lowest currency—a *one*-dollar bill. He starts to put the bill in the offering plate then hesitates as if struggling to let it go! The usher then tries to take the bill from the person's hand. However, the person refuses to release the bill. He holds onto the bill with both hands so tightly it threatens to give him a hernia!)

Does this kind of giving sound like our goal? *"Helping believers grow together in Him through love and forgiveness."*

Ananias and Sapphira secretly kept back part of the money but pretended to give it all! There was no reason to do this except to gain the applause of men! God did not like their actions in the least bit! How do I know? God immediately executed both of them! They died within hours of each other. Their deaths convinced everyone not to try that trick again!

Barnabas needs to be imitated by all of us because he was more concerned with others than with himself! He lived to serve others!

I recall the words of one secretary that were posted on Facebook! She wrote, "I work for a man who wakes up every morning imagining ways he can make people's lives miserable." There are indeed people like that!

But Barnabas was not one of them!

As a matter of fact, his giving spirit was so special the apostles gave him a new name in verse thirty-six. This is a fill-in-the-blank. The Bible says his birth name was Joseph, but his new name became Barnabas! Barnabas means "son of encouragement!" The Greek word for "encouragement" is actually a derivative of *paraklete*. I mention that because *paraklete* is a familiar word to many of you. The Holy Spirit is called the Comforter or *Paraklete* in the book of John.

In other words, Barnabas was a good man to have in your church!

Verse thirty-two says, "the multitude of those who believed possessed one heart and one soul."

That is another way of saying, *"helping believers grow together in Him through love and forgiveness."* It happened in the early church because their membership included people like Barnabas.

I say to you that we need some people like Barnabas in our church, too. I pray that you will ask God to turn you into a Barnabas!

2. Made Everyone Feel at Home

Imagine this particular scenario. A serial killer is in our city. His target is Christians like you and me. He recently killed one of the church's pastors. His goal is to shut down every church. But God gets hold of this serial killer, and the serial killer gets saved. On the next Sunday, he comes through our front door carrying a Bible. He says he would like to become a part of our greenhouse.

What do we then do?

The early church faced a similar situation. Let's read about it in Acts 9:26-27. This passage is about a murdering sheriff named Saul who wanted to stamp out Christianity, but Saul has now been marvelously saved. Incidentally, Saul would eventually become known as the great Apostle Paul. "And when he had come to Jerusalem, he attempted to join the disciples. And they were all afraid of him, for they did not believe that he was a disciple. But Barnabas took him and brought him to the apostles and declared to them how on the road he had seen the Lord, who spoke to him, and how at Damascus he had preached boldly in the name of Jesus." (Acts 9:26-27, ESV)

Let's put this story in the right context. This is a fill-in-the-blank. Everyone is scared of Saul. He was the sheriff who presided over the execution of a Christian named Stephen. He has put many Christians in jail. But Saul meets Jesus and is born again in the early part of chapter nine.

Everyone is now faced with the same question: Is Saul's salvation for real or is he faking it to infiltrate the Christian movement?

Picture Saul being all alone at church. No one will sit with this new convert. No one invites him to sing in the choir. No one invites him to their class or to any church activity. During the greeting handshake, everyone avoids him, and no one shakes his hand.

Saul does not fit in!

Sadly, there are a lot of people who don't fit into our churches because our churches won't let them fit in. Perhaps they have the wrong skin color. I can assure you that racism is still alive in Christianity today! Perhaps they live on the wrong social level. They may be too high socially or too low socially, but they aren't us socially! They may have the wrong background. We reason there is no way they can change! Once a whatever, always a whatever. Or they might even live in the wrong community or section of town. We might reason, "Can anything good come out of Nazareth or out of _____?"

I remember one of my first students in church. He grew up to be a good man. During one of the family funerals, he told me about the problem of finding a church close to where he now lived. He said, "I visited a church you know," and he named the church. He said, "It was the most unfriendly church I have ever seen."

There was nothing wrong with my friend. He had a good job, dressed nice, and had a big smile. He was the kind of person that it was easy to be nice to. But he said, "That is the most unfriendly church I have ever seen." It was also another way of saying, "They don't want me. I will never go back there."

One of the truths we should never forget is that Jesus was known as a friend of sinners! The words, "Neither do I condemn thee. Go and sin no more" were not spoken to a good sinner but to a bad sinner (John 8). It is noteworthy that the unrighteous were more comfortable with Jesus than the righteous Pharisees!

Who comes to Saul's rescue? Barnabas! I am sure that some people questioned Barnabas about his decision. They probably said, "Saul will never last as a Christian." Barnabas would have said, "We'll never know unless we first try." Others probably said, "I can't forgive Saul for what he has done." Barnabas would have said, "We need to forgive as Christ forgave us because it was our sins, too, that murdered Jesus!"

Barnabas even stood up in front of the apostles and said, "Let's help Saul grow in the Lord! Who knows what Saul can become?"

One thing is for certain! Our city is full of Sauls who need a Barnabas to help them grow!

It is a very easy thing to mess up one's life. It is another thing entirely to try to do something about it. And those people need a Barnabas in their lives!

The story is told about Mr. Colgate. How many of you use Colgate toothpaste? You may not know this, but Mr. Colgate began his company selling soap instead of toothpaste. Mr. Colgate belonged to an affluent church where the people joined together to pray for the salvation of sinners. They prayed for several weeks. Mr. Colgate was just as concerned as the rest of them.

One Sunday morning a very poor woman—she was not dressed very well, wore no makeup, nor had she been to the beauty shop—walked down the aisle and presented herself as a candidate for baptism. She told the people that she had received Jesus Christ and would like to become a member of the church.

The pastor of the church hesitated. No one made a motion to receive the woman into the membership of the church. After all, she wasn't one of them!

Finally, the pastor said, "Perhaps it would be good to wait and have some conferences about this applicant."

Mr. Colgate rose to his feet and said, "We have been praying for weeks about lost souls. The Lord has heard and answered our prayers. But I guess we failed to designate to the Lord that we only wanted respectable sinners to be saved."

Do you know what I think? I think Mr. Colgate sounded a lot like Barnabas.

3. Willing to Take Second Place

One of the hardest fights for any Christian is in the area of pride. I remember participating in an association-wide revival as a young preacher. My father directed the association choir. The choir included representatives from every church. Dad assigned one of the popular solos to a person. This assignment created a problem because that solo was sung by more than one person in the association choir.

During one of the practices, the selected soloist sung this very popular song. He did a fine job and then returned to his seat. One of the other soloists couldn't stand it. He immediately leaned over and told the soloist how he would have sung the song and how much the people were blessed when he sang it his way! His ego was so obvious it was comical! Oh, the pride to be number one and to be patted on the back!

I want you to see that Barnabas was just the opposite. It is important to note that being the opposite made Barnabas stand out even more!

Acts chapter thirteen talks about the church at Antioch deciding to send out two missionaries. It says, "While they were worshiping the Lord and fasting, the Holy Spirit said, 'Set apart for me Barnabas and Saul for the work to which I have called them.'" (Acts 13:2, ESV)

Look closely at which person is listed first. Is it Saul or Barnabas? The answer is Barnabas. But which one becomes more important as time passes? The answer is Saul. That means *the pupil will eventually be exalted above his teacher* and yet the teacher's attitude will be, "To God be the glory in His church!"

The attitude of Barnabas is the same as the attitude expressed in John 3:30. By that time the ministry of John the Baptist was in decline. More and more people were flocking to Jesus, and fewer and fewer people were coming to John. The people asked, "John, what are you going to do about this decline in your ministry?" John answered, "He, speaking of Jesus, must increase, but I must decrease. He is the groom, and the bride belongs to Him! I am just the best man!"

The old saying is still true. *It is amazing how much can be done if we don't care who gets the credit!* But that is a hard pill to swallow because it means we have to be willing to not get *any* of the credit!

The 1984 Winter Olympics in Sarajevo included a set of twins by the names of Steve and Phil Mahre. Those twins competed in the men's giant slalom event. It was the day of the Olympic finals. Phil went first and was so good he was in first place.

Steve's turn eventually came. The camera showed Steve on the walkie-talkie getting advice from someone who had already come down the track. The person was telling Steve about the areas that were slick and dangerous. Guess who that person was? It was his brother Phil!

Phil told his brother everything he needed to know. He did not hold anything back. He wanted to see his brother do his very best even if it meant his brother won first place.

You probably want to know how it turned out, don't you? Steve then skied down the mountain and came in second place. Those twins stood side by side at the awards ceremony and received the gold and silver medals.

Everyone was surprised at Phil helping his brother. The reporters asked him to explain his actions. He said, "I was here to perform to the best of my ability. I am in the sport because I love it."

Barnabas could have said, "I am in this church because I love it more than I love me!" What a blessing he was!

Wonder if you can become a Barnabas?

4. Forgiving Others

Let's read our goal one more time. This goal is more than a motto or a saying. It is a true goal in every sense of the word. *"Helping Believers Grow Together in Him Through Love and Forgiveness."* Barnabas demonstrated the skill of forgiving others as well as anyone has ever done.

The Bible says:

> *"And some days after Paul said unto Barnabas, Let us go again and visit our brethren in every city where we have preached the word of the Lord, and see how they do. And Barnabas determined to take with them John, whose surname was Mark. But Paul thought not good to take him*

with them, who departed from them from Pamphylia, and went not with them to the work. And the contention was so sharp between them, that they departed asunder one from the other: and so Barnabas took Mark, and sailed unto Cyprus; And Paul chose Silas, and departed, being recommended by the brethren unto the grace of God." (Acts 15:36-40, KJV)

The disagreement was over a young man named John Mark. John Mark went on a missionary journey with Paul and Barnabas. I have often described the problem as one in which John Mark became homesick for his momma's home cooking. Mark became so homesick that he packed his bags and went home to momma.

The question was, "Will John Mark ever grow up?" The Apostle Paul said no, but Barnabas said maybe, and therefore, Barnabas was willing to forgive John Mark and give him a second chance.

The lesson is clear. *How we deal with the failures of others is often a sign of our own maturity!*

A sixteen-year-old became careless and wrecked her mother's car. She was not injured. She called home to tell her parents about the wreck. She expected an angry reaction. Her father instead asked about her physical and emotional condition.

When the father arrived at the scene, he checked to make sure she was unhurt before checking out the car. Then when it was time to go home, he handed the keys to her and seated himself on the passenger's side. There was no angry speech from the father—just a lot of love and forgiveness and an overwhelming vote of confidence!

John Mark was like that sixteen-year-old. He needed the keys one more time. He needed another chance and another and another and another.

Do you know what Tom Swartzwelder needs and you need? We need another chance and then another and another and another.

One of the most important verses in the book of Jonah is where the Bible says, "The Word of the Lord came to Jonah a second time!" (Jonah 3:1)

Barnabas makes the decision to invest his life in John Mark. Does it pay off? The answer is yes.

The Apostle Paul wrote the book of 2 Timothy from prison just a short time before he was executed. The book is four chapters long. Would you like to guess the person that Paul writes about halfway through chapter four? He writes, and I am paraphrasing, "Timothy, my friend Luke is the only person still with me. I want you to come visit me. When you come, *be sure to bring Mark with you.* Mark will be helpful to me in whatever ministry I have left."

This is a fill-in-the-blank. Paul said, "Mark will be helpful." We could also use the word "useful" or "profitable." Do you know what we call those words? Those words are Paul's confession that he was wrong on rejecting John Mark for his failures.

Paul is saying to all Christians everywhere for the next two thousand years, "I was wrong. I should have forgiven John Mark. *I should have been a Barnabas instead of a Paul.*"

It happened on a cold winter's day. The parking lot to the church was filling up quickly. The church members were whispering as they made their way to the building. All of them saw a man leaning against the outside wall of the church. The man was almost lying down as if he was asleep.

This man was wearing a long trench coat that was almost in shreds; a hat was pulled down so low that you could not see his face. He wore shoes that looked to be thirty years old; the shoes were too small for his feet. His toes stuck out of his shoes.

Once inside the church folk greeted one another for a few minutes. Someone then mentioned the man who was still lying outside. Some of the people snickered, but no one bothered to ask the man to come inside where it was warm.

The church service began with singing. Everyone waited for the pastor to come to the pulpit and lead the service. But the pastor was nowhere to be seen. It was then the church doors opened, and the homeless man walked down the aisle with his head down.

Some of the people gasped. Other people made faces. The homeless man kept walking toward the front row. Someone gasped, "How dare he?" The homeless man reached the front row then walked past the front row and walked behind the pulpit where he took off his hat and coat.

It was then everyone recognized the pastor. He was the homeless man. No one said a word. The pastor took his Bible and said, "I don't think I have to announce my subject today."

Then he started to sing,

> "If I can help somebody as I pass along,
> If I can cheer somebody with a word or song,
> If I can show somebody that he's traveling wrong,
> Then my living shall not be in vain."

Alma Bazel Androzzo

That sounds like a song Barnabas would have written.

Thus, endeth the first lesson in *"Helping Believers Grow Together in Him Through Love and Forgiveness."*

8

WHAT HAS TO HAPPEN BEFORE I CAN GROW?

Which Comes First? Growth or Life?

Preparation: Prepare the stage with two chairs. Recruit six actors.

This is the second message in Section Two of what I call *God's Greenhouse: How to Grow People God's Way*. Section Two is dedicated to helping us accomplish a very important goal. That goal can be stated in the following words, *"Helping Believers Grow Together in Him Through Love and Forgiveness."* In other words, the goal is a kinder, gentler church which knows how to practice kindness and gentleness.

I asked you in our last session how many of you would like to be a member of that kind of church. Everyone raised their hand and said yes.

We like the idea of growing or expanding our horizons. We like the idea of being together instead of apart and lonely. We like the idea of "In

Him" because, "Jesus, Jesus, Jesus, is the sweetest name I know." We like the idea of love and forgiveness because those attributes meet some of our most basic human needs. Heaven help the person who cannot experience love and forgiveness from other people.

But there is something else that precedes all of that. Look again at the ten words in our goal and zero in on word number two. It is the word "believers." The first thing we must do is make sure that every one of you is spiritually *able to grow* and to enjoy every word in the statement, *"Helping Believers Grow Together in Him Through Love and Forgiveness."*

In some ways, the material in this lesson should precede all of the other lessons because it is the most foundational truth of all. After all, which really comes first? Is it growth or life? Can spiritual growth happen if there is no spiritual life? What do we mean when we talk about spiritual life? Is the evangelical emphasis on a born-again experience a genuinely true experience which precedes everything we have previously discussed?

All of us have heard sermons encouraging us to grow by studying more, praying more, surrendering more, witnessing more, worshipping more and on and on the list goes. Indeed, this entire study has focused on how to turn our entire church experience into a greenhouse environment—a place where people can grow up to be just like Jesus.

But, believe it or not, there are some people who *cannot grow* at _____ Church. It does not matter what we do: Sing better, preach better, witness better, teach better, even eat better in our dinners. These people will never be able to grow up to be like Jesus. The reason that is so is because *something must happen in your life before you can grow!*

You ask, "Pastor, why is that so?" Here is your first fill-in-the-blank. It is because you cannot spiritually grow that which is spiritually dead.

John chapter three is perhaps the most important passage that explains this issue.

> *Now there was a man of the Pharisees, named Nico-*
> *demus, a ruler of the Jews; this man came to Jesus by night*
> *and said to Him, "Rabbi, we know that You have come from*
> *God as a teacher; for no one can do these signs that You do*
> *unless God is with him." Jesus answered and said to him,*
> *"Truly, truly, I say to you, unless one is born again he can-*
> *not see the kingdom of God." Nicodemus said to Him,*
> *"How can a man be born when he is old? He cannot enter*
> *a second time into his mother's womb and be born, can*
> *he?" Jesus answered, "Truly, truly, I say to you, unless one*
> *is born of water and the Spirit he cannot enter into the*
> *kingdom of God. That which is born of the flesh is flesh,*
> *and that which is born of the Spirit is spirit. Do not be*
> *amazed that I said to you, 'You must be born again.' The*
> *wind blows where it wishes and you hear the sound of it,*
> *but do not know where it comes from and where it is going;*
> *so is everyone who is born of the Spirit." (John 3:1-8,*
> *NASB)*

There is a flower which grows in our yard every spring which then multiplies itself by leaps and bounds. It is called a dandelion. The flower eventually goes to seed, and the wind scatters the seed everywhere! You end up with even more dandelions!

In our early days, my wife Ruth Ellen made a deal with our youngest daughter, Elizabeth. She promised Elizabeth one penny (a penny must have been worth more in those days) for every dandelion she pulled from the ground. That would prevent the dandelions from going to seed and turning the entire yard into dandelions. In the end, Ruth Ellen paid Elizabeth more than $7.00 for her work. Elizabeth pulled more than seven hundred dandelions and put them in a trash bag.

Three weeks later I needed an illustration for this sermon. I looked at Elizabeth's trash bag and thought about replanting those dead dandelions. But my brain told me there was no reason to do that; those plants were dead, and those same plants would never be able to grow again.

I could plant those dead plants in the ground, give them plenty of sunlight, water them, fertilize them, even give them a constant temperature, but those plants would not grow because those plants were now dead. They were so dead that we could even pronounce it DA-ID with two syllables!

Another fill-in-the-blank. One of the greatest problems in Christianity today is we are trying to grow people who are spiritually dead.

That was true in the case of this man named Nicodemus. Nicodemus was a fine man, had a great reputation, was a member of the Supreme Court of his day known as the Sanhedrin Court, was part of the religious sect known as the Pharisees, taught the Old Testament, prayed, tithed faithfully, attended the Jewish synagogue, and most importantly, he was trying to grow . . . but he was as dead as dead can be!

Let's make sure that all of us understand what spiritual death means.

> *And you were dead in your trespasses and sins in which you previously walked according to the ways of this world, according to the ruler who exercises authority over the lower heavens, the spirit now working in the disobedient. We too all previously lived among them in our fleshly desires, carrying out the inclinations of our flesh and thoughts, and we were by nature children under wrath as the others were also. But God, who is rich in mercy because of His great love that He had for us, made us alive with the Messiah even though we were dead in trespasses. You are saved by grace! Together with Christ Jesus He also raised us up and seated us in the heavens, so that in the coming ages He might display the immeasurable riches of His grace through His kindness to us in Christ Jesus. For you are saved by grace through faith, and this is not from yourselves; it is God's gift—not from works, so that no one can boast. For we are His creation, created in Christ Jesus for good works, which God prepared ahead of time so that we should walk in them. (Ephesians 2:1-10, HCSB)*

Verse one begins by stating we are dead spiritually even though we are alive physically!

I want everyone to turn to your neighbor and repeat after me. "Howdy. You sure are looking good today."

The reason you can communicate is that both of you are alive physically. But if you were lying in a casket, you could no longer do that. You would be dead to the things around you and unable to know what is happening in the world around you. We could take you to Paris, but what would you know? We could take you to Disney World or give you a million dollars, but what would you know?

Pay close attention to the next statement because this is also a fill-in-the-blank. There is another world besides the physical world. That second world is the spiritual world. It is the world where God Himself exists. The Bible says, "God is a spirit and those who worship Him must worship Him in spirit and in truth." (John 4:24) *The spiritual world is a world you cannot know or experience or comprehend unless you have first been born again.*

It is as if you are lying dead in a casket. You are not aware of anything in the spiritual world because you are dead to that spiritual world!

Here is what that means. Before you can grow, you must first have life! Before you can grow *as* a child of God, you must first *be* a child of God! Before you can grow up to look like Jesus, you must first have Jesus living in your heart.

Another fill-in-the-blank. It's letter F on your study sheet. Growth follows life, and that life takes place in the center of your soul! It is an experience called being born again by the Holy Spirit of God! It is also described as being a new creation in Christ Jesus! (2 Corinthians 5:17) Peter writes about us being, "Born again not of corruptible seed but of the incorruptible Word of God!" (1 Peter 1:23)

Let's act it out.

(Note: Bring one man and one chair to each side of the pulpit. The men are seated. Each pretends to be dead (head is bowed, no response to anything around them). However, the congregation does not yet know they are pretending to be dead. Ask the congregation, "How do we grow as Christians?" One individual in the audience will rise and say, "We grow by reading the Bible." That individual then reads John 3:16-18, but there is no response from either man. A second individual will rise and say, "We grow by singing." That individual then sings a verse of "Amazing Grace," but again there is no response from either man. A third individual will rise and say, "We grow by praying." That individual proceeds to read the Model Prayer. Neither man responds. A fourth, very boisterous individual rises and shouts, "We grow by preaching. We need to preach against sin. We need to preach about holiness. We need to preach the glory of God and the Second Coming of Jesus Christ." But, once again, neither man moves!)

We have two individuals who have just heard a lot of spiritual truth, and yet neither individual responded in the least. Can anyone tell me why? (Note: The audience's answers will vary, but eventually someone will suggest the men appear to be dead.)

That is exactly what Jesus is saying to Nicodemus. "Except a man be born again he cannot see or experience or comprehend or even remotely understand the spiritual kingdom of God."

What kind of kingdom is this? What is the kingdom of God that he cannot experience?

Let's fill in the blanks with a list of eight items the unsaved person cannot experience until he is first born again!

1. The Person and Pleasures of the Holy Spirit

First, he cannot experience the person and pleasures of the Holy Spirit. John 14:16-17 says,

> *"And I, [Jesus,] will pray to the Father, and He shall give you another Comforter who is just like Me. The Comforter will continue with you forever. He is also the Spirit of truth. The world is unable to receive Him because the world does not have the ability to see Him nor know Him. But you have the ability to know Him because He dwells with you, and shall be in you."*

Notice the words, "the world is unable to receive Him." The Holy Spirit is described as a gift, but He is a gift to only those people who *can* receive Him, and *those people are the ones who have been spiritually born again* into God's family.

Let me also mention Romans 14:17, "For the kingdom of God is not food and drink; but righteousness, and peace, and joy in the Holy Spirit." In other words, the kingdom of God consists of more than even a Thanksgiving meal with the family. It is the ability to live a righteous life and consistently do what is right! It is the pleasure of having the peace of God rule in your heart when troubles come. It is also possessing something called real joy—joy inexpressible and full of glory!

Those words may sound like concepts, but they are much more than concepts to the born-again child of God! Those words are an *actual reality* that radically changes your attitude toward all of the issues in life.

Being blessed by the Holy Spirit means nothing to the man who is spiritually dead! The overcoming life means nothing to the man who is spiritually dead.

Nicodemus expressed his total frustration when he asked Jesus, "Must a man enter a second time into his mother's womb and be born a second time? Jesus, what do you mean when You talk about being born again?"

2. The Importance of a Church Experience

Second, the spiritually dead man cannot experience the importance of a church experience. Do you ever wonder why more saved people attend church than unsaved people? We might have two hundred saved people in a morning service but only two or three unsaved people in the same service. Some churches don't even have one unsaved person in their services!

The reason is that the attitude of the unsaved person is different than the attitude of the saved person. The unsaved person looks at you and asks, "Why is that person listening to a boring sermon? Why is he taking notes and nodding his head in agreement? Why are these people singing to a God they cannot see? Why are they giving their hard-earned money to something that makes no sense?"

The Bible says, "The unsaved person does not have the spiritual capacity or ability to comprehend spiritual things. They are foolishness or moronic to him!"

I remember a boss who helped me to grow up in my younger years. He was not a believer in Jesus Christ! One day he told me, "I watch Jimmy Swaggart's television program on Sunday morning because I like his style of music. But I turn off the television when he starts preaching. I watch his program for the entertainment."

That word "entertainment" describes how an unsaved person views the church. As for me, I go to church for the spiritual value; the unsaved person can only appreciate the entertainment or some similar value.

3. Cannot Experience the Power of Answered Prayer

Third, the spiritually dead man cannot experience the power of answered prayer. Some doctors say prayer is a sick man's crutch. Others have described prayer as a life preserver. Someone else remarked that prayer is what we do as a last resort when nothing else works!

The Apostle Paul viewed prayer in a much different way. "Do not be anxious about anything, but in everything by prayer and supplication with thanksgiving let your requests be made known to God. And the peace of God, which surpasses all understanding, will guard your hearts and your minds in Christ Jesus." (Philippians 4:6-7, ESV)

I want you to understand there is power—great power—in prayer! Samuel Taylor Coleridge wrote, "The act of praying is the very highest energy of which the human mind is capable; praying, that is, with the total concentration of the facilities. The great mass of worldly men and of learned men are absolutely incapable of prayer!"

I do not say God will 100% never, ever hear the prayer of an unsaved adult or child because our God is a very gracious God. However, we can safely say that such times are an *exception* to the rule because God's Word says, "Your sins have separated you and God so that He will not hear your prayers." (Isaiah 59:2) "If I cherish sin and rebellion in my heart the Lord will not hear my prayers!" (Psalm 66:18) The principle is clear: God's ears are closed to the prayers of the unsaved but are open to the prayers of the saved!

Oh, what a "sweet hour of prayer" belongs to the child of God when he communes one-on-one with His heavenly Father! He can talk freely and openly about every subject to God the Father, God the Son, and God the Holy Spirit! After all, he is a part of the entire family!

4. Cannot Experience the Richness of the Word of God

Fourth, the spiritually dead man cannot experience the richness of the Word of God. Some people describe the Bible as a literary masterpiece, and they are right in doing so! But it is much more to me than a literary masterpiece like *Gone with The Wind*. The Bible is the bread of life to me! Jesus said, "Man shall not live by natural bread alone but by every Word that proceeds from the mouth of God." (Matthew 4:4) The Bible contains those very words!

Let me encourage you to read Psalm 119 this week. The entire Psalm is a tribute to the Word of God! You can sense the writer's deep appreciation for the richness of the Word of God. For example, he wrote in one verse, "God, open my eyes that I may behold and comprehend the amazing things in Your law."

That is so much different than the way Jesus described the unsaved man in Matthew chapter thirteen. Jesus described the heart of the unsaved man as being like a well-traveled, packed-down path that had become hard like concrete. When the seed of the Bible falls upon him, it just bounces off! The Bible means nothing to that man except to perhaps answer a question on Jeopardy! But the Bible means everything to me, how about you?

5. Cannot Experience the Will of God

Fifth, the spiritually dead man cannot experience the will of God for his life. Jesus set the example for all of us. Jesus said:

> *"All that the Father gives me will come to me, and whoever comes to me I will never cast out. For I have come down from heaven, not to do my own will but the will of him who sent me. And this is the will of him who sent me, that I should lose nothing of all that he has given me, but raise it up on the last day. For this is the will of my Father, that everyone who looks on the Son and believes in him should have eternal life, and I will raise him up on the last day."* (John 6:37-40, ESV)

I began the ministry in 1976. Like most pastors, I have not made a lot of money in the ministry. I used to drive hand-me-down cars that had several previous owners. I did not even have central air-conditioning during the years we rented from the Webers. But I have never regretted devoting my life to the ministry.

Let me ask you a question, especially those of you who have given ten, twenty, thirty or even more years to serving God. Some of you have put a lot of time into God's work. Some of you have put a lot of money into God's work. Some of you feel like me—that you have invested your entire life in God's work.

Do you feel like it was a waste? Do you feel like you were wrong and should have abandoned God and gone your own way? How many of you will raise your hand and say, "Pastor, I have tried to do the will of God for my life, and I am glad that I did so!"

I said recently that I'll probably do a final review when I come down to my final days. I am sure I will have some regrets. One regret is that I did not bring more people to Jesus. I have worked hard at it, but I wish the results were more! Another regret is that I did not become a better preacher. Every preacher wants to be a Billy Graham or an Adrian Rogers! But there was only one of them.

But there are several things I will not regret. For instance, I will not regret the many hours I spent in church. I will not regret the thousands of sermons I preached nor the time that went into those sermons. I will not regret the money I put into the Lord's work. I will not regret teaching the Bible to my children. I will not regret the hours spent in prayer!

None of those things make sense to the unsaved man, but it does make sense to me!

Never forget, the unsaved man cannot understand or experience the will of God for his life.

6. Cannot Experience Being in God's Army

Sixth, the spiritually dead man cannot experience being in God's army against an invisible enemy. To be honest, he is just the opposite! He is part of a very organized opposition to the kingdom of God. He may not understand this truth, but it is still true. Two passages of scripture immediately come to my mind.

> *He presented another parable to them: "The kingdom of heaven may be compared to a man who sowed good seed in his field. But while people were sleeping, his enemy came, sowed weeds among the wheat, and left. When the plants sprouted and produced grain, then the weeds also appeared. The landowner's slaves came to him and said, 'Master, didn't you sow good seed in your field? Then where did the weeds come from?' "'An enemy did this!' he told them." (Matthew 13:24-28, HCSB)*

The weeds represent the spiritually dead man! The devil is described in another place as the god of this world. That means he is organizing opposition against the kingdom of God. The principle is very simple: *if God is for something, the devil is automatically against that something.* Thus, the devil plants his own people—spiritually dead people—in the world as part of an organized opposition to God.

The second verse is 1 John 2:15. "Do not love the world or the things that belong to the world. If anyone loves the world, love for the Father is not in him." (1 John 2:15, HCSB)

The English word "world" is a translation of the Greek word *kosmos*. Another fill-in-the-blank. *Kosmos* has the idea of an organized system, one where things have been arranged or put in order. The word suggests the devil has *organized* the current world system against God.

We began this message by reading from Ephesians 2:1. Let me quote it again. "And you were dead in your trespasses and sins in which you previously walked according to the ways of this world, according to the ruler who exercises authority over the lower heavens, the spirit now working in the disobedient." (Ephesians 2:1-2, HCSB)

Yes, the devil is indeed alive and well on Planet Earth!

We should not be surprised when the world encourages immorality and discourages purity. Or when the world encourages a "me first" attitude over a "God first" attitude.

That's why we sing, "Onward, Christian soldiers, marching as to war!" It is because the devil's army is at war with God's army! And vice versa! We have been at war for more than six thousand years! But someday God's Kingdom will finally come. God's righteousness will then rule over the entire world! My reaction to that promise is, "Even so, come, Lord Jesus!"

7. Cannot Escape the Eternal Judgment to Come

Let's add one more difference to our list. Number seven, the spiritually dead man cannot escape the eternal judgment to come. Paul was motivated by what you are writing down. He told the Corinthians, "I know and you know the terror of the Lord; therefore, we seek to persuade men to get right with the Lord." (2 Corinthians 5:11) The Old Testament prophet Amos preached, "Prepare, O Israel, to meet your God." (Amos 4:12) The book of Hebrews teaches, "It is a terrifying thing to fall into the hands of a living God." (Hebrews 10:31) Don't forget these words either. "Death and hell were thrown into the lake of fire." (Revelation 20:14)

Do you know what amazes me the most about our empty seats? It is that we have the best product in the history of the world and yet sinners stay away! Our product promises salvation from hell through the blood of the cross, the blood that washes as white as snow!

We'll sing it, teach it, and preach it, but more sinners insist on rejecting the message than receiving the message!

Why? It is because they are spiritually dead regarding their own future.

One of our country pastors devoted several Saturdays to the work of soul-winning visitation. He went to house after house in his community telling people about Jesus. Sometime later he talked with my father about his lack of success. He said something I have never forgotten. He said, "If I could only find someone to share the message with! In our neighborhood, they don't want to hear!"

After many years of ministry, I have come to a rather startling conclusion. This is a big fill-in-the-blank! All I can do is make an effort to tell them. But only God can open their heart, and only they can believe for the salvation of their soul. I can pull, and I can push, but only they can open their heart to receive Jesus! The Bible says in the book of John chapter one, "God gave the right to become children of God to as many as *received* Jesus!"

8. Cannot Experience the Joy of Seeing Someone Born Again

Number eight, the spiritually dead man cannot experience the joy of seeing someone born again! The 126th Psalm says, "They that sow in tears shall reap in joy. He that goeth forth and weepeth, bearing precious seed, shall doubtless come again with rejoicing, bringing his sheaves with him." (KJV) The Bible also says,

So He told them this parable, saying, "What man among you, if he has a hundred sheep and has lost one of them, does not leave the ninety-nine in the open pasture and go after the one which is lost until he finds it? When he has found it, he lays it on his shoulders, rejoicing. And when he comes home, he calls together his friends and his neighbors, saying to them, 'Rejoice with me, for I have found my sheep which was lost!' I tell you that in the same way, there will be more joy in heaven over one sinner who repents than over ninety-nine righteous persons who need no repentance." (Luke 15:3-7, NASB)

I don't know about you, but we like to rejoice in this church as much as possible!

"Rejoice with Me! A sinner has come home! There's a new name written down in the Lamb's book of life!"

Let me ask you a very serious question. My friend, is your own name written down in heaven? Is your own name written down in God's book of eternal life? Or are you still spiritually dead in your sins, away from God, and without hope for eternity?

Think back to how we began this message. We began with two men sitting on the platform with me. Let's bring them back to their chairs.

(Note: Both men remained close to their chairs during the bulk of the message. At this time, both men return to their chairs and resume their pose as dead men.)

What was their condition? They were both spiritually dead.

But let me now turn to this one and ask him, "Do you now believe in Jesus Christ as your personal Savior?"

(Note: The man raises his hand and says yes. The pastor announces that he has now been born again.)

Ephesians 2:1 was true in this man's life until he received Jesus. But now verse five is true in his life. Verse four says, "But God, who is rich in mercy because of His great love that He had for us, made us alive with the Messiah." (Ephesians 2:4, HCSB) The phrase "made us alive" or "quickened" is the same idea as being "born again."

But notice the other man is still dead.

Notice how different the two of them are now!

(Note: The first individual in the congregation will rise and say, "We grow by reading the Bible." That individual then reads John 3:16-18. The alive man says, "Amen!" and waves his hand as the verses are read. The dead man does nothing. A second individual will rise and say, "We grow by singing." That individual then sings a verse of "Amazing Grace." The alive man rejoices, waves his hand, and sings along! The dead man does nothing. A third individual will rise and say, "We grow by praying." That individual proceeds to read the Model Prayer. The alive person prays the prayer also and rejoices that God has heard his prayer. A fourth, very boisterous individual rises and shouts, "We grow by preaching. We need to preach against sin. We need to preach about holiness. We need to preach the glory of God and the Second Coming of Jesus Christ." The alive man is shouting "Amen" and "That's right!" but the dead man does nothing. Last, the alive man says, "I am persuaded Jesus is the Son of God who died for my sins on the cross. I am persuaded Jesus was buried but rose from the dead on Easter Sunday morning—that Jesus is now alive and able to save anyone who comes to God the Father through Him. I am persuaded Jesus is the way, the truth, and the life. I am persuaded Jesus is also the King of Kings and Lord of Lords! I am persuaded Jesus is able to keep my soul until the day of my resurrection. I can say all those things because I am now a believer in Jesus Christ. I now want to grow to be like Him!")

These two men are as different as day and night!

Which man represents you? Are you the man who is dead and does not believe, or are you the man who is alive and does believe?

Back in the 1800s, there was a convention of the Midwestern Barber's Association in the city of Chicago. Some of the barbers said, "Let's go down to skid row and find a drunk in need of a shave, a haircut, and new clothes. Let's show everyone how we can change him."

The barbers found such a man very quickly. They gave him their best treatment. They shaved him, cut his hair, bought him a new suit along with a new tie and new shoes—the entire outfit! This drunk looked so good!

The convention manager was so impressed he offered the man a job. The man said, "I will report for work at eight tomorrow morning."

Eight o'clock came, but the drunk did not report for work. They later found him in the same place they had first found him. He was dead drunk!

These barbers managed to change the outside of the man by giving him a new suit, but they had not managed to change the inside of the man!

But along comes Jesus, and Jesus offers to put a new man in the new suit!

I ask you the question: *would you rather be an old, unchanged man in the new suit or a born-again new man in the new suit?*

Speaking for myself, I choose to be born again!

Hey, I am born again! January 14, 1965, is the date of my spiritual birthday—the date when I was birthed into God's family.

Guess what that means?

That means I can now grow!

9

HOW THE DEVIL TURNS AN "US" CHURCH INTO AN "I" CHURCH

In the Bull's Eye: Me, Myself, And I

Preparation: bring a one-hundred-piece puzzle.

It happened in Flint, Michigan behind a police station. The Associated Press reported that two officers were wounded in a shootout. The strange thing is that these men were not shot by thieves or drug dealers or some other criminal. These men instead wounded each other as *they argued over who would drive the police car.*

The police report said these two men had just left the morning roll call and were walking to their police car when they began arguing. A few minutes later they drew their guns, shot each other, and both were rushed to the hospital with gunshot wounds.

Their uniforms made them look like they were together, like they were one, but their actions told an entirely different story.

That brings us to our text, and it is a text those two police officers needed to hear. It is a text which we also need to hear. Psalm 133:1-3 says,

> *"Behold, how good and how pleasant it is for brethren to dwell together in unity! It is like the precious ointment upon the head, that ran down upon the beard, even Aaron's beard: that went down to the skirts of his garments; As the dew of Hermon, and as the dew that descended upon the mountains of Zion: for there the Lord commanded the blessing, even life for evermore." (KJV)*

The writer is King David. David could remember times when his nation was not together, when his government was not together, and when even his own family was not together.

That brings us back once again to the goal for our church. Let's read it together. *"Helping believers grow together in Him through love and forgiveness."*

Can you imagine how great this church would be if every single one of us were committed to this goal? Everyone in our membership would know about it, everyone in our city would know about it, and even everyone in the Tri-State would know about it! Why? It is because there is something very special about "helping believers grow together in Him through love and forgiveness."

Now here is the first key question for this message: What is the one word which brings all of these individual words into unity? It is the one word "together." If there is no togetherness, there will be very little growing or love or forgiveness.

For instance, there will be very little growing because we will come to church talking about our problems rather than coming to church to celebrate Jesus. As a result, whatever we are doing won't be happening "in Him," because we will be choosing sides and following each other rather than Jesus.

Furthermore, there will be very little love and forgiveness because we will be questioning each other's motives and why they do what they do, whether they really mean what they say and, heaven forbid, what are they planning to do next?

Let me ask you to look closely at the fourth word in our goal. Think about what it means. Think, also, about whether you are personally willing to do *whatever it takes to keep our church together* so that people might be won one by one and then also grown one by one to look just like Jesus!

That is what happened in the early church because the Bible says in Acts chapter two, "and all that believed were together." The same chapter ends with the words, "The Lord was adding to them daily those who were being saved." If we want the same thing to happen to us, we must make togetherness a very high priority.

But yet the fact remains that every church's biggest problem is just getting everyone to pull together—to be on the same team serving the same God in the very same way.

Now, why is that so? Why is it so difficult for God's people to come together? What is in me—what is in you—that rebels against togetherness and makes it so difficult for us to come together?

The problem is bigger than we can adequately develop in one message. Therefore, let's take *two* messages and make a thorough examination of this entire issue. This first message will provide an in-depth look at the **problem** (why it is so hard for churches to stay together). The second message will focus on the **solution** and how we can keep our church together no matter what comes our way.

Let's look at the problem and begin with a very important question. How does the devil exploit us and ruin our togetherness? How does the devil turn an "us" church into an "I" church?

Before listing the three largest reasons, I want you to see where the problem begins. The Bible says,

And the fifth angel blew his trumpet, and I saw a star fallen from heaven to earth, and he was given the key to the shaft of the bottomless pit. He opened the shaft of the bottomless pit, and from the shaft rose smoke like the smoke of a great furnace, and the sun and the air were darkened with the smoke from the shaft. Then from the smoke came locusts on the earth, and they were given power like the power of scorpions of the earth . . . They have as king over them the angel of the bottomless pit. His name in Hebrew is Abaddon, and in Greek he is called Apollyon. (Revelation 9:1-3, 11, ESV).

The demons of hell are described in this passage like locusts, but the most important thing to remember is the demons have a king over them. That king, of course, is Satan whom we know as the devil or *diabolos*. Satan is not called Satan in this passage of scripture, but he is given a very distinct title that defines his character. This new title is Abaddon in the Hebrew language and Apollyon in the Greek language. Both of those names mean destroyer. You'll want to write the word "destroyer" in your second fill-in-the-blank.

The Bible says the devil is a destroyer, not a builder! He tears down and never builds up! He discourages rather than encourages!

I want you to repeat four statements with me.

1. The devil wants to destroy my church.
2. My church stands for God and the truth.
3. The devil hates God, and he hates the truth.
4. The devil wants to destroy my church.

Don't you ever forget the devil's number one goal is to destroy everything that God is trying to build and that includes our very own church! The devil doesn't want our church to be a Bible-based church because a Bible-based church is a Jesus-first church, a soul-winning church, a praying church, an all-members serving church, a church where we kick out the devil, and we let God move in!

The devil and his demons and his partners want this church to be divided! Why? Because the devil cannot defeat a church which is together, but he can almost always defeat a church which is divided.

Jesus taught in Matthew 12:25, "A divided kingdom is headed for destruction. A divided city cannot survive. A divided home cannot stand." Based upon that principle, we can also say, "A divided church cannot stand either."

How then does the devil attack a church like ours? Is it through the homosexual movement? Not really. Is it through the government? Not really. Is it through Hollywood, the ACLU, the school system, and the drug dealers? Not really. The truth is I have never been in a church where those people were a threat.

How then does the devil attack a church like ours?

That brings us to 1 Corinthians 3:16-17. Allow me to refresh your mind on a very important truth. The Bible says, "Are you aware that you . . . " No one can know this by reading an English translation, but the Greek word for "you" in verse sixteen is plural. That means we are not talking about you as an individual but you as a group, as all of us. Let me hit F5 and refresh the verse!

"Are you aware that all of you are the one temple of God and that God's Holy Spirit dwells in this one temple of God which we call _____ Church." In other words, this verse teaches that God has combined all of us in this church to be His temple! Collectively, we have become God's temple! Collectively, _____ Church is God's temple.

One of you may be like a brick in that corner while another person may be like a brick in the far corner. God makes us into a temple by stacking us wherever He wants us.

In other words, we are not only standing on holy ground, but we actually *are* holy ground! We are God's temple where God is doing a spiritual work in the hearts of people.

But then along comes the destroyer and his henchmen.

The next verse, verse seventeen says, "If anyone destroys God's temple, God will destroy that person. Why? It is because the temple of God is holy to the Lord and your local church is that temple."

I want you to fill in the next blank on your study sheet. The number one goal of the devil is to divide our church, and the devil will begin with me.

(Note: Ask the congregation to repeat that sentence.)

The devil must begin with someone, and who better to begin with than each one of us? Why? It is because each one of us has the potential to destroy _____ Church.

So how does the devil operate? There are three basic ways the devil will approach you—I am talking about you personally—and try to divide our church.

1. Different Personalities

First, the devil creates divisions using the different personalities in the church. We sometimes think it is bad today, but it was also bad in the early New Testament church.

> *Now I urge you, brothers, in the name of our Lord Jesus Christ, that all of you agree in what you say, that there be no divisions among you, and that you be united with the same understanding and the same conviction. For it has been reported to me about you, my brothers, by members of Chloe's household, that there is rivalry among you. What I am saying is this: Each of you says, "I'm with Paul," or "I'm with Apollos," or "I'm with Cephas," or "I'm with Christ." Is Christ divided? Was it Paul who was crucified for you? Or were you baptized in Paul's name? I thank God that I baptized none of you except Crispus and Gaius, so that no one can say you were baptized in my name. (1 Corinthians 1:10-15, HCSB)*

Amazing! The divisions were so bad that Paul was glad he had not baptized all of them! Can you imagine a pastor saying, "I sure am glad I didn't baptize you!" but that is exactly what Paul did.

Verse twelve says:

> *"Now this I say, that every one of you says (in other words, the devil's goal is to divide our church. The devil will begin with me just like he began with every member in the church at Corinth) - every one of you says, I am of Paul, but another says, I am of Apollos, and others say, I am of Cephas or Peter, and there are even a few of you who say, I am a follower of Jesus Christ."*

Talk about a first-class mess! It is as if you had a pastor election and you were able to vote for whomever you desired. Paul got the highest number of votes, Apollos came in second, Peter came in third, and the Lord Jesus Christ, well, He barely got any votes at all!

You say, "Pastor, it sure is strange that Jesus came in fourth place." My friend, that may sound strange to you, but that is the way it always is when a church divides over personalities. *The church then talks more about the personalities than Jesus Christ!*

Now listen to what happened and tell me if you have ever fallen into this trap. What kind of men were Paul and Apollos and Peter and Jesus? The answer is they were all preachers!

Do you know what this squabble was over? It wasn't over preaching the truth because all four of them were doing that. It is likely that the fight instead was over *how to present the truth*. In other words, what kind of style do you have? Does your style fit my own personal tastes?

Each of these four men had a different personality; that personality expressed itself in how they preached.

Let's think first about the Apostle Paul. Paul was the deep, organized theologian who probably had a squeaky voice, a crooked nose, and a bald head. Plus, he was short. Paul is the kind of preacher who would take four years on Sunday mornings to preach through the book of Romans. Paul loved that book, and he believed that book was so very important!

Paul would say, "Here is my outline. Point number one, write down so-and-so," then he would say "Here is letter A under point number one," then he would say, "Here is subpoint 1 under letter A under point number one," and on and on it would go because that is the way Paul wrote his books of doctrine! He was known for his deep preaching. If you didn't agree with him, there was the door. Many of the people liked that kind of deep, scholarly preaching.

The seminary students would have loved Paul because he was one of those deeeeeeep preachers!

Now listen: Paul didn't preach anything different than the other three, but he did have a different style than the other three!

Let's look next at Apollos. The Bible does not tell us much about this great preacher, but what it does tell us is that Apollos was "an eloquent man and mighty in the scriptures." (Acts 18:24) In other words, Apollos was the most polished preacher you have ever seen—he was like greased lightning!

There is an old saying, "Speech sweeter than honey flowed from his tongue."

Some of you have problems with public speaking. You get tongue-tied. You shake in your boots. But not Apollos! If he had been an Englishman, we would have said that he really knew the King's English! He was the kind of guy who never said, "ain't." His nouns and verbs were always in agreement. He never left a hanging sentence.

He was the kind of preacher you would expect to see in a polished church where everything is done prim and proper! Some of the people at Corinth loved that kind of preaching!

Now listen: Apollos didn't preach anything different than the other three, but he did have a different style than the other three!

Who came in third place? His name was Peter. Peter appealed to those people who like emotion in their preaching! The Bible indicates that Peter was a very spontaneous individual. Peter might preach behind the pulpit, or he might run up and down the aisles.

Peter didn't care about how he got it said as long as he got it said! Today we would describe Peter as a "Pentecostal Baptist" because of his style. He got excited when he preached! There were probably some people who got excited with him! They said, "Give us Peter and forget about Paul and Apollos."

Notice Peter didn't preach anything different than the other three, but he did have a different style than the other three!

Then along comes Jesus, and poor Jesus ends up in fourth place. Why? These folks are more obsessed with preaching styles than they are with the personal presence of the Lord Jesus Christ.

The sad truth is we have not progressed even one inch in the last two thousand years. We are no different than the Corinthians, and so we divide along the lines of Billy Graham, Charles Stanley, David Jeremiah, Chuck Swindoll, Rick Warren and on and on the list goes.

We are no different than the Corinthians because there are times when we actually find the preacher or the teacher or the singer even more interesting than we do the Lord Jesus Christ. How do I know? It is because we leave the service talking more about *them* than we do the *Lord*.

I am just wondering: has that ever happened to you personally? If it has, then you know how easy it is to divide the church over personalities. It is an issue which must be overcome by every one of us because every one of us is different with different preferences.

We need to totally change our mindset in how we approach the hearing of God's Word. We need to adopt a spirit of desperation, that we are desperate to hear the Word of God, that *any style will suffice as long as you give us the Word of God!*

The people in deepest Africa don't get to choose a style. They count themselves blessed to have *anyone* tell them the Word of God.

I want you to understand you're blessed to have *anyone* tell you the Word of God!

So be thankful someone is teaching you! You are being blessed more than most of the people who have ever lived on Planet Earth!

Let me say it one more time. It is easy to divide the church over personalities. Guess what? The devil knows this lesson even better than any of us.

So beware!

2. Leadership Control

Second, the devil creates divisions over the issue of leadership control. That's a technical name for three common-sense words. Those three common-sense words are words we know very well. They are the words, "thirst for power" or "thirst for control."

Let me begin with a positive statement. There are some people in every church who will never cause this division because it is not in their nature to be number one and run the show. They have no desire to control the organization. They have no desire to make all the decisions!

But there are other people who have this potential in their nature!

To be honest, we need to thank God for those people. If it weren't for them, we wouldn't have any leaders! And if we didn't have any leaders, we would never get anything done.

But there are times when we leaders cross the line, and the church becomes "MY Church" instead of "the LORD'S Church," it becomes "MY Way" instead of the "LORD'S Way," it becomes "MY Will" instead of "The LORD'S Will."

Neil Tyson wrote, "If your ego starts out, 'I am important, I am big, I am special,' you're in for some disappointments when you look around at what we've discovered about the universe. No, you're not big. No, you're not. You're small in time and in space. And you have this frail vessel called the human body that's limited on Earth."

But we sometimes lose sight of how little we are! We begin to think instead about how lucky the world is to have someone like us.

It may start out as a very simple decision such as who gets to mow the yard, but even more important, who gets to make the decision about who gets to mow the yard?

The devil whispers in our ear, "Don't you think so-and-so is getting a little too important at the church, so-and-so is singing a little too much, or so-and-so is getting patted on the back a little too much?" Sure enough, our ego gets hurt. We then have to show them who is really the boss.

We need to be reminded of Paul's words to the Philippians, "Allow the same attitude to be in you which was in Jesus Christ. He is God—no one is bigger than Him—and yet He took on the form of a servant, became a lowly man like us, and even humbled Himself to the point of letting inferior men nail Him, the Creator, to a cross." (Philippians 2:5-8) One can only ponder, "What happened to His rights? To His reputation?" But He conquered those issues by adopting the attitude of a servant!

The book of 3 John mentions a man by the name of "Diotrephes who loves to be given first place." The KJV uses the word "preeminence." The Bible does not mention if Diotrephes was the pastor, deacon, teacher, music director, or just a regular member. What we do know is that he divided the church because he wanted to be in charge. He wanted to be the top dog!

One man said, "Pastor, this is the way I am. The rest of the church just has to put up with me."

But that is not so, and it is equally wrong for anyone to excuse his behavior in such a manner! Let's look at two Bible examples. You'll write both of these men's names on your study sheet. First name—do you remember the story of Moses? Hopefully, everyone does! I ask you, was Moses a weak man or a powerful man? Of course, the answer is "powerful." In terms of power, Moses didn't have to take a back seat to anyone!

But the Bible (Numbers 12:3) actually describes Moses as the meekest man in all the earth. That means he was notable for being humbler than any man of that age!

First, notice what the Bible does not say! It does not say Moses was the weakest man because that would have been a lie! Moses was anything but weak! God made Moses strong! Just ask Pharaoh!

Second, pay careful attention to what the Bible does say! It refers to Moses as a meek man. How can a powerful man be considered meek? The answer is more than skin deep! Let's fill in the blank. The idea behind meekness is that one keeps his power under control! That makes sense when you think about the example of Moses. Moses was a man of tremendous power who kept that power under control.

(The most notable exception was when Moses became frustrated with Israel and disobeyed God. Per God's instructions (Numbers 20:11) Moses was supposed to strike the rock only once, but he struck the rock twice! Of course, he later paid for that sin in the harshest of ways. God did not allow Moses to enter the Promised Land. Moses died looking *into* the land but not being actually *in* the land.)

Now listen: you may be a person—man or woman—who has one of those natures that likes to run the show. You are a take-charge person. You like to be in the middle of things.

Do you know the truest measure of your Christian maturity? It is not in how much we get done (we'd like to think it is), but it is in whether others can say that "he is the meekest man, or she is the meekest woman I have ever met."

The Bible says, "Blessed are the meek for they shall inherit the earth!" (Matthew 5:5) That's just the opposite of Wall Street which says, "Blessed are the go-getters for they shall inherit the earth!" It's just the opposite of the educators who say, "Blessed are the smart for they shall inherit the earth!" The truth is those last two methods always fall short!

"Blessed are the meek for they shall inherit the earth!" means power, ego, and self-promotion have been brought under the control of the Holy

Spirit, thereby enabling us to have a servant's attitude in everything we do!

It is God answering my prayer, "Lord, save me from myself! Lord, put 'I' behind the cross so that I am crucified with Christ and it is no longer 'I' that is living my life, but rather it is Christ living out His own life in me and through me!"

Example number two is the Apostle Paul. The Apostle Paul was a man who liked to be in charge, but he also identified that thirst to be one of his biggest weaknesses. Paul even wrote in 1 Corinthians 9:27, "I fight my body—my power-seeking ego—every day . . . I beat it black and blue . . . and bring it under subjection lest I should be disapproved by God!" Paul said, "The secret to winning this battle is always seeking first the approval of God instead of the applause of men."

Paul even went so far as to say, "I die daily." (1 Corinthians 15:31) Why? "So that self and my thirst for power might be crucified with Christ, and I might live the Spirit-filled life! Lord, save me from myself!"

That's why Paul was able to describe himself as "the least among the apostles" even though he wrote more of the New Testament than anyone else!

I suggest Paul's way is a good way to begin every day! Before we see anyone or talk to anyone, let us pray, "Lord, save me from myself today!"

The world will be thankful! The church will be thankful! Even the dog will be thankful!

3. Different Priorities

Third, the devil creates divisions over different priorities. This is one of the smartest attacks of all. Why? It is because the devil takes the way I'm made and turns it against the way you're made.

That line of attack often works for the simple reason that we don't see things the same way. Our experiences are different, our education is different, our income is different, our hobbies are different, our clothing is different, our politics are different, our background is different, and yet somehow, we are supposed to agree.

Quite honestly, it's a miracle that we're able to get anything done when you consider how different we are!

Those differences have the power to divide us and then defeat us!

Problem area number three is different priorities.

Another word for priorities might be the word *obsessions*. Write that word down somewhere. Sometimes our priorities become obsessions which totally control the way we live and the way we think. Sometimes we become so obsessed with our own priorities that we actually think God is as obsessed as we are!

For example, the Bible mentions the apostles were so obsessed with ministering to adults that they actually tried to keep the children away from Jesus! Jesus, though, rebuked the apostles and said, "Do not stop the little children from coming to me because their spirit is very much like the spirit in the kingdom of heaven." (Mathew 19:14)

It is so easy for us to make the same mistake as the apostles! Here is another fill-in-the-blank. We believe in our ministry so much we think our ministry ought to be the highest priority in the church. If our ministry is a music ministry, it makes sense to us that the music ministry ought to be the most emphasized ministry. If our ministry is oriented to the children, it is reasonable that such a ministry ought to be the church's number one focus. After all, the youth of today is the church of tomorrow!

On the other hand, we may be so wrapped up in the senior adult ministry that we designate our tithes and offerings away from everything else and instead direct the money to a comfortable bus for us seniors! After all, let's not forget who gives the biggest dollars to this church! On and on the list goes.

What we forget, though, is that it takes all of it working together for people to "grow together in Him through love and forgiveness."

It is like a puzzle. I have in my hand one piece from a one-hundred-piece puzzle.

This piece is critically important to our success as a church. This piece represents one ministry in our church. Let me say it another way. Each ministry in our church is represented by one piece in the puzzle. Pardon me, but let me say it an even different way. Each ministry in our church is represented by *just one piece* in the puzzle.

Your own piece may look really big to you. You may wave it at the church and say, "This ministry of mine ought to have the highest priority!" But can you imagine what a one-hundred-piece puzzle would look like if all one hundred pieces looked exactly like this one piece?

The fact is, it takes all of us working together for people to "grow together in Him through love and forgiveness."

Let me give you an example. One of our area churches began ministering to children in the neighborhood. The church vans picked up a full load of children on Sunday morning, Sunday night, and Wednesday night. The children were very rowdy and hard to control.

One group in the church was bothered by those children disrupting the services. But they tolerated it because they knew those children needed help. The other group was obsessed with taking care of those children. Their philosophy was, "We'll die for these children. They are our highest priority."

Sure enough, in time some of the children got saved. The church had a good ministry to some very needy children.

Then came the big disagreement. The first group said, "We need to have at least one decent service per week for us adults. Let's not run the vans on Sunday night so we can have a service all of us can enjoy. The children are keeping us from enjoying any of the services."

The second group said, "Not on your life. We'll die for these children. They are our highest priority."

Do you know what happened? The church split in half, and the group in charge of the children left the church. They left the children even though their philosophy was, "We'll die for these children. They are our highest priority."

The first group—the group which wanted a quiet Sunday night service—well, they now have a quiet Sunday morning service, a quiet Sunday night service, and a quiet Wednesday night service, also.

Neither side was willing to submit to the other and look for a more reasonable solution. Surely such a solution existed! Goodness, I can think of a few possible solutions! As a result, the entire church was ruined. Sad to say, the church never regained those glory days.

We now reach the most interesting question of all. I can read your mind. You want to know, "Pastor, what happened to those children?" Ah, my friend, who knows and who really cares because in the end, *both* sides' priorities were more important than the souls of those children!

Always remember this:

> *"All together the links make the chain,*
> *All together the cents make the dollar,*
> *All together the bricks make the wall,*
> *All together the shingles make the roof,*
> *All together Christians can do great things."*

10

WHEN TOGETHERNESS BECOMES REAL TOGETHERNESS!

In the Bull's-Eye: Others, You and Me

Preparation: You'll need flower seed, a water jug, a planter, and a pan to collect excess water flowing from the planter. Ask everyone to bring a plant which best represents their personality. Suggest that someone bring a cactus. We will explore the question, is there room in God's greenhouse for me?

Y ou never met the man I am about to quote, but you need to listen closely to his quote and add it to your study sheet. James Cash Penney often said, "Growth is never by mere chance; it is the result of forces working together." James Cash Penney knew what he was talking about. He opened a store in 1902 that was so successful he decided to open more stores. He kept opening stores until he died in 1971.

The one big problem was the 1929 stock market crash. Penney lost just about everything. He had to borrow money against his life insurance policies to meet the payroll. His health then suffered a severe decline. Penney checked himself into the Battle Creek Sanitarium for treatment.

One day he went to a church service in the hospital's chapel and heard someone sing the hymn, "God Will Take Care of You." Penney believed the words in that song, and he became a born-again Christian.

Now look again at the quote. "Growth is never by mere chance; it is the result of forces working together."

Many of you have shopped in one of his stores. Does anyone know the name of his company? It is J. C. Penney!

But that's not the entire story.

This is a rabbit trail, but it is a good rabbit trail! In 1940 Penney visited a store in Des Moines, Iowa. He trained a young man on how to wrap packages by using a small amount of paper and ribbon. The young man's name was Sam Walton. Have any of you ever shopped at Sam Walton's store? It's called Wal-Mart.

Look again at the quote. "Growth is never by mere chance; it is the result of forces working together."

The Bible gives us an example of that quote.

> So those who received his word were baptized, and there were added that day about three thousand souls. And they devoted themselves to the apostles' teaching and the fellowship, to the breaking of bread and the prayers. And awe came upon every soul, and many wonders and signs were being done through the apostles. And all who believed were together and had all things in common. And they were selling their possessions and belongings and distributing the proceeds to all, as any had need. And day by day, attending the temple together and breaking bread in their homes, they received their food with glad and generous hearts, praising God and having favor with all the people.

And the Lord added to their number day by day those who were being saved. (Acts 2:41-47, ESV)

Fill in the second blank on your study sheet. It comes from verse forty-four, "and all who believed were together . . . "

Sometimes the church of the Lord Jesus Christ gets a black eye that really hurts. I remember reading this article in the newspaper some years ago. You may not believe it, but it's true!

"A minister in Mississippi was charged with firing a pistol to chase off dissident members of his congregation before he began preaching. The Rev. _____, pastor of _____ Missionary Baptist Church, was charged with pointing, aiming, and discharging a deadly weapon. He was freed on $1,000 bond.

"A church member said the church had voted out the pastor on three occasions and about twenty-five people confronted him outside before Sunday services.

"The church member said the pastor told them he would leave and went to his car but returned with a pistol and fired two shots into the crowd. No one was injured. Afterward, she said, the group dispersed, and the pastor went into the church and conducted his regular service. He was arrested afterward.

"Church members reported the incident stemmed from a long feud between two factions, one that wanted to keep the pastor and one that didn't."

The Associated Press reported a long feud between two factions. Neither was willing to submit to the other. Neither was willing to leave and let the remainder be at peace. As a result, not just half the church was ruined, but the *entire* church was ruined.

No wonder the Bible talks so much about God's people coming together. The book of Ephesians urges us to "endeavor (the Greek word *spoudazo* means do our best or work hard) to keep the unity created by the Holy Spirit in the bond of peace." (Ephesians 4:3) In other words, God wants us to be together in the Holy Spirit!

The Apostle Paul said to the Corinthians, "I beg you that all of you speak the same thing and that there be no divisions among you but that you be perfectly joined together in the same mind and in the same judgment." (1 Corinthians 1:10, KJV)

The psalmist said, "Behold, how good and how pleasant it is for brethren to dwell together in unity." (Psalm 133:1, KJV) Wouldn't you agree that it is both good and pleasant when brethren dwell together in unity?

Let's add Ecclesiastes 4:12. "And though a man might prevail against one who is alone, two will withstand him—a threefold cord is not quickly broken." (Ecclesiastes 4:12, ESV) Yes, there is strength in numbers!

The old saying is so very true:

> *"All together the links make the chain,*
> *All together the cents make the dollar,*
> *All together the bricks make the wall,*
> *All together the shingles make the roof,*
> *All together Christians can do great things."*

That is exactly what happened in the early church! Verse forty-four says, "and all that believed were together." That doesn't mean they agreed on every specific thing, but it does mean they had learned how to agree on the really important things and how to disagree agreeably on the less important things!

Then you read about how God blessed their efforts because they performed those efforts *together* in the power of the Holy Spirit! Look at chapter one and verse fifteen: their number is only one hundred and twenty. Look at chapter two and verse four: and they were all—all implies togetherness—filled with the Holy Spirit! Look at chapter two and verse forty-one: many gladly received the word of God and were baptized. Also, the original number of one hundred and twenty has now expanded to three thousand! Look at chapter two and verse forty-seven: they were together praising God, and the "Lord added to them daily such as were being saved!" Look at chapter four and verse four: but many of them who heard the word believed and the number has now grown to five thousand! Look at chapter five and verse fourteen: "believers were added to the Lord, multitudes both of men and women."

Sure enough, the devil didn't like what was happening. It upset the devil that too many people were getting saved, too many people were being baptized, and too many people were being changed! The people were excited, but the devil was mad!

The devil then decided to put a stop to it once and for all!

The devil may have consulted all the demons of hell to find the right strategy to stop what was happening! It may have taken the devil a few weeks, but he eventually came up with the perfect strategy. Based on the record of history, this strategy should have worked!

The devil's strategy was to divide the church down the middle by telling the Jews they shouldn't worship with the Gentiles nor should the Gentiles worship with the Jews. In other words, the devil appealed to their *racial bias and historical bias* (both are still very powerful in today's society) because the Jews didn't like the Gentiles and the Gentiles didn't like the Jews.

It was then the Apostle Peter stood up at the Jerusalem church council and said, "Brethren, this is the issue which will make us or break us as the church of the Lord Jesus Christ. The Bible says that God has made both Jew and Gentile to be one in Jesus Christ! Not two like we were in the Old Testament but now one! One spiritual new man! The devil, though, does not want the church to be one, but he wants the church to be divided in two!

"The devil knows the Gentiles don't think like us Jews. They don't dress like us Jews. They don't even sing like us Jews. The devil wants the Gentiles and us to go our own separate ways!"

Try to picture this argument in your mind. Imagine how it would look to have two churches sitting side by side! The sign over the first church says, "The First Jewish Baptist Church of Jerusalem." The sign over the second church says, "The First Gentile Baptist Church of Jerusalem."

The two churches preach the same Bible, believe the same doctrine, sing the same songs, pray to the same Jesus, baptize the same way, even treat Communion in the same way as a symbol instead of a sacrament! But one church is named, "The First Jewish Baptist Church of Jerusalem" and the second church is named, "The First Gentile Baptist Church of Jerusalem."

I have a question which must be answered: Will the devil win or will God's purpose win?

Peter then finished his appeal. He said, "People, the Bible says the church is one body, and one doesn't mean two!" Some dear brother said, "Amen!" and another dear brother said, "I'll amen that, too!" Before you knew it, the Jews and the Gentiles were worshipping *together* in the very same church service even though they were two totally different kinds of people!

Do you know what I think? I think the early church was committed to this goal, *"Helping believers grow together in Him through love and forgiveness."*

They beat the devil where it really counted. **Together** they moved the church forward, **together** the church evangelized the world, and **together** the church made the world a better place for all of us!

It's time to do some thinking.

What exactly does this word "together" mean? Most important of all, how can you help our church to be "together?" There are four meanings associated with this word "together." Let's fill in the blanks in our study sheet!

1. Submissive Togetherness

One of the most important verses for a healthy church is found in the book of Ephesians chapter five where Paul says, "Be not intoxicated with wine, but be filled with the Holy Spirit." Everyone is acquainted with those words in verse eighteen, but I suggest Paul's words in verse twenty-one are just as important. Paul explains in verse twenty-one what it means to be filled with the Holy Spirit, and he says, "submit yourselves one to another in the fear of God."

It should go without saying that a Holy Spirit-filled church is a church that is experiencing submissive togetherness. Be sure to write the word "submissive" on your study sheet.

I believe the Bible gives us a definition of this concept in Romans 12:10. The Bible defines submission like this: "Be kindly affectioned one to another with brotherly love, in honor preferring one another." The Holman beautifully translates it as, "Show family affection to one another with brotherly love. Outdo one another in showing honor." (Romans 12:10, HCSB)

God calls us to prefer one another or lift up one another even above ourselves because we are *not afraid* to "submit ourselves one to another in the fear of God."

The Greek word *hypertasso* speaks of submission in the sense of a humble, voluntary yielding (not surrendering) of ourselves in love to our brothers and sisters in Christ. It is the opposite of self-assertion or self-promotion.

In other words, the focus is not on who is in control or even of my seeking control. It is not saying, "I have the higher position, so you have to submit to me." It is not saying, "I am the boss in this house, or I am the boss on this committee, or I am the boss in this church." The focus instead is on "kneeling before each other (as in John chapter thirteen's footwashing example) and seeing how we can best serve one another in voluntary love." It is thinking in terms of all of us actually becoming the servants of one another rather than being served or administrating a department.

It is the idea that I treasure you so much I will promote you even above myself! That is true love!

Guess what? That is not an easy thing to do!

I heard about a church whose auditorium was always too dark. One man stood in a business meeting and said, "I make a motion we buy a chandelier." Another man stood to object. He said, "I'm against it for three reasons. No one knows how to spell it on an order form. Second, there isn't anyone in the church that can play it. Third, what we really need is more light in here!"

No, submissive togetherness is not an easy thing to do!

Warning: The church which functions based on rank—in other words, I have a higher position than you, so you must do this—that church is in serious trouble.

Let me show you what happens to the church where there is no submissive togetherness. (Note: Choose four men from the audience.) These four men are our actors for today. Let's pretend that each one of these men represents a different point of view. Neither one is willing to give an inch to preserve the unity of the Holy Spirit.

Notice what happens when each man goes his own separate way.

(Note: Have the men walk to four opposite corners in the auditorium.)

Take a good look at these four men and answer me this: How much can these men do *together*? Not much. Let's suppose these men are our four leaders. Let's choose sides. One-fourth of you choose to go with each man to his corner. How much can this church do together if we are divided into following each of these men? The answer is not much. We will be like a man who has lost two legs and one arm and is barely able to function. *No church should operate at one-fourth of its capability, but many churches try!*

You say, "Pastor, what if the church is wrong? What should I do then?" My friend, it is then you show your true spirituality because the church has the right to be wrong! Let me say that again: The church has the right to be wrong. *I can safely make that statement because most of the time the issues are very trivial.* The issue is probably not so much a choice among right and wrong as much as it is between two rights. The truth is that today's mountain will look like a molehill in eternity! We would not divorce our spouse over such minor differences! At least, I hope not!

We need to keep such issues in perspective. Let me pose a question of a different sort to you. How many of you have worked outside the home for an employer? How many of you sometimes disagreed with the employer? How many of you stayed awake at night, feuding in your mind with the employer? We've all been there!

How did you ultimately respond? Once or twice you might have left for greener pastures only to learn later that greener pastures aren't always greener! Employers have a way of being the same everywhere. Eventually, you learned to grin and bear it, and you persevered through the problem.

The church is no different. It makes mistakes just like any business makes mistakes. It makes mistakes just like the politicians make mistakes. It makes mistakes just like our school system makes mistakes. The bumper sticker correctly says, "Life happens." Church mistakes, too, are a part of life.

It is even then that God calls you to "submit yourselves one to another in the fear of God" and to say, "I may not agree this time, but this is my church. I will do everything I can to help my church for the glory of God."

That is what submissive togetherness is all about!

2. Organized Togetherness

Second, the word together suggests organized togetherness. I am known as a very organized person. Therefore, it will not surprise you that one of my favorite Bible verses is 1 Corinthians 14:40, "Let all things be done decently and in order." That is the same way God created the heavens and the earth. In seven days, God made something out of nothing and then made that something into a very organized place where we can live.

The pattern of creation is the same way God expects His church to conduct His business of "winning sinners one by one and growing them one by one!"

All of you are part of a family. Hopefully, it is a functional family rather than a dysfunctional family. You are now in a position where you receive the benefits of being in that family. But you must also remember that you are now in a position where you need to contribute benefits to the others in your family.

That begins with identifying your role in your family. For example, are you the mother? If the answer is yes, there are certain things which a mother should do. Are you the father? If you are the father, there are certain things which a father should do. Are you perhaps the child? If the answer is yes, there are certain responsibilities which belong to you! In our family, it is the children who go to grade school then high school, how about yours?

Each one of us has our own role in life; the same is true for our church. Each one of us has a certain role in this church. We are organized with one group doing a certain work and another group doing a different work so that all of us together can get the work done as efficiently as possible!

When everyone is in their place, minding their own business, dedicated to their work—what a tremendous blessing that is to God's church!

But let me show you what happens when we don't have organizational togetherness—when someone insists on doing it his own way and changing the rules to fit his own point of view!

(Note: Place the planter in a pan so, later in the illustration, water doesn't leak onto the furniture or carpet. The point of this illustration is that you normally put dirt in the planter followed by seed then add water. Doing the reverse pattern results in chaos!)

Part of the work I do as a pastor is planting the seed of God's Word in the hearts of people. It is like planting a seed in this planter and letting God start the growing process.

(Note: Someone in the audience interrupts and says, "Pastor, I know how to do that better than you. I'm an expert at growing flowers. The church should have put me in charge a long time ago.")

(The person puts the seed in the bottom of the planter then pours water into the planter. Naturally, the water washes out the seed through the holes in the planter. The person ignores the wasted seed and proceeds to put dirt in the planter. The pastor kindly points out that the seed is no longer in the planter nor is the water. The person admits he made a mistake and goes back to his seat. The pastor then asks the custodian to clean up the mess after church. The custodian remarks, "Pastor, one of my duties is to clean up all of the messes around here!")

What really happened in this illustration? Something very simple and yet very profound! *What just happened was a lack of respect for God's process.* It is similar to sinning against the church because someone refused to submit to the will of the church. Such a person then creates chaos and confusion!

(Note: The same person raises his hand from his seat in the congregation and meekly says, "Pastor, I know this is not my department, but may I be a part of the process? I'm excited about this idea, and I'd just like to be a part. I'll try not to mess it up.")

(Note: The pastor asks the congregation for a decision.)

What does everyone think? Has this man's attitude changed? Will there be any hard feelings? Will there be a mess this time? Speaking for myself, I think he might now be a good addition!

In the same way, our church has established a way to do things. We try very hard to get the round pegs in the round holes and the square pegs in the square holes. Do you know which kind of peg describes you? We need you to do what you're good at!

Let's do our best to have organizational togetherness in our church.

3. Doctrinal Togetherness

One of the most overlooked requirements for genuine togetherness is in the area I describe as doctrinal togetherness. We believe the Bible is the manual for everything regarding our church. The Bible plainly teaches what we are to believe and what we are not to believe. Those basic Bible teachings are called doctrines.

Someone said, "Doctrine *divides* churches." The Bible, though, says doctrine *unites* churches.

You can think of doctrine as being the skeleton in your body. If you take away the skeleton, you're in deep trouble! Without the skeleton, the body cannot be held together or accomplish anything of value.

Let me give you a brief overview of how important doctrine really is. The book of Ephesians is one of the greatest books in the New Testament. The book is six chapters in length. The first three chapters are full of doctrine—things we are to believe. The last three chapters are full of what we should do with our doctrine. In other words, the last three chapters are focused on how we should live. Chapters one, two and three are about what we should believe! Chapters four, five, and six are about how we should live!

The Apostle Paul believed very strongly in the principle that you practice what you believe. That means *practice follows beliefs!* So be sure to get your beliefs right!

Chapters one, two and three are about what we should believe! Chapters four, five, and six are about how we should live! Would you like to guess what is in the middle of the book? Look at the opening verses of chapter four.

> *I therefore, a prisoner for the Lord, urge you to walk in a manner worthy of the calling to which you have been called, with all humility and gentleness, with patience, bearing with one another in love, eager to maintain the unity of the Spirit in the bond of peace. There is one body and one Spirit—just as you were called to the one hope that belongs to your call—one Lord, one faith, one baptism, one God and Father of all, who is over all and through all and in all. (Ephesians 4:1-6, ESV)*

Notice the emphasis on the word "one." The word "one" appears eight times in that passage. That "oneness" depends upon us being one in doctrine. That oneness in doctrine then allows us to be one in practice—in maintaining the unity of the Holy Spirit in the bond of peace.

A man once asked me, "Are you proud to be a Baptist?" I answered, "Yes, I am. To quote one of the old-time preachers, 'I was Baptist born, and Baptist-bred and when I'm dead I'll be Baptist dead.'"

One dear old woman was very denominational in her thinking. She was asked, "What happens if you find out at the Rapture that the Lord isn't a Baptist?" The elderly saint thought for a moment then said, "I'd know it wasn't the Lord." The elderly saint said those words with conviction because she believed the Bible confirms what mainline Baptists have always believed!

Let me explain why this issue is so critically important for our modern churches.

Some people say, "It doesn't matter what you believe as long as you are sincere." The Apostle Paul clearly disagrees with that idea in the books of Ephesians, Galatians, Philippians, and Colossians. The first half of those books is dedicated to doctrine—to what you must believe. The second half of those books is dedicated to your sincerity—how you behave. *The worst thing you could ever do is be sincere about the wrong belief!*

Maybe doctrine doesn't excite you! But you need to think of doctrine as your skeleton and learn to appreciate the importance of doctrine!

Let me say it one more time: you cannot have true togetherness unless you also have doctrinal togetherness. Why not? It is because "endeavoring to keep the unity of the Spirit in the bond of peace," is built upon the foundation of these seven unifying doctrines in verses four, five, and six.

I remember preaching in a church which tried to have togetherness *without* doctrinal togetherness. Those people ignored the Bible warning in the book of Amos 3:3, "Can two walk together except they be agreed?" This particular church tried to walk together without being in agreement.

I was asked to speak on a Sunday night at this church. It was my first time at this church so I preached a sermon that all mainline Baptists could agree on. The subject is not really important, but what happened is. I noticed halfway through the sermon that half of the church seemed to disagree with it.

During the sermon I was asking myself, "Have I made a mistake? What was the denominational name on the church sign?"

When the service was finished, I asked the pastor what had happened. He said, "Tom, we have been trying to put together a doctrinal statement for our church—a statement about what we believe—but we cannot do so because we don't have togetherness on some of the most important doctrines of the faith."

Needless to say, that church wasn't getting much done for the Lord Jesus Christ because they couldn't agree on what to teach or what to preach.

The story is not over. Fifteen years passed. I met one of their members in a store and asked him if the church had finally figured out what they believed. He said, "No, we still haven't. We still have as much confusion today as we did fifteen years ago. The only difference is there are a lot fewer of us than when you were with us."

My friend, pardon me for meddling, but the name over the door ought to settle some issues before you ever walk through the door!

In our case, we are a mainline Baptist church, and we believe what mainline Baptists believe. We will believe it today, we will believe it next year, and we will believe it when King Jesus comes again!

Never forget the importance of doctrinal togetherness! It is the foundation of our church!

4. Inclusive Togetherness

Number four is what I term "inclusive togetherness." You have probably figured out that togetherness is an attitude thing! John Maxwell taught us in a seminar, "People may hear your words, but they feel your attitude." This is particularly true in the issue at hand!

One of the marks of the early church is how they took in people from every walk of life. They took in the rich like Barnabas. That may seem sensible to us, but there are some churches which would have taken a pass on Barnabas. After all, "He's not one of us!" The early church took in the poor such as the beggar. Someone said, "God must love the poor! He made a bunch of them!" They even took in a murderer known as Sheriff Saul and, thank God, they did! We noted in the last chapter that they even took in those Gentiles which had once been identified as dogs, people they would previously have done anything to avoid!

There is no question the early church was able to overcome an exclusive bias and adopt a spirit of inclusive togetherness.

Sometimes, though, we forget to love as Jesus loves. We no longer are as inclusive as we should be. So-and-so isn't accepted at the church because we already have our own little group.

A woman wrote a letter in response to an article which appeared in a Christian magazine. The letter said:

"You missed a painful reality for many of us who just don't fit in or seem to be accepted in our evangelical churches. My husband is not a believer. Another woman I know, who is feeling the same way I do, is a young, divorced mother (her husband walked out on her against her will). The church seems filled with every kind of comfortable group— seniors, families, singles—but there doesn't seem to be any place for us.

"I teach Sunday School, and there is no small-group Bible study for working women, so I 'give' but receive only from the preaching. It's very lonely not having any Christian friends or fellowship. I have been praying and studying scripture for some time, trying to decide whether I should leave.

"At this point, I don't feel any strong leading, so I just keep praying, sitting alone at church, and skipping the other activities because it's

painful to go when people don't even speak to someone outside their lit-
tle homogenous groups."

I wonder if we would like to have that woman in our church. If the answer is yes, then someone must volunteer to be her friend. Who would that someone be? She said, "It's very lonely not having any Christian friends or fellowship." We must really ask ourselves if we would like to have that woman in our church.

Let's make this even more personal. You can't get any more personal than you personally. Wonder if there is room in our church for people who are just like you? People who are the same age as you, have the same problems as you, sin the same sin as you, are as poor or as rich as you, sing like you, are as talented as you, and especially need help just as much as you?

Yes, is there room for other people who are just like you?

I asked everyone to bring a small plant to this service. I would like for each one of you to now bring that plant to the front of the church.

(Note: Have the people come to the front and face the audience with their plant. Each plant represents a different personality. Is there room in God's greenhouse to grow a plant like them? Is there room for that personality?)

One truth is absolutely certain—there was room in the early church for each one of these people. That's why we read that "all that believed were together, praising God and having favor with all the people."

Let me remind you one more time of the poem:

> *"All together the links make the chain,*
> *All together the cents make the dollar,*
> *All together the bricks make the wall,*
> *All together the shingles make the roof,*
> *All together Christians can do great things."*

11

HOW TO BE AN EFFECTIVE CO-WORKER WITH GOD

A Sower Went Forth to Sow

Preparation: Distribute a lapel label as people enter. The label says, "Co-Worker with God." Instruct the person to write his/her name on the label and to stick it to his/her clothing.

How good are you as a gardener? Let me share some quotes about gardening that you might know something about.

Doug Larson from Green Bay, Wisconsin, wrote, "A weed is a plant that has mastered every survival skill except for learning how to grow in rows." Amazing, isn't it?

Quote number two: "When weeding, the best way to make sure you are removing a weed and not a valuable plant is to pull on it. If it comes out of the ground easily, it is a valuable plant." I have a lot of experience in that area.

The comedian Jerry Seinfeld said, "I have no plants in my house. They won't live for me. Some of them don't even wait to die; they commit suicide." I'm sure some of you have the same problem!

Then the question of the ages: If a man is alone in the garden and speaks, and there is no woman to hear him, is he still wrong?

Let's get down to business. Our main text for this series is 1 Corinthians 3:5-9. The Bible says, "I, Paul, have planted the seed, my friend Apollos has watered the seed and in due time God has seen fit to give the increase." Paul goes on to say, "It is true the one planting has only a minor role, and it is also true the one watering has only a minor role because it requires a power above our own to get the increase. So, Paul plants the seed, Apollos waters the seed, and the mighty God of heaven gives the increase, and the seed then becomes a full-grown plant."

What then is my job title? Also, what is your job title? Believe it or not, you are wearing your job title. The Apostle Paul says in verse nine, "we are coworkers with God in God's cultivated field or greenhouse!" In other words, we are coworkers with Almighty God Himself in God's Greenhouse. We are coworkers with God the Father, God the Son, God the Holy Spirit, along with the Apostle Paul, Apollos, 19th century preachers like D. L. Moody and Charles Spurgeon, 20th century people like Billy Graham and the pastor who taught me about Jesus, 21st century people like Charles Stanley, Chuck Swindoll, David Jeremiah, plus the previous members in this church along with everyone sitting around me today.

God has come down to the earth to do His work, and He has enlisted each one of you to be His own special co-worker.

Jesus said it like this. This is a fill-in-the-blank on your study sheet. "Take My yoke upon you." He said, "You get in one side of the yoke, I'll get in the other side of the yoke, and *together* we'll plow the field. I'll use your energy, you'll use My energy, and together we'll get the work done."

I may be insignificant to you, but I am significant to God because I am a co-worker with God. I may not be the star quarterback, but I thank

God that He has allowed me to be on His team, how about you? I'd rather be a water boy on Jesus' team than be the president of Amazon!

What do I need to know to be the best co-worker I can be?

Our text is found in Matthew chapter thirteen. It is the well-known parable of the seed and the sower. It is a story about us as coworkers doing the work of God.

> *Then He told them many things in parables, saying: Consider the sower who went out to sow. As he was sowing, some seed fell along the path, and the birds came and ate them up. Others fell on rocky ground, where there wasn't much soil, and they sprang up quickly since the soil wasn't deep. But when the sun came up they were scorched, and since they had no root, they withered. Others fell among thorns, and the thorns came up and choked them. Still others fell on good ground and produced a crop: some 100, some 60, and some 30 times what was sown. Anyone who has ears should listen! (Matthew 13:3-9, HCSB)*

This parable gives us the secret to how you and I can be an effective co-worker with Almighty God.

1. Sow Yourself in the Lives of Others

If you want good results in your ministry, you must first learn the importance of sowing yourself in the lives of others! The first words out of Jesus' mouth are the words, "Consider the sower!" The entire process begins with a person accepting the responsibility of sowing the seed outside of himself!

Most of you Bible students know this parable frontward and backward. You have heard many sermons on this parable. The preacher focuses his effort on the four different kinds of soil and how each kind of soil responds to the seed.

Let's say the sermon is forty minutes long. The preacher will talk thirty-nine of those forty minutes about the soil. In so doing the preacher refers to this passage as "The Parable of the Seed and the Four Soils."

I want you to notice that is *not* the way Jesus characterized this parable. Look at verse eighteen. Jesus says in verse eighteen, "Listen to the parable of the *sower!*" Jesus begins with the sower! The sower is where this entire process begins!

Who is the sower? The sower is Jesus along with all of His coworkers and who are His coworkers? The coworkers are all of us!

The same principle carries over into so many areas of life. I spent twenty-nine years in the accounting profession. I remember a recurring theme that appeared in numerous books oriented to personal finance. "If you want to get ahead in the world be an investor rather than a loaner. Own something that has the potential to make you money rather than put your money in the mattress." In other words, you can't reap unless you first sow. *You have to be a sower to get ahead in the world!*

Jesus believed in sowing, also, but His version was that of sowing in *people* rather than dollars. Notice the first words of the parable are, "behold the sower—the one who is actively sowing," because God's law says you don't reap unless you first sow!

God is saying, "Take your life and sow yourself in the lives of others. Those other people are represented by the four types of soil. The goal is to help those other people know Jesus and become like Jesus. Jesus can make everyone better than they already are! Everyone needs Jesus! They won't find Jesus on their own. They need one of My coworkers to introduce them to Jesus!"

Let me give you three passages which talk about the importance of the sower. Each passage is a fill-in-the-blank on your study sheet. "When he saw the crowds, he had compassion for them because they were harassed and helpless, like sheep without a shepherd. Then he said to his disciples, The harvest is plentiful, but the laborers are few; therefore pray earnestly to the Lord of the harvest to send out laborers into his harvest." (Matthew 9:36-37, ESV)

The second passage is in Psalm 126. "Those who sow in tears shall reap with shouts of joy! He who goes out weeping, bearing the seed for sowing, shall come home with shouts of joy, bringing his sheaves with him." (Psalm 126:5-6, ESV)

The third passage is in Mark chapter sixteen. I spent the late 1970s studying for the ministry in Chattanooga, Tennessee. This verse was written in big letters across the choir loft at Highland Park Baptist Church. The verse says, "Go ye into all the world, and preach the gospel to every creature." I want you to know the mission is just as big as the mission field. Both are as big as the world itself!

Write this down in your notes: Nothing positive can happen without me sowing!

It begins with me. It will end with God giving the increase, but God can't give the increase if it doesn't begin with me!

Do I want to be successful as a co-worker with God?

It begins with sowing myself in the lives of others.

2. Sow the Right Seed.

The Bible says the sower sowed some seed. Let's identify what the seed is. Verse nineteen says the seed is "the word of God's kingdom." That sounds like the Bible to me. Verse twenty says the seed is the "word." That sounds like the Bible to me. Verse twenty-one says the seed is the "word." "Problems arise because of the teachings of the Word." Again, that sounds like the Bible to me. Verses twenty-two and twenty-three mention the "word" three more times, and every one of those times is consistent with the "word" being the Bible.

Some people question whether the Bible is now outdated and should be replaced. They say in ridicule, "Who needs that born-again message? Who needs the Ten Commandments? Who wants to hear about one way to heaven rather than many ways to heaven?"

It reminds me of the atheist who visited an island in the South Pacific. Of course, the atheist did not accept the Bible as God's Holy Word. The natives told him that every one of their homes had a copy of the Bible. The atheist laughed at them. He told the natives they needed a

215

replacement for the Bible. He said the Bible was outdated in his home country and would soon be outdated in their country, too. One of the tribal leaders then rose and said, "Mister, if the Bible was outdated here, you would have been eaten a long time ago!"

But a sower had sown the Word of God in that village and what a difference it made!

The Apostle Paul went forth as a sower, and he testified, "For I determined not to know anything among you, except Jesus Christ, and him crucified." (1 Corinthians 2:2)

Paul boldly stated, "I am not ashamed of the gospel or good news associated with Jesus Christ: the good news of the cross is the power of God unto salvation to every person that believes; first to the Jew, and second to the Gentile." (Romans 1:16)

The book of Hebrews teaches, "For the word of God is living and active, sharper than any two-edged sword, piercing to the division of soul and of spirit, of joints and of marrow, and discerning the thoughts and intentions of the heart. And no creature is hidden from his sight, but all are naked and exposed to the eyes of him to whom we must give account." (Hebrews 4:12-13, ESV)

Whatever you do, *don't ever sell the Bible short!* The Bible still has the right message and the necessary power to do whatever God wants to do!

Someone asked, "But suppose the people don't accept the authority of the Bible?" The situation is similar to what happened to a fool! This fool was facing an intruder who held a sword! The intruder threatened to kill the man if he did not reveal the hiding place of his money. The fool laughed and said, "That play sword of yours can't harm me! Run me through!" Which the intruder proceeded to do!

The atheist may say, "That sword called the Bible can't harm me! Run me through!" I say in all sincerity, "Run him through! His armor is only skin deep. The Bible is able to pierce through the skin and even separate the joints from the marrow! It is able to reveal the hidden thoughts of the heart! Go ahead and run him through!"

Isaiah 55:11 gives a promise to every sower. It is a fill-in-the-blank on your study sheet. God promised, "My Word shall not return to Me void or empty. My Word will accomplish whatever I please!"

The question is not whether the Word of God will work! The question is, do we believe enough in the Word that we will put it to work? Rest assured, there is no substitute for the Word of God! Simply put it to work and let God do what He does best!

Billy Graham told about one of the greatest dilemmas in his own ministry. In his early days, Billy questioned the authority of the Word of God. He kept asking himself, "Is the Bible wholly inspired by God or only partially inspired by God?" He could not determine which part to believe and which part to not believe. Well, that eventually changed! Someone later remarked, "From the way Billy preaches now, it is obvious he believes in every word in the Bible!"

What phrase did Billy use many times in his sermons? It was the three words, "The Bible says!" Billy could say those words because he was convinced of the genuineness, complete inspiration of the Word of God!

Do you want to be an effective sower? You must first have total confidence in the Word of God. I do, but how about you?

3. Sow Abundant Seed

Every farmer knows the principle of sowing abundant seed! Why? It is because some seed will never produce fruit. This was especially true before modern technology. In his early days, my father would sow three seeds in the same hole with the hope that at least one seed would germinate! Dad was satisfied with only a 33% success ratio!

Unfortunately, God's co-worker can expect the same results as the sower in this parable. Would to God that everyone appreciated our message! Would to God that everyone who hears the message also believes the message! Would to God the sun shone equally on everyone, too, and no one ever experienced heartache or sorrow or death!

The prophet Isaiah cried out in agony of soul, "Who has believed our report or message? Is there anyone anywhere to whom the arm of the Lord has been revealed?" (Isaiah 53:1) You can sense his unwritten words, "Is there anyone out there who believes our message?" Of course, the answer was yes. But sometimes we need to be reminded of this truth. The reason we need to be reminded is that the naysayers outnumber the yes-sayers.

Elijah was a mighty man of God in the Old Testament! He lived in a day similar to Isaiah. Elijah prayed one time and asked God to withhold rain from rebellious Israel. As a result, it did not rain for three years and six months! It sounds to me like he must have been really upset with rebellious Israel!

John the Baptist began the New Testament with a fantastic ministry! It wasn't long until he was imprisoned for sowing abundant seed. John reached such a level of despair that he dispatched coworkers to Jesus with the question, "Are you truly the Christ? Are you really the Messiah?"

The Bible is full of coworkers who experienced rejection similar to the rejection experienced by our own Lord and Savior Jesus Christ. Isaiah 53:3 says about Jesus that he was "despised and rejected of men!"

The truth is we must get over our expectation that everyone will respond positively to our message. Let me repeat what I just said. We must get over our expectation that everyone will respond positively to our message. I have been in the ministry more than forty years. Yet I *still* struggle with this issue. Why? It is because I fail to understand how anyone—even one person—can reject Jesus. It simply makes zero sense to me. Jesus is the best thing to ever happen to me! Surely everyone wants Jesus!

But the fact remains that everyone does not want Jesus. That is the purpose behind the parable of the sower.

Actually, there is a twofold purpose. First, the parable teaches us that everyone does *not* want Jesus. Second, and this item is critically important, it teaches us that some people *will* want Jesus! So keep sowing because a harvest time is coming!

The lesson is clear. This is a fill-in-the-blank. Some seed will *not* produce, but God guarantees some seed *will* produce.

Jesus gives us the seed of the Bible and then sends us out to sow. We sow into people's lives in every church service, every small-group meeting, and every church activity. We also sow into people's lives at work, home, recreation, Wally World, and throughout the neighborhood.

We are constantly sowing our lives and the Bible into others.

What kind of results can we expect? This parable teaches the results will fall into four broad categories. Let me briefly cover the four categories with you.

Category number one is what we'll call the closed-minded hearer. The King James Version describes him as the wayside hearer. To quote one such person, "I already know what I believe and am not interested in what you have to say."

It reminds me of the train engineer whose train was moving down the track at sixty miles an hour. The engineer saw a man ahead of the train who was waving his arms and shouting. The train's noise drowned out the man's words. The engineer responded to the man by waving back and smiling. The train went around the next bend, rolled onto the bridge, but the bridge was no longer there. The bridge had been washed out by a flood. The train went over the edge, and that was the end of the engineer.

The first hearer is described as a type of soil that can never produce any fruit. His heart is likened to that of the wayside or the path that people walk on day after day. The soil may have been good at one time, but now it is as hard as concrete.

As a matter of fact, that is a good way to think about this man. Imagine sowing seed on the interstate highway. How much of that seed would ever produce fruit? The answer is none. The concrete is so hard the seed can never penetrate to the soil beneath.

The closed-minded hearer is like a concrete highway. His mind is so closed to new truth that he never considers the new truth.

But we sow the seed anyway. After all, we don't know the true condition of this man's heart. The closed-minded hearer may tell us he is not interested; therefore, don't talk to me. Or he may listen patiently, so he does not hurt our feelings. But his mind is already made up.

There is nothing you or I can do to change the closed-minded hearer. The truth is God must first change his heart. God must first plow up the soil before our seed will have any success. This person is like the soil by the wayside.

Let me say it again so you don't let this problem discourage you. There is nothing you or I can do to change the closed-minded hearer. Learn, therefore, to wait on God!

The second type of soil is what I call the emotional-minded hearer. The text describes this person as being a type of soil that contains an abundance of small rocks and stones. This soil is almost as bad as the soil in the closed-minded hearer, but there is some small potential here for better results.

The seed is sown in the emotional-minded hearer, and that seed actually begins the process of germination. It is similar to a pre-salvation experience such as Jesus described in John 16:7-11. This may be considered the "enlightenment" stage in the salvation experience. Verse twenty says the person responds to the seed with joy—with great emotion.

This is an improvement! The closed-minded hearer slammed the door (his heart) in our face, but the emotional-minded hearer actually listens!

But there is no depth to the experience. The seed never penetrates deep into the soil. No root develops. Difficulties arise. The person's original emotions disappear . . . and so does the person.

Bible scholars struggle in understanding this soil as well as the third soil. *Our understanding is clouded by the realization that our faith falls into the fourth soil category.* We are bewildered at these lack-of-true saving faith categories. The experiences seem similar to John 2:23-24. The King James Version says, "Many believed . . . when they saw the miracles which He did but Jesus did not commit Himself unto them because He knew all men." In other words, Jesus knew the true condition of their hearts!

Perhaps the emotional-minded hearer is the one who shouted "Hosanna" to Jesus on the day of the triumphal entry (also known as Palm Sunday) and who, a few days later, changed his opinion and cried out, "Crucify Him! We will not have this man to rule over us!"

I want you to understand that emotions are much more shallow than faith! Faith goes deep! Faith goes so deep that it perseveres when the storms come! I say again, I can't produce such faith in people.

The songwriter said,

> *I know not how the Spirit moves, Convincing men of sin,*
> *Revealing Jesus thro' the word, Creating faith in Him.*
> *But "I know whom I have believed, And am persuaded that He is able*
> *To keep that which I've committed Unto Him against that day."*
> *Daniel Webster Whittle*

My job as God's co-worker is to sow the Word and leave the consequences up to God . . . and, of course, to the individual! The Bible says, "As many as *received* Him, to them He gave the right to become children of God!" (John 1:12)

The third hearer is the worldly minded hearer. Verse twenty-two explains the problem with this soil. The seed has potential, but it is overcome by three adversaries. The first adversary is the many concerns of life such as the worries and anxieties associated with everyday living. The routine of everyday life consumes the individual. In his way of thinking, Jesus Christ is something to be compartmentalized rather than be the controlling philosophy for how he conducts his life.

The second adversary is termed "the deceitfulness of riches." During my many years as a part-time pastor and part-time finance director, I saw these four words in action! "The deceitfulness of riches" is one of the most profound terms in the Bible to me. "The love of money is indeed a root that tends to all kinds of evil." Interestingly, in this particular case, the root associated with money goes deeper than the seed! The rich young ruler was not the only person to fail in this matter. He liked everything Jesus said until Jesus made an issue of his money. It turned out that his money was his god! That exposed which side he was really on, and, no, it wasn't the side of Jesus.

The third adversary is implied but not stated. It is the love of worldly pleasures rather than a love for God. Paul described men as "lovers of pleasure more than lovers of God." In many ways, it is the great sin of America, but it is not confined just to America! 1 John 2:15-17 warns,

> *"Do not love the world or the things that belong to the world. If anyone loves the world, love for the Father is not in him. For everything that belongs to the world—the lust of the flesh, the lust of the eyes, and the pride in one's lifestyle—is not from the Father, but is from the world. And the world with its lust is passing away, but the one who does God's will remains forever." (1 John 2:15-17, HCSB)*

The Bible doctrine of repentance is part of a genuine salvation experience. The simplest definition of repentance is "changing one's mind." The person hears the Word, considers the claims of Jesus, then becomes fully persuaded to commit his soul (nothing is dearer to a person than his own soul) to Jesus as Lord and Savior. *It is a conscious decision which originates in the human will, agrees with one's intellect, and tends to bring emotional sorrow over sin.*

Let's say it in a theological way for you Bible teachers. Genuine born-again salvation affects three parts of your being: the intellect, the emotions, and the will. I can't do that. You can't do that. Only God can do that.

The fourth seed, though, falls on what the Bible calls good ground. This ground pictures the prepared-minded hearer. This person's heart is described as "good ground" or "plowed ground" or "prepared ground." The sower keeps sowing, and some of the seed falls upon ground that is ready to receive the seed. The seed then does what it is supposed to do, and salvation comes to that person.

And the reason salvation comes is because the sower went forth to sow and he sowed *abundant* seed!

That brings us to the fourth secret to how you and I can be an effective co-worker with Almighty God.

4. Sow Expecting a Harvest!

Psalm 126:5-6 says, "They that sow in tears shall reap in joy. He that goeth forth and weepeth, bearing precious seed, shall doubtless come again with rejoicing, bringing his sheaves with him." (KJV) Underline the word "doubtless" on your study sheet. The word "doubtless" means "without a doubt."

We can read the verse like this, "without a doubt the sower will return rejoicing, carrying an abundant, overflowing harvest with him."

The sower went out sowing very tiny seed, but he comes again carrying a much greater harvest than what he sowed.

This part of the parable is the most amazing part to me. *The sower has invested his life in the lives of others.* It has cost him time, it has cost him money, it has deprived him of many worldly pleasures, but he has stayed at it for many years.

I suspect there were many times when the devil whispered in his ear, "You are wasting your time with this Jesus stuff. No one is listening. No one cares."

But he keeps on year after year as a co-worker with God. He hears Paul saying, "Your labor is not in vain if your labor is expended in the Lord's strength."

Sometimes the results look mighty slim. The sower might even wonder if the devil is right. But down deep in his heart, he keeps sowing because he sees himself as a co-worker with God! He may not be Billy Graham, but he can do what God has called him to do!

The same is true with us. You and I are coworkers with God.

Let me share with you something that is very, very important.

Do you know what our biggest problem is? It isn't the devil. It isn't God. It isn't the people we deal with. It is one critical issue! *The issue is we cannot yet see the true results of our ministry.*

Look closely at verse twenty-three. Eventually, in God's own time, the sower's effort brought forth some fruit, but notice it wasn't just some fruit. It was abundant fruit, more fruit than we could ever anticipate.

"Some results were a hundredfold, other results were sixtyfold, and the smallest results were thirtyfold."

How much is a hundredfold? You're going to write the number on your study sheet. It's a percentage. Don't write anything yet.

Onefold means you doubled your investment. Think of it in terms of money. I recently bought a certificate of deposit that paid a 3.5% interest rate. Onefold does not mean a 1% interest rate. It means a 100% interest rate. It means you start out with one and end up with two. In effect, you double your money! Which result would you rather have? A 100% interest rate or a 3.5% interest rate?

There are some spaces on your study sheet in front of the percentage sign. Go to the far left space and write the number 1 then write the number 0 in the next space and then write the number 0 in the third space. In other words, onefold means 100%.

But Jesus did not say He would multiply our seed onefold. Let's assume it's a tenfold return. Tenfold is ten times onefold. That means we need to add a 0 in the fourth space. That is the measure of a tenfold return. How much is it? It is 1,000%.

But Jesus did not say He would multiply our seed tenfold. He said some efforts would get a return on their investment of one hundredfold. One hundredfold is ten times tenfold or ten times what you have already written. Add another 0 in the fifth space. You are now looking at the measurement of a hundredfold return. How much is it? It is 10,000%. *No one on earth can multiply your money or your time or your effort like Jesus.*

You start out with one, and you end up with a hundred. That is a return on your initial investment of 10,000%.

Now, pay close attention! During your ministry, you will sow seed in the lives of the people you meet. Some of that seed *will*, not might but definitely will, fall on the wayside soil, other seed will fall on the rocky soil. Still other seed will fall on the thorny soil, but God guarantees some of your seed will fall on the good soil.

That seed will affect a life this year and next year and next year. Should I stop or should I keep saying and next year and next year and next year and next year? Long after you are dead and gone that seed will still be multiplying in the lives of others. As a matter of fact, it will keep multiplying until the earth comes to an end and eternity begins!

It is a shocking thing to realize that three-fourths of the seed produced nothing of lasting value. *But it is even more of a shock to realize that just one-fourth of the seed produced results that can only be measured by God Himself!*

The largest return on the initial investment is 10,000%. The smallest return on the initial investment is still 3,000% or thirtyfold.

I ask you, where on God's earth can I get a return on my investment like that? The answer is nowhere except in God's work!

I was mentored in my early ministry by Leo Gibson, one of the best preachers in Wayne County, West Virginia. Leo preached two revivals for me. One night he preached directly at a young discouraged preacher named Tom Swartzwelder.

Leo said, "In my early years I worked so hard at getting people saved. I would lay awake at night praying for them! Lay awake thinking about what I could say that would cause them to get saved. The agony of that experience nearly broke me. *But then I realized that it was not my business to save them. It was only my business to tell them!* I couldn't save them! Only God could save them! I finally realized that truth. From that time on, I was able to sleep at night."

"Behold, a sower went forth to sow."

That sower is God's co-worker.

That co-worker is you!

12

WHERE TOGETHERNESS BECOMES HEAVENLY TOGETHERNESS – Part 1

In Him – Answers 1-3

Preparation: You will need a large cookie and one actor.

In the year 1765, a young preacher named John Fawcett was called to pastor a very small church in the land of England. This church loved their new pastor, but it was a very poor church. The church was not able to properly care for this young pastor's family. As a matter of fact, the family almost starved to death. In their case the old saying was true, "The church wanted a whale but did not have enough water for a minnow."

Seven years passed. John Fawcett then received a call from a much larger church located in the great city of London. There was no doubt that this church could take care of his family. John Fawcett accepted the call to pastor this much larger church.

The day came for the pastor's family to move. The church people helped them load their few possessions into a wagon. The church people then begged the pastor to stay.

The begging was so intense that it caused the pastor and his wife to begin weeping. Finally, Mrs. Fawcett said, "O John, I cannot bear this! They need us so badly here!"

John said, "God has spoken to my heart, too! Tell them to unload the wagon! We cannot break these wonderful ties of fellowship!"

So it was that John Fawcett stayed as the pastor of that little church. Some years later John Fawcett then wrote a song which was based upon that very experience:

> *Blest be the tie that binds,*
> *Our hearts in Christian love!*
> *The fellowship of kindred mind*
> *Is like to that above.*

But there is one item which holds a church together even more than Christian love because this one item is the source—the ultimate source—of all true Christian togetherness. They are probably the two most important words in the entire Bible. What are those two words? Why are they so very important? What do they mean to me and also to our church?

Our text is repeated over and over again in the first two chapters in the book of Ephesians. Let me read the verse, but I won't read the most important part of all. I'll simply pause, and I want you to fill in the blank.

Chapter 1:1 says, "Paul, an apostle of Jesus Christ by the will of God, to the saints which are at Ephesus, and to the faithful _____ (in Christ Jesus)." The two key words are "in Christ."

Chapter 1:3 says, "Blessed be the God and Father of our Lord Jesus Christ, who has blessed us with all spiritual blessings in heavenly places

_____ (in Christ)." This is the first fill-in-the-blank on your study sheet. The two key words are "in Christ."

Chapter 1:4-7 says, " According as he hath chosen us _____(in him) before the foundation of the world, that we should be holy and without blame before him in love: Having predestinated us unto the adoption of children by Jesus Christ to himself, according to the good pleasure of his will, To the praise of the glory of his grace, wherein he hath made us accepted _____(in the beloved). _____ (In whom) we have redemption through his blood, the forgiveness of sins, according to the riches of his grace." I count the idea of "In Him" three times in that passage.

Chapter 1:10 says, "That in the dispensation of the fulness of times he might gather together in one all things _____ (in Christ), both which are in heaven, and which are on earth; even _____(in him)." The concept is contained twice in that verse.

Chapter 1:13 says, "_____ (In whom) you also trusted, after that you heard the word of truth, the gospel of your salvation: _____ (in whom) also after that you believed, you were sealed with the Holy Spirit of promise."

Chapter 2:5-6 says, "Even when we were dead in sins, has made us alive together with Christ, (by grace you are saved;) And has raised us up together, and made us sit together in heavenly places _____ (in Christ Jesus)."

Chapter 2:10 says, "For we are his workmanship, created _____ (in Christ Jesus) unto good works, which God has previously ordained that we should walk in them."

One more time! Chapter 2:13 says, "But now _____ (in Christ Jesus) you who were previously far off have been brought near by the blood of Christ."

Let's repeat our goal one more time. The goal is written at the bottom of your study sheet. The goal is, *"Helping Believers Grow Together in Him Through Love and Forgiveness."* Underline the middle two words. They are the words "in Him."

Ten words in all and all ten words have a lot of meaning. The middle two words are critically important to this particular study. Please notice that symbolically those two words join together the first four words and the last four words. You can't join the first four words to the last four words unless you go where? Through Him!

Let me remind you of the title for this message. The title is "*Where* Togetherness Becomes Heavenly Togetherness." This subject is not about "how to get togetherness" or "what is togetherness" but "*where* is togetherness."

The reason that is so significant is that you will never experience true spiritual togetherness if you take out the two words "in Him". *Remember this: True spiritual togetherness is both a vertical and horizontal relationship.* Vertically it rises to heaven itself; it makes God Himself part of the fellowship. Horizontally it reaches from the back row to the front row; it makes every single one of us part of the fellowship.

In plain English, and this is a fill-in-the-blank, true spiritual togetherness is with both God and each other.

It is like taking your right hand and holding the hand of your brother. Would you like to guess whose hand you are holding with your left hand? You are holding the hand of Almighty God.

Thus, our togetherness is both horizontal and vertical. It is a togetherness which exists with each other, but most importantly, it exists with God Himself!

To attempt to have togetherness without including God is an insult to God! And it's also a very poor substitute for God's kind of togetherness.

Think again about the title of the message. I do not claim inspiration for any sermon title, but I believe those words communicate what we need to experience in our church.

"Where Togetherness Becomes Heavenly Togetherness" means it is *not* a togetherness created by this world, but it is a togetherness which comes from heaven itself!

How exactly do we come together as a church? We come together many times, and we talk about the church being together, the church is in unity, the church is enjoying peace, and the church is one.

But the interesting thing is that many times we come together and never realize the true source of our unity. Furthermore, sometimes we think we are united, but we are not united in the right way. That kind of unity becomes a very shallow unity.

There are three basic errors in the way we often think about togetherness. These errors will be fill-in-the-blanks on your study sheet.

Error #1: Some people think we are spiritually together because we are united in an activity. It may be an activity like Vacation Bible School or the fall festival or a senior adult celebration. The outside world may look at us and say that we were one because we were all together in the same place. We were all enjoying the same activity! But that is not necessarily so because you can be one in an activity and yet still not have the heavenly togetherness that this study is about.

Error #2: Others will say that a well-written church constitution will bring spiritual togetherness. Some of you may not even know what I am talking about so let me explain. A church constitution explains how the church is to be operated. It lays out the duties of the different offices and how we are to function. That is very important because the Bible says, "Let all things be done decently and in order." Some think, though, that you will automatically have unity if everyone submits to the constitution!

I remember one of my early experiences at Tucker Memorial Baptist Church. I was the new pastor. I wondered who to visit first. I chose to visit Mrs. Fowler. She taught the biggest class in the church. I remember sitting in her living room. Her first words were, "Pastor, it's nice to meet you. But I won't get to know you very well because I'm moving to a different state in a few weeks." My heart sank when I heard that because I needed good workers.

Mrs. Fowler then said, "Pastor Tom, I have just one word of advice for you. Tell them to quit changing the constitution. They think the solution to every problem is changing the church rules."

She taught me something that night. *It's not what you put on paper that counts, but it's the spirit of the people that counts.* If the spirit of the people is wrong, you're in trouble regardless of what is on the paper.

You can put anything you want in the constitution. Indeed, all of us can even agree on its contents, but that won't guarantee you'll experience heavenly togetherness.

Error #3: Spiritual togetherness is the result of all of us being members of the same church. In other words, all of us believe the same teachings, all of us sing the same songs, and all of us worship the same way. But, once again, that unity may fall far short of heavenly togetherness.

Dr. B. R. Lakin once said, "Ninety percent of the work which is done by the so-called Christian church could be done by an atheist." That is likely an exaggeration, but the truth is much of the work will be done regardless of whether the Holy Spirit is present or not present.

One of the great preachers said, "The church of the future will not be a lazy church, but rather it will be a very busy church." That means there will be all kinds of activities! The future church will be built around activities and yet may totally miss this idea of heavenly togetherness.

What then is heavenly togetherness? This is a fill-in-the-blank. It is a togetherness which is rooted in the right source—it absolutely must be rooted in the right source—and out of that one source comes this heavenly togetherness.

Remember our goal again. The goal is at the bottom of your study sheet. The goal is, *"Helping Believers Grow Together in Him Through Love and Forgiveness."*

I want you to know that *the middle two words determine if our togetherness becomes heavenly togetherness.* They are the two words "in Him."

Never forget: the highest form of togetherness takes place in Him! God's version of togetherness is the togetherness we should always seek, and that togetherness always takes place in Him—in His Son, Jesus Christ.

Coming together "in Him" means that our minds are focused on Him, our hearts are dedicated to Him, and our affections are yielded to Him! Everything we do, along with everything we believe, is being controlled by Him! It is then that you can experience God's heavenly togetherness!

The key is tapping into the *source* of true heavenly togetherness, and that source is "in Him!"

What then is this heavenly togetherness all about?

1. Heavenly Togetherness Means We Have the Same Nature.

Answer #1: Heavenly togetherness means we have the same nature. That means you have the same nature as I do and the same nature as the people sitting around you. Based upon us having the same nature, we can now experience heavenly togetherness!

The Bible is a nature book, but not in the same sense as the naturalist thinks. The Bible is a book which reveals facts to us about the old nature we call the Adamic nature and the new nature we call the new creation, or the new man, or Christ living in me.

The Bible says in Galatians 2:20, "I have been, with the result that I am still, crucified with Christ. The old nature has been judged and crucified. As a result, it is no longer I that live but Christ lives in me! The life I now live in this body is a life I live by faith in the Son of God who loved me and gave Himself for me!" Paul says, "I have a new life . . . a new nature . . . a life in the Holy Spirit. I now have a desire to live for Jesus Christ and to experience Jesus Christ in my daily life."

The Bible says in Colossians 3:1-4,

> *"Since you have been raised with Christ, set your heart on things above where Christ is enthroned at the right*

hand of God. Set your mind on things above and not on things down here on the earth. For you have died and your life is now hidden with Christ in God. Therefore, when Christ who is now your spiritual life shall appear, then shall you also appear with Him in glory."

Let me give you one more verse. 1 John 5:12 says, "This is God's record, that God has given us eternal life, and this eternal, spiritual life is in His Son."

I read all of those verses not to take up your time but to prove this point is supported by plenty of scripture. The Bible is very plain that I am now indwelt with the spiritual life and the spiritual attitude and the spiritual desires of God the Son.

Let me pose a question. What do we mean when we say that Christ lives in me and I am in Him?

Let's act it out. (Note: Have a man represent Jesus Christ. Let a cookie represent one of the older members. Ask that member for the date of his salvation. Picture that person coming to Jesus for salvation. The Bible teaches we are then united with Jesus Christ in His death, burial, and resurrection. It says we are crucified with Him, buried with Him, and resurrected with Him to walk in newness of life. We have been united with Jesus. *The Bible says we are now "in Him!"* How can we illustrate this truth? Very simply! Jesus has "swallowed" us and united us to Him. Have "Jesus" swallow the cookie.)

Let's read one more verse which explains what just happened. This is a fill-in-the-blank. Ephesians 5:30 says, "We are now members of His body!" We are now in Him!

The cookie can no longer be seen; the cookie is hidden. All we can see is Jesus! The cookie is now being absorbed into the body. Likewise, we have been vitally united to the life of Jesus Christ! The life of that cookie has now been absorbed into someone bigger than it, and that bigger someone will now overwhelm the smaller person!

That means I am alive! Alive in Him!

It is important you understand that Jesus Christ is now living in me! I can now live a different kind of life!

The Bible says, "No longer I but Christ lives in me!" Christ now wants to live His own life through me! From this point on, I need to be submissive to Him. If I am submissive to Him, your attention will not be on Tom Swartzwelder but on Jesus Christ!

All of us who are saved have Christ living in us! No one can say, "I have more of Jesus than you do." All of us have the same Christ living in us! *That means we can now grow together because we now have a common bond!*

2. Heavenly Togetherness Means We Have the Same Head.

Answer #2: Heavenly togetherness means we have the same head. What is a head for? A head is for thinking. A head is for planning. It is for giving direction to the rest of the body.

When I was a boy they would often say, "Tommy, use your head. You know better than to do that." Did anyone ever talk to you like that?

Nick's Barber Shop had a sign on the wall which said, "Be sure brain is in gear before putting mouth into gear." That's good advice for any age!

The head is very important because the head tells the rest of the body what to do.

My wife and I were lying in bed one night at about two a.m. when the dog started barking. We had a sixteen-week-old Labrador puppy. The head of the house said, "Go check on the dog before it wakes everyone up. It probably has its chain wrapped around the tree."

I put on my house shoes, got the flashlight, and went out to check on the dog. The dog was asleep in the doghouse. She looked at me as if to say, "Don't you know what time it is?" It turned out it was the neighbor's dog that was barking!

The head tells the rest of the body what to do.

Now follow closely. Answer #1 taught us that every believer is now in Christ. That means every one of us has the very same head to tell us what to do! I want you to know this head is much smarter than any of us!

Ephesians 1:22 says, "God the Father has placed all things under the feet of Jesus Christ. Furthermore, God the Father has made Jesus Christ to be the head over all things to the church."

There are times when we don't know what to do. We need direction! We're not smart enough!

We're like the arm. The arm has no brain. It doesn't know whether to make a fist, raise itself higher or go lower. But the head expresses its will to the rest of the body. My head says, "Raise your left arm" and my left arm goes up.

The instruction did not originate within the arm but within the head.

The same truth applies spiritually. The Head has a will for each one of us as well as for our church. *All of us can know that will because we have the very same Head!*

It is not a case of me saying, "You go pray to your God, and I'll pray to my God," because we are praying to the very same Head! The God that listens to me is the very same God that listens to you!

We don't go to God the Father through a man like the Roman Catholic Pope or the Virgin Mary or some other saint, but we go directly to God the Father through His Son Jesus Christ!

We need to continually seek Him because we are in Him. His life will then be lived through you. Not only is that true, but His will can also be expressed through you!

This is another reason we can have heavenly togetherness. It is because all of us are in the same body, we have the same nature, and we have the same head! We are together in Him!

3. Heavenly Togetherness Means We Have the Same Blessings.

Answer #3: Heavenly togetherness means we have the same blessings. This is one of the reasons why we are Baptists and not some other denomination. You need to listen very closely to this point. Ephesians 1:3 says, "Blessed be the God and Father of our Lord Jesus Christ, who has blessed us with all spiritual blessings in heavenly places in Christ." Three words stand out in that verse. The first word is the word "all." The little boy said, "All means all, and that's all all means!" If you say "all", you are including everything without exception. That verse means God has made everything available that is necessary for me to do the work of God.

Let me run a rabbit trail with you. In my early days, I worked three years as a motor bank teller in Portsmouth, Ohio. One of my customers was a wonderful Pentecostal man. One night he came to the window to cash a check. I gave him the money, then he asked me a question I had never heard before. He asked, "Have you received the second blessing?" I had never heard of the second blessing. I did not know how to respond.

I went home and told my father about our conversation. I said, "Dad, he asked me if I had received the second blessing, and I did not know what to say."

Dad said, "If he asks you again, just tell him that you have received the second blessing and the third blessing and the fourth blessing and the fifth blessing and the sixth blessing and the seventh blessing and all the other blessings, too, but you received all of them when you were saved, and God sealed you in the Anointed One!"

The Bible says that every born-again child of God automatically receives the same Holy Spirit along with **all** of the blessings that are connected to the Holy Spirit. Romans 8:9 says, "If any man claims to be saved but does not have the Holy Spirit that man is none of Christ's—he has never been saved."

From the moment of salvation to the moment of our homegoing, the believer does not need to receive *more* of the Holy Spirit. He already has *all* of the Holy Spirit that he needs. The issue is no longer one of my getting more of Him but of *Him getting more of me!*

The Holy Spirit is mine. The Holy Spirit is yours, too. The blessing of being filled with the Holy Spirit is mine. The blessing of being filled with the Holy Spirit is yours, too. The blessing of praying in the Holy Spirit, of being led by the Holy Spirit, of producing the fruit of the Holy Spirit are all mine. Guess what? They are also yours, too.

"My God shall supply all of your needs according to His riches in Christ Jesus" is just as true for you as it is for me. "The Lord is my Shepherd, I shall not want," is just as true for you as it is for me. "Cast your worries upon the Lord for He cares for you," is just as true for you as it is for me. "Therefore, we can come boldly to the throne of grace and find mercy and grace to help us in our time of need" is just as true for you as it is for me.

The good news is that God has blessed us with all of the necessary spiritual blessings in Christ Jesus.

2 Peter 1:3 says "God has given to us *all things* pertaining to life and godliness." In other words, nothing has been left out.

End of the rabbit trail!

Second, notice where all of the blessings are located. The Apostle Paul says all of the blessings are located "in Christ." Two very powerful words! These blessings are not in a book nor in a church nor in the world but in a person—they are in Christ!

Here is what that means. Since God has put all of us in the same place—"in Christ"—then every single one of us has the same spiritual blessings as the other person.

Bill Gates, the founder of Microsoft, is worth billions of dollars. His worth changes by a billion dollars every week depending upon the value of Microsoft's stock. By contrast, many of you barely make ends meet despite living on Social Security. You consider yourself fortunate if you finish the month with a few dollars left over. And yet to imagine having a billion dollars!

I want you to know that Bill Gates's billions of dollars are just a penny when compared with all of the spiritual blessings which God has given me in Christ Jesus. Bill Gates can go to the White House, ask to see the President, and the President will gladly see him. I, though, can get down on my knees, go past the White House, go to the very throne of

God Himself and my God is able to do "exceedingly abundantly above all that I ask or think."

Bill Gates can count his money at night then go to sleep and not worry about having food on the table. Well, so can I because "my God shall supply all of my needs according to His glorious riches by Christ Jesus."

Bill Gates can write a computer manual which talks about config.sys and autobat and MS-DOS and confuse everyone, but I am able to open the Book of Books and understand more than Bill Gates because the "natural, unsaved man receives not the things of the Spirit of God for they are moronic to him, neither can he know them because they are spiritually understood." (1 Corinthians 2:14)

What does it mean to be in possession of "all spiritual blessings?" *It means that God has given you everything you need to live the Christian life.* Do you need peace in the midst of the storm? That peace is now yours. Do you need grace for the trial you are now facing? That grace is now yours. Do you need wisdom to know which way to go? That wisdom is now yours. Do you need power to witness to that lost family member? That power is now yours. Do you need a teacher to learn the Word of God? That teacher (the Holy Spirit) is now yours!

You may never be rich in terms of physical money, but God has made you richer in Christ Jesus than you can ever be in money!

God has given you everything you need to live the Christian life!

I came across a special poem many years ago. I need to share it.

> *I was walking down life's highway a long time ago,*
> *One day I saw a sign that read 'Heaven's Grocery Store.'*
> *As I got a little closer, the door came open wide*
> *And when I came to myself, I was standing inside.*
> *I saw a host of angels, they were standing everywhere,*
> *One handed me a basket and said, "My child, shop with care."*
>
> *Everything a Christian needed was in that grocery store,*
> *And all you couldn't carry, you could come back the next day for more.*
> *First, I got some Patience, Love was in the same row,*

Further down was Understanding, you need that everywhere you go,
I got a box or two of Wisdom, a bag or two of Faith,
I just couldn't miss the Holy Ghost, for He was all over the place.

I stopped to get some Strength and Courage to help me run this race,
By then my basket was getting full, but I remembered I needed some Grace.
I didn't forget Salvation, for salvation was free,
So I tried to get enough of that to save both you and me.
Then I started up to the counter to pay my grocery bill,
For I thought I had everything to do my Master's will.

As I went up the aisle, I saw Prayer and I just had to put that in,
For I knew when I stepped outside, I would run right into sin.
Peace and Joy were plentiful, they were on the last shelf,
Song and Praises were hanging near so I just helped myself.

Then I said to the angel, 'Now how much do I owe?'
He just smiled and said, 'Just take them everywhere you go.'
Again, I smiled at him and said, 'How much do I really owe?'
He smiled again and said, 'My child, Jesus paid your bill a long time ago.'

Ron DeMarco

And all of it is now yours and mine because we are now together in Him!

13

WHERE TOGETHERNESS BECOMES HEAVENLY TOGETHERNESS – Part 2

In Him – Answers 4-6

Preparation: Place a chair near the pulpit. You'll need one actor.

Two men met on an ocean liner in the middle of the Pacific Ocean. One man was an American; the other man was Japanese. Neither man could speak the other's language, so they had no means of communicating with each other.

But each man carried a book. It was obvious to each man that the book was a Bible even though neither man could read the other man's Bible. (Bibles have a way of looking like Bibles.)

The two men just looked at each other because they didn't know how to share their faith. Finally, the American said, "Hallelujah, Jesus!" The Japanese said, "Amen, Jesus!" They then hugged each other and rejoiced in the Lord Jesus Christ even though neither one could speak the other's language.

What was it that made that togetherness possible? Was it nationality? No. Was it a common language? No. Was it a common background? Again, no.

Where then does true Christian togetherness begin? The answer, of course, is to be found in the inspired, inerrant Word of God!

Our text begins in 1 Corinthians 12:12-14. The Bible says,

> *"For even as the body is one and yet has many members, and all the members of the body, though they are many, are one body, so also is Christ. For by one Spirit we were all baptized into one body, whether Jews or Greeks, whether slaves or free, and we were all made to drink of one Spirit. For the body is not one member, but many." (1 Corinthians 12:12-14, NASB)*

1 Corinthians 12:25-27 continues the thought,

> *"so that there may be no division in the body, but that the members may have the same care for one another. And if one member suffers, all the members suffer with it; if one member is honored, all the members rejoice with it. Now you are Christ's body, and individually members of it." (1 Corinthians 12:25-27, NASB)*

Keep this phrase in your mind, "you are Christ's body" meaning we have been united with Him!

Ephesians 1:1-3 says,

> *"Paul, an apostle of Christ Jesus by the will of God, To the saints who are at Ephesus and who are faithful in Christ Jesus: Grace to you and peace from God our Father and the Lord Jesus Christ. Blessed be the God and Father of our Lord Jesus Christ, who has blessed us with every spiritual blessing in the heavenly places in Christ." (Ephesians 1:1-3, NASB)*

On your study sheet write the key phrase, "in Christ."

Someone asked me which subject I like to preach upon the most. They expected me to answer "prophecy" or the book of "Revelation" or "Daniel," but I surprised them by saying that my favorite subject for either personal study or pulpit preaching is wrapped up in these two little words "in Christ."

It has been said that the entire ministry of the Apostle Paul could be wrapped up in these two words "in Christ," because Paul wrote entire chapters about who we are and what we can now do based upon our position in Jesus Christ. The truth is no one yet has plumbed the depths of what it means to be "in Christ."

One writer pointed out that Paul used this little phrase "in Christ" or its equivalent a grand total of twenty-seven times in just the little book of Ephesians. That means these two words contain some very powerful teaching!

Think about it like this. This is a fill-in-the-blank. When Noah went inside the ark, God shut the door. The storms then came, but Noah was safe. He lived for 371 days inside the ark. During that time, God met every single one of Noah's needs because Noah was *inside* the ark of safety.

That is exactly what happens when you believe in Jesus Christ. God then places you *inside* the ark of safety; that ark of safety is His Son, Jesus Christ. It is *in* the greater ark of His own Son that God has promised to meet every single one of your needs.

That is why Paul makes such a big deal of these two little words "in Christ." Always remember this: Being in Noah's ark in the Old Testament is the same as being "in Christ" in the New Testament.

"In Christ" is the place where God has made all of us to be one whether we "be Jew or Gentile, free or slave, male or female, God has made all of us to be one with one another."

That is why the American and the Japanese could have fellowship with one another even though they could not even speak the same language. It was because they were both one in Jesus Christ! This meant they were able to enjoy a heavenly togetherness unlike any other togetherness which this world can create!

The key to making that happen is continually seeking the Lord Jesus Christ! When we seek Him, there are a number of things which automatically happen. Those things bring us together in Him.

We have already identified three facts that are true of all of us who believe in Jesus Christ as our Lord and Savior. These facts are fill-in-the-blanks on your study sheet.

What is heavenly togetherness?

Answer #1: Heavenly togetherness means we have the same nature. That same nature is the life of Christ now being lived through us—not just through the preacher but through every one of us! This is the first reason for our togetherness!

Answer #2: Heavenly togetherness means we have the same head. Christ's will is now being expressed through us. It is a will which binds us together in winning the lost and teaching them in the ways or disciplines of Jesus Christ.

Answer #3: Heavenly togetherness means we have the same blessings. It is like being in a supermarket, and everyone has enough money to buy whatever they need. God's supermarket includes everything we need to live the Christian life! The best part of all is that everything is free!

That's why the Bible can say the gates of hell shall not prevail against God's people. It is because we are laborers together in Christ and "if God be for us, who is there that can possibly stand against us?" This truth is shouting ground for the child of God!

But remember it is only in Him—in Christ—that togetherness can actually become heavenly togetherness.

So what else happens to all of us because we are together in Christ?

4. Heavenly Togetherness Means We Have the Same Relationship.

Answer #4 –Heavenly togetherness means we have the same relationship. This is new material so listen closely. All of us know what a relationship is. We have relationships in the military called privates, sergeants, and captains. We have relationships in the factory called workers, foremen, and supervisors. We have relationships in the government called mayors, governors, senators, and a president.

But what kind of relationships do we have now that we are in Christ Jesus?

The Roman Catholic Church is led by a man called the pope. It is customary for people to kiss the pope's ring when they meet the pope. In their religion, the pope is treated as someone distinct from the rest of the people. The pope never kisses anyone's ring, but everyone kisses his ring!

It is interesting that the Bible says just the opposite should take place in God's church. The Bible talks instead about "greeting one another with a holy kiss." The phrase "one another" includes everyone seated around you. "One another" is a good way to describe all of us who think we are important and all of us who think we're just ordinary. The truth is God sees all of us as having the same title and that title is "one another." That is a fill-in-the-blank! Our title is "one another." What a title to describe everyone who thinks they are important!

I hope that title does not bother you because that's exactly what you are to me. You are "one another" to me, and I am "one another" to you!

The Bible says, "For this reason I bow my knees before the Father, from whom every family in heaven and on earth derives its name." (Ephesians 3:14–15, NASB) The Bible makes it clear that we enjoy a family relationship.

What kind of relationship does a family enjoy? Is it a military relationship? How about a factory relationship? Maybe a government relationship? No, it is a brother and sister relationship.

(Note: Go to several people of different ages in the congregation. Choose one who is old enough to be the other's grandparent. Point out that they are brothers and sisters in Christ.)

(Note: Have everyone look at their neighbor and say, "Hello, brother" or "Hello, sister." Point out that there may be many years between their ages.)

Let me ask you a question. How do you treat members of your family? Like dogs? No, they are family, and you treat them like family!

We read earlier from 1 Corinthians 12:25-26. The passage talks about us having the same care for one another. Why? It's because we're a family and these folks are very precious to us!

It reminds me of when our daughters were still at home. When one family member goes to the hospital, all of us respond and are hurting. When one gets a special honor at school, all of us attend the celebration and are proud. When someone has a special need, all of us pray about that need. When a person wrongly criticizes one of us, the whole family rallies together.

Why? It is because we are a family and that's what families are for! Families are for encouraging one another! Not for tearing down one another! Families are for loving one another! Not for hating one another! Families are for praying for one another! Not for slandering one another! Families are for helping one another! Not for pushing down one another!

That's the way our church ought to be, also! Our church is a family which is made up of our brothers and our sisters! These people are just as much a part of our family as our own natural family!

They need just as much encouragement, love, prayers, help, and attention as the members of your own family!

That brings me to something very important. When I seek Jesus, I will also seek your best interest. I cannot seek Him without seeking your best interest, too. God has made us a part of the same family. You're my brother. You're my sister. I welcome you to my family. I trust you will welcome me and the people around you to your own family.

5. Heavenly Togetherness Means We Have the Same Anointing.

Answer #5 —Heavenly togetherness means we have the same anointing. Everyone senses their own weakness when God lays on our heart a new way to serve Him. For example, someone asks us to serve in a new area. Our first reaction is, "I can't" because we sense our own weakness. We hear a sermon on the subject of witnessing or praying or Bible study or taking a stand. Our first reaction is, "I can't" because we sense our own weakness.

We say, "If I had an anointing like so-and-so, then I could really serve the Lord Jesus Christ."

The King James Version sometimes uses the very old word "unction" in place of "anointing," but the two words mean the same thing!

In the years before the Civil War, a slave preacher was asked, "What does the Bible mean when it talks about the unction?" The preacher barely knew how to read. He said, "I don't know what the unction is, but I sure know what it isn't—what it's like when the unction is not there." The preacher could say that because he sensed that he was too weak to do the work of God on his own.

Look at your study sheet and fill in the blank. I have the same anointing as the best Christian I know. That person may be your pastor, teacher, deacon, even a D. L. Moody or Billy Graham!

Listen to what the Bible says, "For by one Spirit we were all baptized into one body, whether Jews or Greeks, whether slaves or free, and we were all made to drink of one Spirit." (1 Corinthians 12:13, NASB) Catch the last phrase and don't let it go. "We were all made to drink of one Spirit." The Bible teaches God has anointed or poured out the Holy Spirit into your life! It is just like an Old Testament priest taking a cup of oil and pouring the oil upon your head as happened in the Old Testament anointings.

247

You have been anointed just like Jesus was anointed at His baptism. The dove representing the Holy Spirit descended upon Jesus. The symbolism was clear: The Holy Spirit had been poured out upon Jesus. The next verse (Luke 4:1) says, "Jesus being full of the Holy Spirit returned from Jordan."

God has made that same fullness of the Holy Spirit available to every one of us! Jesus promised, "You shall receive power when the Holy Spirit comes upon you." (Acts 1:8) That same Holy Spirit has come upon you *if* you are in Jesus Christ like the rest of us!

As a matter of fact, you cannot be in Christ without being in the anointing!

Let me run a short rabbit trail with you and explain why that is so. 1 Corinthians 1:3 says, "Grace to you and peace from God our Father and from the Lord Jesus Christ." That verse provides three different names or titles for our Savior. I want you to know that each of those titles has a very specific meaning. The name Lord means "Master." The name Jesus means "Jehovah saves" or "Savior." No doubt, you'll remember the verse, "He shall save His people from their sins." The name Christ is critical to our current study because the name Christ means "Anointed One." Anointed with what? Not a what but rather a whom! The answer is the Holy Spirit!

Here is the conclusion of that rabbit trail. You can't be in Christ without also being in the anointing of the Holy Spirit because that is where the Holy Spirit is located! He is positioned in Christ! If you are in Christ, you are also immersed or saturated in the anointing of the Holy Spirit!

Here is what that means. First, you don't have a different Holy Spirit than I do! You have the same Holy Spirit that Jesus had, that all the great evangelists have, and that I have. Second, God didn't put you on a lower level than other Christians. Oh, my! God did not give you just a trickle of the Holy Spirit but give someone else a river of the Holy Spirit. Jesus promised, "He that believes on Me out of his belly or out of his innermost being shall flow rivers of living water." (John 7:38) Not just a trickle but rivers, and those rivers are a reference to the Holy Spirit! Third, it also means you can be filled with the Holy Spirit just like Jesus was filled! You can be filled for praying, filled for witnessing, filled for Bible study, filled for parenting, filled for encouraging, filled for anything that will honor God.

One of my shortcomings is that I often forget the Bible describes the Holy Spirit by the symbol of oil. The Bible scholars refer to that kind of symbol as a type.

Sometime ago I could not make a piece of metal slide into a deep hole. My construction had left me with a not-so-good fit. I cheated by putting oil on the metal. The oil served as a lubricant and the metal then slid easily into the hole.

Do you remember what the slave preacher said? He said, "I don't know what the unction is, but I sure know what it isn't." Everyone eventually learns the Holy Spirit oils everything! Everything works better with oil! Everything works better in God's work with the oil of the Holy Spirit. Things have a way of falling into place when the Holy Spirit is involved. That means we need to make the effort to get Him involved *before* we begin rather than waste a lot of time.

Someone complained and said, "I can't serve God because that person has more of the Holy Spirit than I have." I'm sorry to disappoint you, but no, he doesn't. It is not a question of whether he has more of the Holy Spirit but whether *the Holy Spirit has more of him*. Perhaps he is more yielded and saying, "Here I am, Lord. Come and use me in any way you wish for Your glory."

Someone else objected and said, "God doesn't use me like He used Billy Graham." My friend, maybe God doesn't want you to be a Billy Graham! Maybe God wants you to be yourself but to also be filled with the Holy Spirit so that He can touch others through you!

The truth is you can touch my life with the touch of the Holy Spirit just as much as the greatest Christian you know! It is a touch which all of us can provide because we all have the same anointing.

6. Heavenly Togetherness Means We Have the Same Victory.

Answer #6: Heavenly togetherness means we have the same victory. The victory is ours because of our position in the triumphant Christ!

The Apostle Paul's writings make it clear that Paul was a triumphant man. The enemy beat him in the city of Philippi, threw him into prison, and tried to ruin his ministry. The Bible, though, tells us that at midnight Paul was heard praying to God and singing praises to God.

The circumstances did not matter to Paul. The beating did not matter to Paul. The chains did not matter to Paul. Even the fact that he might be executed did not matter!

This was possible because Paul knew that heavenly togetherness means we have the same victory, and that victory is greater than any circumstance we might face!

Ephesians 2:4-6 tells us we already have the most important victory of all. It says,

> *"But God, being rich in mercy because of the great love with which he loved us, even when we were dead in our trespasses, made us alive together with Christ—by grace you have been saved—and raised us up with him and seated us with him in the heavenly places in Christ Jesus."*
> *(Ephesians 2:4-6, ESV)*

Count the blessings with me. We have been made spiritually alive or born again. We have been joined together with Christ. We have also been saved from the wrath to come. "O to grace how great a debtor daily I'm constrained to be!" Also, we have been raised up or undergone a spiritual resurrection to newness of life. And last, we are now seated together with Him in the heavenly places at the Father's right hand where our destiny is certain!

Picture it like this. Where is Christ today? He is seated at the Father's right hand.

(Note: Place a chair next to the pulpit. Hopefully, the chair is higher than the audience. The chair will illustrate Christ being seated at the Father's right hand. Have a man sit in the chair. The man represents Christ.)

Picture Jesus seated in heaven. Tell me this: Is Christ bothered by the circumstances down on earth? Down on your level? No. He is above that and so are we because we are in Him!

Let me explain what this actually means to the child of God. I'll give you the point then I will support the point with scripture. These are also fill-in-the-blanks on your study sheet.

First, God sees us as already being in heaven. That statement may surprise you, but it is an accurate statement! Romans 8:28-30 is one of the most complete presentations of doctrinal truth that is found anywhere in the Bible. It says,

> "And we know that for those who love God all things work together for good, for those who are called according to his purpose. For those whom he foreknew he also predestined to be conformed to the image of his Son, in order that he might be the firstborn among many brothers. And those whom he predestined he also called, and those whom he called he also justified, and those whom he justified he also glorified." (Romans 8:28-30, ESV)

Notice the English tense of the words called, justified, and glorified. All three of those words are in the past tense meaning it has already been done. That tense is the same tense in the Greek text. I say this because I want you to know these tenses are not a translation mistake but a biblical fact. The Greek tense is called the aorist tense (the aorist tense describes completed past action). It is true this activity has not yet been finished in my life, but *it is already as good as done in the mind of God.* I may still be on earth, but God sees me as already being glorified in heaven. That is how certain my salvation is.

During my years at Tennessee Temple University, we were blessed to hear many great speakers. One experience stands out to me. The speaker (I do not recall his name) said, "Someone told me that salvation was like swimming. If you commit sin, you will then sink and drown and lose your salvation. I told him that will never happen to me because *how can a man drown when his head is always above water?* The Bible says Jesus is my Head, My Head is in heaven, and that means my salvation is already settled!" I say amen to that line of reasoning and you should, too!

Second, the devil sees us as already being invincible. Look at our Jesus for a moment. Does Jesus have to listen to the devil anymore? No. Nor do we. The Bible says, "Resist the devil and he will flee (that means run, not walk) from you." (James 4:7)

Third, sin sees us as no longer being under its control. Sin may pull on my heart, but I am now joined to Jesus in heaven and, "greater is He that is in me than he that is in the world." (1 John 4:4)

Fourth, the world now sees us as belonging to another world. The Bible says we are different because we are, "pilgrims and strangers looking for a city which John saw coming down out of heaven." We are nomads, just temporary residents with no permanent home on earth! Our citizenship is in heaven; someday heaven will be just a real as being here at this very moment is real.

The Bible says there is a place reserved in heaven for me! There is a place reserved in heaven for you!

Albert E. Brumley taught us to sing, "This world is not my home, I'm just a passing through! My treasures are laid up somewhere beyond the blue. The angels beckon me from heaven's open door, and I can't feel at home in this world anymore!"

Rest assured, the victory is already ours because we are *already seated* in heavenly places in Christ Jesus!

You say, "The circumstances of life have dealt me a hard blow. I don't feel like praying, like worshipping, like studying."

Here is what you need to remember. You are now seated in heavenly places. You are now positioned in Christ who has risen victorious from the grave, who has defeated every foe and is now seated at the right hand of God. Those heavenly places are far above the circumstances of this life! I have been joined to the victory Man! And you, too, have been joined to the victory Man!

Your circumstances, though, are tied to this world! Every one of your problems is tied to this world.

So ask yourself, "Is Jesus fretting and worrying about my circumstances?" The answer is no!

The Apostle Paul taught us, "Rejoice evermore! In all things give thanks!" He wrote those words from the prison in Rome because he knew that heavenly togetherness means we have the same victory. *The final victory has already been won and someday you, and I will experience it for ourselves!*

You are familiar with the famous author, Robert Louis Stevenson. Robert's father was a passenger on an ocean liner. One night the ship was caught in a great storm just a short distance from the coastline. It appeared the ship would run into the rocks, and everyone on board would be killed.

The passengers were frightened. They asked Mr. Stevenson to go to the pilothouse and check with the pilot of the ship.

Mr. Stevenson fought his way along the railing then up the ladder to the pilothouse. He opened the door. The pilot looked at him and smiled. Not a word was spoken. The look on the pilot's face was enough.

Mr. Stevenson then fought his way back to the passengers. He said to them, "It is all right. I have seen the pilot's face and he smiled."

Here is the point of the story. It doesn't matter how rough your storm may be. Our pilot is smiling because the victory is already ours.

All I can say is "Thanks be to God who gives us the victory—the VICTORY—through our Lord Jesus Christ!"

We are now in Him—in Christ—and that means we have the same nature, we have the same Head, we have the same blessings, we have the same relationship, we have the same anointing, and we have the same victory!

We are IN HIM! God help us to now put our common position into common practice!

Everyone read with me the goal which is the last line on your study sheet. *"Helping believers grow together in Him through love and forgiveness."*

We can actually accomplish every word of that goal because all of us are now IN HIM!

14

THE TEETER-TOTTER OF SUCCESS!

Hallway Theology

O liver Cromwell was one of the most important leaders in England during the early part of the 17th century. It was during this time that England developed a very bad shortage of currency, of coins like pennies and nickels and quarters.

Oliver Cromwell selected a group of men to search for some silver which could then be melted down and turned into currency.

The men searched for several months then came back to Cromwell and said, "We have searched the empire in vain to find silver. To our dismay, we have found no silver except in the great cathedrals. That silver is contained in the statues of the famous church saints."

Cromwell thought for a moment about the preciousness of the statues but also about the need of the country. He then said, "Let's melt down the saints and put them into circulation."

One of the greatest needs of this present hour is for God to melt down the saints such as you and me and put us into circulation in our church, in our community, in our workplaces, and in every area of society.

But what has to happen for us to minister to our fullest potential?

Let's go back to the theme of this teaching series.

The Bible says, "Behold, a sower went forth to sow, to work in God's Greenhouse." It says, "Paul sowed, Apollos watered" and we are coworkers with God in this work we call God's Greenhouse. We are sowing our lives into the lives of other people so they might experience God in all of His fullness.

We have looked at many subjects. We are closer to the end of our study than the beginning. But there is one more major section we need to think through. It is the one section in which we absolutely must succeed. If we fail in this last area, everything else will be in vain.

I will give you a clue: It is an attitude thing. As we all know, our attitude will always determine our altitude or how high we fly.

Here is the key question. What does the sower need in order to do his job? Is it more Bible study? Is it more courage? Is it more planning? Is it a combination of all of these factors?

With God's help, I want to walk you through *three rooms* in God's Greenhouse that we *must* master. That is your first fill-in-the-blank.

Our text is three entire chapters in the Bible. Let's turn to the book of 1 Corinthians and read the first verse in chapter twelve, the first verse in chapter thirteen along with the first and fortieth verses in chapter fourteen.

The first verse in chapter twelve says, and I am paraphrasing, "Regarding how you are to put your spiritual gifts into practice, I do not want you to be ignorant or unlearned or unskilled." I'll explain how that applies to you in just a moment.

The first verse in chapter thirteen says, "If I speak with those languages spoken by foreign men and even the angels of heaven but have not love I am nothing but a noisy gong or a clanging cymbal." Someone suggested, "I am just the creaking of a rusty gate." Don't waste your oil on me! That is another way of saying I am a nobody!

The first verse in chapter fourteen says, "Chase after love and at the same time earnestly desire the use of spiritual gifts, especially the primary gift of prophecy," or what we think of as preaching or *forthtelling* the truth.

The fortieth verse in chapter fourteen ends this section of three chapters by saying, "All things should be done decently or appropriately as well as done in the proper order."

It is not common for a pastor to take three entire chapters as his text, but these three chapters are linked together. These three chapters actually form one unit. Therefore, it needs to be studied as one unit.

These three chapters are like an old-fashioned teeter-totter. How many of you can remember riding a teeter-totter? Can you ride a teeter-totter by yourself? No! It takes someone on the other end to counterbalance you. But it also takes something in the middle to balance *both* of you.

That is exactly what these three chapters are. They represent God's teeter-totter to making you an effective sower in God's Greenhouse.

One chapter—chapter twelve—is on one end. If you don't add anything to the opposite end, your end of the teeter-totter will do nothing but sit on the ground. Chapter twelve will have nothing to counterbalance it.

Chapter fourteen, though, is on the opposite end. It has the same weight as chapter twelve.

Guess what is in the middle? That is chapter thirteen.

If you emphasize chapter twelve and chapter thirteen but leave out chapter fourteen, your teeter-totter will never work. If you emphasize chapter twelve and chapter fourteen but leave out chapter thirteen, your teeter-totter will just sit on the ground. You can sit on it, but you won't go up or down! It won't be long until your legs are cramping!

Don't miss this next statement. *It is absolutely imperative that you include all three parts in your personal teeter-totter for your teeter-totter to work*. Likewise, you must include all three chapters in your own sowing ministry for your ministry to be truly effective.

God does not want you to have a one-sided ministry that sits on the ground all day and accomplishes nothing. No, God wants you to have a well-balanced ministry because a well-balanced ministry is the key to effective Christian service.

That brings us to this question. What does your teeter-totter need for you to have an effective sowing ministry?

1. An Effective Sowing Ministry Begins with a Classroom.

Answer #1: An effective sowing ministry begins with a classroom. I'm talking about a classroom like you experienced during your school days. For some of us that was a long time ago. For some of us that is an ongoing experience. You may still be in school, or perhaps you're a teacher, or perhaps you're taking a class at work.

When I was a kid, the teacher would challenge us and say, "It's time to put on your thinking cap." Do any of you remember those days? We reached under our desk, picked up an imaginary hat and put it on our head. That hat was called our thinking cap. You may laugh, but it looked like a baseball cap to me! We were then ready to think and to learn.

I am not going to ask you to reach under your seat and pick up an imaginary hat, but I am asking you to really focus on what I am about to say!

What is a classroom for? A classroom is a place for teaching. It is a place for study. It is, also, a place for learning.

Most jobs require a high school diploma or its equivalent. Why? It is because there is a minimum level of education required to do the job. Other jobs require a college degree, some jobs require a master's degree and some jobs even require a doctorate degree.

Remember: a classroom is a place for teaching, for study and, most importantly, for learning.

The sower is no different. He needs to understand the laws of nature regarding agriculture to improve his performance from being the class clown to becoming a successful farmer. It is not enough to just give him a hoe and a bucket and say, "Figure it out on your own!"

Many universities even offer degrees in agriculture. My brother-in-law Richard went to Ohio State to study agriculture and learn how to be a better farmer! He had been raised on a farm, but he knew he needed to know more. So he went to the classroom, and he learned more than he already knew. In my case, I am out of my depth in discussing the subject of farming with him!

We have missionaries go to foreign countries to teach people how to farm better. They teach things like which crops will grow best in that environment, when to plant those crops, and how much fertilizer to use. One missionary said, "It amazes me that these people have farmed for so many years and yet know so little about farming! They could improve their lives immensely if they were better educated in the art of farming!"

Sowing may not seem like much, but in my way of thinking, it is both an art and a science!

One of the best comedy television shows of all time was *Green Acres* with Eddie Albert and Eva Gabor. Eddie played a lawyer named Oliver Wendell Douglas. The two of them left the skyscrapers of New York City to try farming in a place called Hooterville. The reason it was a comedy is that neither one of them had a clue about what they were doing.

Here is why I mention *Green Acres*. They tried farming without first passing through the classroom. That's why the show was a comedy.

That's the way it often turns out with us, too. If we don't pass through the classroom, we turn our life and our ministry into a comedy!

Let me share a secret. It is a fill-in-the-blank, too. Chapter twelve represents the classroom experience for all of us. It is the chapter which answers the biggest question of most Christians. It is the question, "What does God want me to do?"

When the Apostle Paul got saved, his first question was, "Lord, what do You want me to do?" A short time later God sent Paul to Arabia for three years of schooling at the hands of the Holy Spirit. (Galatians 1:17) It was in a classroom called Arabia that Paul learned what God wanted him to do and how he should do it. It is obvious to me that Paul learned his lessons very well!

When the apostles got saved, Jesus said, "Come, follow me and I will make you into fishermen who know how to catch men." (Matthew 4:19) The apostles went to school with Jesus, learned what God wanted them to do and how they should do it! It is obvious they learned very well, too!

The saddest thing in the field of Christian service is that Christian who does not know what God wants him to do. Therefore, he spends his entire life doing nothing or practically nothing for the Lord Jesus.

I read about a man who stopped by a business one day to see his friend named Sam. The boss said, "I'm sorry, but Sam no longer works here." The man said, "Do you have someone in mind for his vacancy?" The boss thought for a moment then said, "When Sam left, he didn't leave a vacancy."

Chapter twelve is the classroom where we learn what God has called us to do. Therefore, we are able to leave a vacancy when we leave this world because we truly amounted to something for God!

The classroom of 1 Corinthians 12:4 says, "There are varieties of spiritual gifts or spiritual abilities, but the same Lord is the one giving the gifts." Verses eight, nine, ten, and eleven list *some but not all* of those spiritual gifts or abilities.

> *To one is given a message of wisdom through the Spirit, to another, a message of knowledge by the same Spirit, to another, faith by the same Spirit, to another, gifts of healing by the one Spirit, to another, the performing of miracles, to another, prophecy, to another, distinguishing between spirits, to another, different kinds of languages, to another, interpretation of languages. But one and the same*

Spirit is active in all these, distributing to each person as He wills. (1 Corinthians 12:8-11, HCSB)

Write on your study sheet, everyone is someone for Jesus.

We often describe a pianist or an athlete by saying, "He is so gifted." That is our way of saying that he has a special ability.

We learn in God's classroom of chapter twelve that every Christian has at least one special ability! You say, "Me?" I mean especially you!

There are several things we need to learn in the classroom of chapter twelve. First, this special ability to serve Jesus is called a spiritual gift. Both words are very important. It is called a gift because you didn't earn it by good behavior. It is called spiritual because it is a spiritual ability rather than a physical ability like singing or playing a piano.

We will not take the time to look at every passage dealing with spiritual gifts, but items like playing an instrument and public speaking are not mentioned among the gifts. Those are important items for the ministry, but they technically fall into a different category called physical abilities.

We recognize there are plenty of physical abilities or talents in this church. Every physical ability or talent should be used for Jesus just as much as your spiritual gift. There are also different personalities, different likes and dislikes along with different experiences in this church. All of those items should also be used for Jesus.

I want you to recognize that you are a very unique person. No one has ever existed just like you! That means you bring something very special to our church. We need you to be what God made you!

Let me give you a word of advice. Many years ago, I made the mistake of getting hung up on identifying every spiritual gift and then defining every spiritual gift. I bought books dedicated to that very subject. I could tell you what this writer believed and what another writer believed. I no longer do that.

My current strategy follows the K.I.S.S. formula of "Keep It Simple, Stupid." When in doubt always drop back to the K.I.S.S. formula! So here is the K.I.S.S. formula that you need to follow. It's a fill-in-the-blank. Whatever I am good at is what I need to do for Jesus. Let's say it together. Whatever I am good at is what I need to do for Jesus.

Let me add two more things before I move on. First, don't be surprised if someday you start doing something for Jesus that you have never done before.

Also, somewhere within you lies a supernatural, spiritual ability to be a spiritual blessing to everyone you meet. *It is so special that it is beyond the realm of the physical, and it exists in the realm of the spiritual.*

Let's move further into our outline. Second, we receive this spiritual ability when God saves us. We know that is so because you are one part of the body of Christ. Every part has a purpose and contributes to the whole body. We know without a doubt that you are placed into the body of Christ at the moment of salvation. Therefore, logic says you must receive your spiritual gift at the very same time.

In my own case, the ability to gab or talk comes with being a Swartzwelder. Dad liked to talk. Mom liked to talk. We sometimes sing, "when this poor, lisping, stammering tongue lies silent in the grave." That will be the *only* time when we Swartzwelders stop talking. But that is not the same as the spiritual gift of teaching the Word of God because you can't do that without the Holy Spirit.

Third, God Himself made the decision about which spiritual gift you and I should receive. This decision was not based upon your good looks, your education, your family reputation, or anything pertaining to you. It is called a gift because it is not something you earn! It is something God freely gives you! God made the choice, and God's choice is always the best choice for you and me both!

Look again at verse eleven. Paul says it is the Holy Spirit who distributes the gifts. Notice also that Paul says a spiritual gift is given to all of us. The emphasis is on all of us.

During the early 1980s, I ministered at Leatherwood Baptist Church. In those days I was not so much a minister as I was an experimenter. I was still experimenting with how to teach. I just kept trying and trying.

To be honest, I am still trying today! Sometimes I hit a single, sometimes I hit a double, and a few times I hit a home run.

I remember teaching a Tuesday class meeting about spiritual gifts. A wonderful lady named Betty stopped my lesson and said, "I cannot do anything for Jesus." I showed her verse eleven then she said, "Well, I am obviously wrong, but I still don't know what I can do."

That may be so, but Betty took what she had and did a good job for Jesus. You can do the same!

Let me share an astonishing number with you. I conducted a Saturday morning workshop in 2006 for a church which was averaging one hundred and twenty people for Sunday morning worship. During that workshop, we made a list of every necessary ministry for the next twelve months. For example, this list included every necessary role such as doing crafts in Vacation Bible School. Our final list of the next year's ministries exceeded three hundred and twenty ministries! In other words, there is no shortage of work to be done. The only question is whether we have enough workers to do all that needs to be done!

Let me add a word of caution at this point. Do you remember the K.I.S.S. formula? Those three hundred and twenty ministries do not line up precisely with the Bible's list of spiritual gifts. Therefore, don't overcomplicate chapter twelve. *Just do what you're good at, and we will all be blessed!*

D. L. Moody was a great evangelist but very uneducated. They said Moody was the only man who could say, "Jerusalem" with just two syllables. I would love to have heard him say, "Jerusalem!" His ministry, though, was enormously successful because God was in it. On the other hand, a college professor may be a brilliant teacher in biology but may not have the spiritual gift of teaching. He may instead have the very valuable gift of helping or serving. He may be the guy who puts oil on everything and makes everything fit and run smoothly.

One thing is certain: We can be confident that the choice of our particular gift belongs to God, and God will always make the right choice!

Rest assured, your ministry will be a ministry worth sowing in the lives of the people you meet!

What might your own ministry be? The Bible mentions several spiritual gifts which are still at work in the church today. By contrast, some ministries like speaking in tongues are no longer with us. You may not know this, but the gift of speaking in tongues is another name for speaking in an *unlearned* foreign language. It is called a gift because you have never learned the language on your own. The ability to speak in that unlearned foreign language was a miracle from God. We do not believe that miraculous gift is in use today, but almost every other ministry is still with us.

Let me give you some examples from this list in chapter twelve. There is the gift of wisdom or spiritually knowing how best to do the work of God. This gift of wisdom was a requirement for selecting the first deacons in Acts chapter six. There is another gift called knowledge. Do you ever wonder how some people can be so smart about the Bible and yet be so dumb about everything else? It's because spiritual knowledge is not the same as knowledge in the natural world. There is also a special gift called faith. One application is in how God uses these people to help the church step out of its comfort zone and try something new. There is the gift of administration. The King James Version refers to it as the gift of governments in verse twenty-eight. God uses this person to organize God's people for the best results. There is also a unique gift called mercy. These people have been spiritually anointed to be a spiritual blessing to the sick and the homebound. The gift of mercy is a super ministry!

On and on the list goes because God has many, many opportunities for us to serve Him!

Again, don't get hung up on the specifics or even what you call it. Just ask yourself, what am I good at? What do I have a desire to do? That's what I ought to be doing for Jesus.

That's why chapter twelve is in the Bible. *It is the chapter where you learn that you can make a big difference for Jesus.* It is the chapter where God shows you how to sow your life in the lives of others.

Remember this: An effective sowing ministry begins with a classroom.

2. An Effective Sowing Ministry Requires a Laboratory.

Answer #2: An effective sowing ministry requires a laboratory. What is the purpose of a laboratory? This is a fill-in-the-blank. A laboratory is a place where you take what you have learned in the classroom, and you put that learning into practice.

One of my daughters taught a chemistry lab class for Ohio State University and Indiana University. The students learned in that class to put their studies into practical application.

My own experience in a laboratory was Abysmal with a capital A. During my years in junior high school, the girls took a class in home economics. The boys took a class in shop, or a better name might be industrial arts. We learned how to use shop tools and even made a few things. As for me, I was all thumbs! I have become better through the years due to repeated experience, but that is not how I began!

All of us have seen the movie of the student who sits in the classroom, supposedly learns everything, but doesn't follow the instructions. The story ends with the student blowing up everything in the laboratory.

Let's hit the refresh button regarding the purpose of the first two rooms. The classroom is the place where you *learn.* You should never stop learning! But the laboratory is the place where you put your learning into *practice.* In other words, the classroom accomplishes nothing unless we progress to the laboratory!

It is important you understand the next statement. That is why it is a fill-in-the-blank on your study sheet. *Chapter fourteen represents the laboratory where we learn how to use our gift or ability in the service of the Lord Jesus Christ. In other words, it represents our church experiences or our ministry experiences.*

The Corinthians had a problem. Well, they actually had a lot of problems. One of those problems was in the area of spiritual gifts. 1 Corinthians 1:7 states the Corinthian church was blessed in abundance with all of the spiritual gifts. They had every imaginable gift in their church.

Some of you may not know your own gift. The Corinthians, though, apparently had a good idea about their gifts! As a matter of fact, they were so obsessed with their gifts that they treated the church like a stage to show off their gifts. Furthermore, once they got on the stage, they wouldn't give equal time to anyone else. They instead used their gift to monopolize the church service.

They knew *what* to do, but they didn't have a clue about *how* to do it. As a result, their teeter-totter was lopsided—it was weighted on the chapter twelve end. They were just sitting on the ground wondering why their teeter-totter would not work!

The Corinthians had some knowledge, but they kept blowing up the laboratory! The end result was worse than the beginning!

Therefore, Paul gave them some rules regarding the proper use of the laboratory. That's what chapter fourteen is to the Corinthians.

Let me give you a modern example. It is common for people to enter a college laboratory and see a list of dos and don'ts posted on the wall. If you violate the rules, your laboratory experience will be very brief. Those rules are designed to keep everyone safe plus more.

Chapter fourteen is a similar experience for the Corinthians. Follow closely in your Bible. There was a rule about the use of tongues. The gift of tongues was widespread in the early church due to the world's use of so many different languages. Verse nineteen says, "In God's church I would rather speak five words that I clearly understand so I can plainly teach others rather than speak ten thousand words in an unlearned, foreign language that I don't understand at all."

There was also a rule regarding the number of times a gift could be used in a single service. Verse twenty-seven says, "If any man wishes to speak in an unlearned, foreign language, he should do it, first, in an organized way, and second, with a maximum of two or three people exercising that gift. Plus, someone has to be present who can interpret what is being said. Otherwise, stay silent and stay seated."

Verse twenty-nine has another rule which pertains to the prophets or what some consider to be modern-day preaching. "Let no more than two or three prophets speak, and let the others judge if the speakers are telling the truth."

Verse thirty-four has a rule about women and their role in the church. "Let your women keep silence in the churches: for it is not permitted unto them to speak; but they are commanded to be under obedience, as also saith the law." I once had a deacon who used this verse to teach that a woman should not be allowed to sing a solo in church! I, along with the vast majority of Christians, beg to disagree! In my way of thinking, the idea is not to prevent women from singing and praising the Lord. Rather the idea is that women should not be permitted to take over a church service. Pastor Chuck Stewart taught me years ago, "There is nothing wrong with women serving in the church. But if the women are doing the job of the men, it will be a very weak church because that means the men aren't doing their job." He was right!

Verse forty includes a rule about how to organize a church service. The Bible says, "Let all things be done decently and in order."

Be sure to add this statement to your study sheet. God has rules for everyone to follow!

Here is why that statement is so very important. If you want to have an effective sowing ministry, you must learn to serve God by His rules! God's rules are like guard rails which prevent your car from driving over the hill or driving into oncoming traffic.

Everyone needs rules. That includes the deacons as well as the pastor. There is an old saying that, "Absolute power corrupts absolutely." That's very true. That's why you need rules.

Rules also include the idea of accountability. Steven Covey once said, "Accountability breeds response-ability." He was right! Many televangelists have failed because they were considered too powerful to be accountable to anyone, until one day their moral or financial failures made them accountable to everyone!

The rules in the laboratory chapter are just a sample of many more rules expressed throughout the Word of God. Chapter fourteen was not written to express *all* of the rules, but only to indicate the *importance of rules*. Rest assured, you need rules, or you will eventually go off the rails.

The sower may have the best seed in the entire world, but he will fail if he refuses to follow God's rules for sowing, watering, and reaping.

If you want to be an effective sower in *any* church, there are certain rules you must follow! If you don't follow the rules, you will blow up the laboratory. We will then have to do damage control and call in the clean-up crew. The same is true for the big church down the street and the little church up the street.

I have known people who said, "I don't like the rules at my church, so I'll go to another church." To their surprise, the other church had rules, too!

There once was an entertainer who got saved. He told his pastor he wanted to do something great for God. The pastor knew the immaturity of this entertainer. He suggested the entertainer get into church, get grounded in Bible teachings, and learn how to use his gift for the glory of God.

The entertainer, though, didn't want to follow the rules. He insisted on starting his own ministry and going on the road. The entertainer's ministry lasted less than six months and ended in a divorce.

The pastor said, "It was all because he wouldn't play according to the rules. *His branches went out further than his roots."*

Look again at the teeter-totter. On one end we have the classroom, and on the other end, we have the laboratory.

Now we come to what I believe is the most important part of this message.

What balances the teeter-totter so it can become a good experience?

3. An Effective Sowing Ministry Is Completed with a Hallway.

Answer #3: An effective sowing ministry is completed with a hallway. It is not merely connected, but I want you to think in terms of the ministry being completed or matured.

Everyone knows the purpose of a hallway. This is a fill-in-the-blank. A hallway connects rooms so that you can pass from one room to the next.

We began this study a long time ago. The study eventually progressed to the point where we were able to establish a goal for implementing God's Greenhouse. That goal is written at the bottom of your study sheet. I want you to read it with me then I will explain what is now happening.

The goal says, *"Helping believers grow together in Him through love and forgiveness."*

Here is where the rubber meets the road! If you want to "help believers grow together in Him" you must pass through the hallway of "love and forgiveness." Think again of those words because it is critically important you understand this point. It's a fill-in-the-blank. If you want to "help believers grow together in Him" you must pass through the hallway of "love and forgiveness."

1 Corinthians chapter thirteen is "The Hallway to Being an Effective Sower" or "The Hallway To Effective Christian Service." It is the hallway which joins chapter twelve with chapter fourteen. It is the hallway which joins the classroom with the laboratory. It is the hallway which joins what you learn with what you practice. It is the center part or the fulcrum of the teeter-totter which makes the whole thing work and gets you off the ground!

Take away the center part, and your ministry will never work! "Love and forgiveness" is the part that will make your ministry work!

It is not enough to know your gift or ministry! It is not enough either to know how to play by the rules. It is only enough when you love others just like Jesus Christ loves them and you forgive others just like Jesus Christ forgives them.

May I ask a question? What makes you do what you do in this church? Is it because someone has to do it? Is it because you were raised by your parents to do a work? Is it because you are trying to earn God's blessings? Is it because you can be someone important here?

Follow along in your Bible in the hallway of chapter thirteen. Verse one says, "Though I—we're talking about a great apostle. Though I, a great apostle and greater in rank than all of you Corinthians, speak with the languages of men and even of angels, am the most eloquent teacher you have ever heard, and yet have not the love of God in my heart and ministry, I am like a noisy gong or a clanging cymbal. Though I have the spiritual gift of prophecy—I can explain everything about the Revelation and the future and I understand all mysteries and possess all knowledge; though I have the kind of faith that says 'Rise up, mountain and be cast into the sea,' and yet do not have the love of God in my heart and ministry I am nothing. I profit neither you nor me in even one thing. Though I donate all of my worldly possessions to feed the poor—though I am the biggest giver in the church—I even donate my body to be sacrificed for the cause and yet I do not have the love of God in my heart and ministry I am nothing. I accomplish nothing. I have nothing to show for everything I have done." WOW! That's tough stuff.

How can I best show you what a well-balanced teeter-totter is really like? On one end is the classroom, on the other end is the laboratory, and in the middle, balancing the entire ministry is the hallway of love and forgiveness.

A man served as the superintendent of a city rescue mission for forty years. They asked him why he dedicated his life to working with dirty, abusive, drunken people.

The man said, "All I am doing is giving back to others a little of the love God has shown to me."

He explained further that as a young man he had gone the way of the drunkard. One night he went into a city mission for a bowl of chili. He heard a preacher say that Christ could save sinners. He stumbled down the aisle and accepted Jesus Christ as his personal Savior.

His brain was confused by the alcohol, but he felt a weight lifted from his shoulders. God changed his life.

Sometime later God called him to go back to the gutter and reach the people who were still wallowing in sin. That is exactly what he did.

For him, it wasn't enough to know what God had called him to do. That was the classroom. For him, it wasn't enough to know how to do the work. That was the laboratory. It was only enough when he knew how to love the people like Jesus loved them and to forgive the people like Jesus forgave them.

That is what the "Hallway to Being an Effective Sower" is all about!

15

WHERE LOVE BEGINS BUT DOES NOT END

God Is Love

Preparation: Bring an arrow.

A mother and her totally worthless son stood in the courtroom before a judge and waited on the judge's sentence. This was not the first time this worthless son had been in court. The judge had previously tried to help the son, but all of his efforts had been in vain.

The judge thought long and hard about what to do with this boy. He then said, "I can do nothing more for your son. I have done everything I can do. I give up. Mother, I advise you to do the same."

The mother could not speak at first. She then wiped the tears from her eyes and said, "Judge, I don't blame you. You have been more than kind to us. You have gone out of your way to help us. I don't blame you for giving up. But I can't give up on this boy. I gave him his life. I have taken care of him. I cannot go back on him because he is still my boy, and he will always be my boy!"

How can you explain a love like that? It is a love which continued to love in spite of everything that son had done including his backtalking, his insults, and even his criminal behavior!

How can you explain a love which is as *unending* as that?

The Bible teaches some great lessons about love in 1 John chapter four. Let me begin at verse seven. "My beloved friends, let us continually love one another with an *agape*, selfless kind of love. This kind of *agape* love originates with God. Everyone who loves in this selfless way is born again of God and knows God in daily experience. The one who does not love in this way does not know God because God Himself is love."

Love is discussed in the following verses down to verse nineteen. Verse nineteen is one of the most profound scriptures in the Bible, but I warn you, it may look very shallow on the surface. Trust me, verse nineteen is very deep! Let me quote verse nineteen from the King James Version because that is the way most of you memorized this verse. Verse nineteen says, "We love Him because He first loved us."

Let's step back for a moment and see the big picture before we zero in on the little picture. Or, as I like to say, let's look at the puzzle box and see what the puzzle looks like before we open the box and look at the little pieces.

Here is the big picture. Where are we in our study? The title of this entire study is *God's Greenhouse: How to Grow People God's Way.* We have studied extensively about how God expects His church to be a greenhouse environment where He can grow people. The Bible says in 1 Corinthians 3:9, "We are co-laborers with God in God's cultivated field," or as I like to call it, God's Greenhouse.

We spent a great deal of time conceptualizing the greenhouse. That means we identified those characteristics that make a greenhouse effective for growing plants. We learned those same characteristics can be reproduced in a church environment. Every church, whether it be small or large, can be a spiritual greenhouse that grows people. As a matter of fact, our ultimate success will be determined by whether we become a spiritual greenhouse.

We then moved to a new section that focuses on a ten-word goal for our church. That goal appears at the bottom of your study sheet. *"Helping believers grow together in Him through love and forgiveness."* That statement has five main advantages. First, the goal is understandable. Second, the goal is biblical. Third, the goal will encourage a godly attitude. You will be much easier to get along with! Fourth, the goal can be achieved by everyone of every age. Fifth, the goal provides focus for everything we do.

"Helping believers grow together in Him through love and forgiveness." That leads me to the following questions. Look closely at the goal and think through these questions with me. Are we helping *believers*? Are we helping believers *grow*? Are we helping believers grow *together*? Are we helping believers grow together *in Him*—in Christ who is the life giver for the entire greenhouse?

Now we come to the final part of our goal. The last four words of our goal state, "through love and forgiveness." The word "love" and the word "forgiveness" are critical to the creation of a greenhouse environment or atmosphere.

In many ways, we have saved the hardest part until the last. We are asking people of different ages to love and forgive one another. We are asking people with different political beliefs to love and forgive one another. We are asking people with different levels of education to love and forgive one another. We are asking people whose only connection is through this church—we are asking those people to love and forgive one another. We are asking people who have different backgrounds, different experiences, and different skin color to love and forgive one another. We're not asking for much, are we? That's why I say we have saved the hardest part until the last.

But obviously, it can be done because Jesus taught (and this is a fill-in-the-blank), "Through the action of loving one another all men shall know you are my disciples." (John 13:35)

We will take a good look at the subject of love over the next several studies. It is my hope you will learn how to love your brothers and sisters more, love your spouse and children more, and especially love your God more.

One of the greatest hymns of the faith says,

There is a name I love to hear, I love to sing its worth,
It sounds like music in my ear, The sweetest name on earth.
O how I love Jesus, O how I love Jesus,
O how I love Jesus because He first loved me.

Frederick Whitfield

That song is based on the words in verse nineteen, "We love Him because He first loved us."

A lady was walking past a church one day and saw a little girl come out of the church by herself. It was not Sunday, so the lady asked, "Was there a church service today?"

The little girl said, "No, I was just praying."

The lady thought the little girl might have a problem. She asked, "What were you praying for?"

The little girl said, "Nothing. I was just loving Jesus."

The little girl could do that because the love of God is being poured out in our hearts by the Holy Spirit.

But the truth is, verses seven through twenty-one are actually bigger than just loving Jesus because they actually deal with how we can love others *with* the love of Jesus.

If the Apostle John were to write a song on this entire passage, he would change the song from "O How I Love Jesus" to "O How I Love Others Just Like Jesus Loves Them" because He first loved me.

We talk so often about how much God loves us, but we often forget that God wants us to experience that same love for one another!

Look again at our goal of ten words at the bottom of your study sheet. *"Helping believers grow together in Him through love and forgiveness."* Those last four words turn every greenhouse into a very special greenhouse.

Your third fill-in-the-blank says love and forgiveness are not only an attitude, but they are also actions. They are the actions that allow the first six words in our goal to actually happen in every single one of us.

How is it possible for us to experience the love of God in our church, in our homes, and in our lives?

It is time to fill in some blanks on your study sheet.

1. The Originator of Love

An elderly man counseled a young person with the words, "Let's do first things first." If we do first things first on this issue of love, we must begin with the originator of love. That is, what or who is the originator of love? The first six letters of the word "originator" make up the word "origin." Origin means "the beginning, the root, the source." Who or what is the originator of love? Someone said love begins with a mother, but that is not what the Bible says!

Let's take a deep look into verse seven. The first word in the Greek text is *agapetoi*. Most of you are acquainted with the Greek word *agape* which is the Greek word for the highest form of sacrificial love. It is the love expressed in John 3:16, "For God so *agape* the world that He gave His only begotten Son."

John begins verse seven by describing his readers as deeply loved. Based on the context, the sense is that they are deeply loved by God. In my view, the translation "dear friends" is too shallow a translation. Based on the surrounding context, we could even translate it "God's loved ones" or "divinely loved ones." The sense is that these people are very, very special. These words also mean that you are very, very special.

We begin with "Dearly beloved!"

Someone said that their church's Sunday night attendance was very, very small. As a matter of fact, the attendance was so small that when the pastor said, "Dearly beloved," an old maid blushed because she thought she was receiving a marriage proposal!

We may not be receiving a marriage proposal in verse seven, but we are very special! We are divinely loved. You can't be treated any better than that!

Let's probe deeper into verse seven and complete two more fill-in-the-blanks. The verse says, "love is of God" which is another way of saying love comes from God. That means God Himself is the *source* of love. He is the *origin* of love. You need to understand this truth because if there is no God, there can be no love!

Let me repeat what I just said and be sure you let it sink in. If there is no God, there can be no love!

Verse eight ends with the very deep statement, "God is love." The idea is not so much that God loves but that God is love itself. God Himself is the embodiment of love. He is love personified!

We come next to verse nineteen and something very important that you may not know! The word "Him" is not found in what is generally considered to be the best manuscripts. As a result, the word "Him" is missing from practically all of the newer translations (NIV, NASB, ESV, HCSB, NLT, CEV, etc.).

At first, it might seem that something is lost by leaving "Him" out of this verse, but *the longer you think about it, the more obvious it becomes that something is actually gained.*

It would be better to translate the verse, "We love because He first loved us!" We love . . . period! That is different than saying, "We love Him." Literally, the verse is teaching that we have the ability to love—to love our spouse, our children, our parents, even anyone for one sole reason! *It is because God gave us the capacity to love in the first place!*

Why is it that creation takes care of its own offspring? For instance, a dog has a litter of pups. Instead of walking away and letting them die, that mother will nurse those pups, wash them, keep them warm, and provide for their safety. It has a motherly instinct to be very protective.

Where did that female dog learn to love its puppies? Was it taught by the owner? Was it taught by the veterinarian? The answer, of course, is no. The dog somehow has an inbred ability to love! From what source, though, did that love originate? Such a capacity to love originates with God, the Creator and Designer of all! *God has placed within all of His creation the capacity to take care of their young!*

That is what verse nineteen is telling us! We love—animals love, birds love, humans love—all of creation loves because He loved first! *God demonstrated this love by giving each one of us the ability to love!*

That is why it is natural for you to love your children, your parents, your spouse, your friends, and your coworkers. Your first instinct when you are born is not to hate, but your first instinct is to love because that is the way God designed all of His creation to be!

"We love because He first loved us!"

There was a little girl who attended one of my churches. She came from a very poor family. The father worked forty hours a week, but he only made minimum wage. The family was so poor that they had cereal for supper, and sometimes they did not even have cereal. (Unfortunately, that was in the days before schools provided breakfast to the students!) The family lived in a rented house (actually more like a shack) just over the hill from the church. They only took a bath once a week. They really had it rough!

This girl would come to church all the time. We gave her food, clothes, and someone bought her a new watch for Christmas. She was so proud of that watch!

Then came time for the fall revival. This little girl came every night. One night her mother came to church with her.

This girl's mother had attended our church only once before. The mother had been drunk on that occasion. The smell of her alcohol had almost reached the pulpit.

But on this night her mother came for a second time. The mother smelled, she was dirty, and she was sitting on the back row with her little girl.

We were an old-fashioned country church which practiced what is commonly referred to as a united prayer. This may seem strange to some of you, but it was traditional for everyone to gather at the front of the church for a united prayer. Everyone would kneel and pray aloud. Yes, it was noisy and, no, you couldn't make out what any one person was saying. Some prayed in a loud voice, and some prayed in a low voice. I am sure God had no trouble sorting out what was said. I am also sure God enjoyed hearing the prayers of His children.

We had our united prayer just before the sermon. This happened more than thirty years ago. I can still see it clearly in my mind. We were taking prayer requests. This little girl left her mother, came up front, tugged on our clothes, and pointed back at her mother. Over and over again she would say with pride, "That's my mommy. I love my mommy."

We wondered, "How can she be so proud of her mother? How can she love her mother that much?" The reason was God had put love in her heart for her mother.

That is the reason mankind has the ability to love! It is because love originates with God!

2. The Distorter of Love

But something has obviously gone wrong with the world in general and humanity in specific. Main point number two on your study sheet is the Distorter of Love. The word "distort" has the idea of twisting something from its original meaning. It keeps the same spelling, but it creates a new definition. The new definition is not consistent with the original meaning of the word.

Here is the problem. If God designed all of creation to love, why then do we have so little love in the world? Instead of loving one another we are killing one another, cursing one another, tearing down one another, lying about one another and on and on the list goes.

Someone said, "Every war ends not with a peace treaty but rather with a truce treaty until the next war begins!"

God's original plan was for this world to be a world of total love, but that plan has now been distorted by the enemy.

The Bible says one of the names for the devil is Apollyon which means destroyer. (Revelation 9:11) One of the ways the devil destroys the program of God is by *distorting* the program of God!

We have already learned love is only possible because God makes it possible. God put that instinct to love deep inside every part of His creation. But when Adam sinned, that ability to love, as God Himself loves, became distorted. The result of Adam's sin is that love in our homes, communities, and our own lives became less than what God designed it to be!

How many of you have ever gone bow hunting or shot an arrow? Henry Wadsworth Longfellow wrote, "I shot an arrow into the air, it fell to the earth I know not where." One fellow did that, and his arrow came down through the roof of one guy's pickup truck. I am not sure who was more surprised: the archer or the truck owner. But I'm glad I wasn't there to see what happened next!

Have you ever shot an arrow? Tell me this, what kind of arrow did you shoot? Was it straight or crooked? Hopefully, it was straight! But why would you want it to be straight? It is because you wanted to hit the target!

(Note: Hold up an arrow. A straight arrow is worth a thousand words! The arrow's owner may want to share something about the arrow.)

You will notice this arrow is straight. Everything about this arrow is right including the balance. A good archer can hit the bull's-eye with this arrow.

This arrow represents what we were in our creation. We were straight. Adam loved Eve with a straight love, with no waves or distortions. Eve loved Adam like no man has ever been loved since. The arrow of their love was uninterrupted by fighting or anger. She had eyes only for him, and he had eyes only for her! The old saying, "They lived happily ever after" could have been true of them.

But the devil caused them to sin against God. This is a fill-in-the-blank. That sin *distorted* the arrow. Sin *twisted* the arrow. I like to say that sin *bent* the arrow!

That means our arrow can no longer reach the bull's-eye of God's love! It seems that every time the world tries to love, its arrow goes off course. Its arrow falls short of the true love of God. That's why we have a distorted view of love in today's society.

The kind of love in today's world falls far short of the kind of love in the Garden of Eden! The devil has used sin to distort love into something less than it should otherwise be.

Let's identify what the devil has done to God's kind of love. These are fill-in-the-blanks on your study sheet.

First, the devil has distorted love into lust. Titus 3:3 describes the modern-day world like this: "At one time we were senseless, out of control, disobedient, deceived, a slave to all kinds of lusts and pleasures, living in evil and envy, hateful to the point of hating one another." That doesn't sound like the Garden of Eden to me.

Sin changed the Garden of Eden's four-letter word "love" into the four-letter word "lust." Lust represents sexual lust in this passage.

One day I was flipping channels on the television. I happened across one of the evening lust operas. You know what I mean! The star woman was taking off her clothes and said to the man, "Now let's see how well you can perform." That is the way the world defines love. Love is no longer spelled l-o-v-e but is spelled l-u-s-t. When lusting for one person fades away, it's time to lust for someone new. "Get me a new partner!"

Today's television is full of shows where lust is the main subject. It is very rare to have a show where love is the main subject.

The difference is enormous. Lust is only skin deep, but true love is heart deep. Which one would you rather experience in your own life?

There is one more item worth noticing about that verse. Can a person who is full of the love of God also be full of hatred for the people around him? No. But notice in this verse that *lust can exist at the same time* that you are "hating one another." That tells you there is a great difference between love which is *not* mentioned in this verse and lust which *is* mentioned in this verse.

Second, the devil has distorted love for others into love for self. The Bible says in 2 Timothy 3:2, "People will be in love with themselves and their money." It goes on to talk about people being "boasters, egocentric, and blasphemers." The word sacred is not in their vocabulary.

You probably have noticed that this is the age known as the "love for self" age. Everything is focused on "me" and what "I" want.

Too many pregnant women say, "I don't want this baby. It will ruin my figure, cost me money, and tie me down at the house. I have my own life to live." What does she then do? She has an abortion and ends an innocent life. Unbelievable, but that is what happens!

Then again, too many children abandon the parents who gave them life and raised them. One mother told me that she was glad to receive just a simple birthday card from her children. This mother had not seen her children or talked to them in several years. They viewed mom as a bother! They had written her off.

I knew one mother who walked into the living room and said to her husband and three children, "I'm tired of all of you. I want some space. I want my freedom." She then walked out without any regret!

I want you to know the Garden of Eden did not operate that way! But those ways are the accepted way in the "love for self" age.

Third, the devil has distorted love for the opposite sex into love for the same sex. This is a difficult issue in our modern world, but that does not change the truth of God's Word.

Paul wrote in Romans 1:27, "the men abandoned normal sexual relationships with their women and burned with lust for other men." The problem of homosexuality and similar behavior is not a modern-day problem. It is a problem which has existed throughout the history of sinful man. God classified this sin as an abomination in the Old Testament. (Leviticus 18:22) I see no reason for Him to re-classify it now!

Today's world accepts this distortion of love. This acceptance extends to some in our religious community, too. The president of one mainline denomination examined this matter and asked, "Can we always know the clear meaning of scripture?" In other words, are we sure this behavior is wrong? That president put a question mark where there should have been an exclamation mark. His question was reminiscent of Satan's words to Eve, "Has God really said, or did you put words in God's mouth?"

I wonder what Paul would have said to that religious leader! Romans chapter one and verse twenty-seven states such behavior is unseemly. In other words, *it does not seem right because it is not right!* Call it by any name you wish, but God still calls it wrong and sin.

Why is this behavior accepted by the world? It is because sin has given us a distorted view of love. This distorted view extends across the entire spectrum of worldly activity!

3. The Restorer of Love

Is the situation hopeless? Not by a long shot. That brings us to main point number three on your study sheet. It's time to look at the restorer of love. Who is it that is able to bring the true, undistorted love of God back into our lives? Back into our world? Back into our community? It is evident our world has lost it, so how can our world regain it?

Do you remember the arrow? We know the arrow is now crooked or bent instead of straight. We need someone to restore the arrow to its original design so we can experience love in its highest form!

Who is the person that can restore the highest quality of love to our lives? Is it our spouse? Maybe it is the pastor! How about a marriage counselor?

We come back again to our text in 1 John 4:7. My version reads like this, "My beloved friends, let us continually love one another with an *agape*, selfless kind of love. This kind of *agape* love originates with God. Everyone who loves in this selfless way is born again of God and knows God in daily experience. The one who does not love in this way does not know God because God Himself is love."

Look carefully at the second sentence and notice where we get this kind of love. The Bible makes it very plain that *agape* love originates with God, that "love is of God." Those words mean that *agape* love does not come from a marriage manual or a *Woman's Day* magazine or at a grocery store or at Walmart or even at a wedding! The literal way of reading verse seven is to read, "love is *out* of God"—not merely from God but out (Greek *ek*) of God. It is like taking ice cream out of a container. The ice cream is *in* the container then it is *out* of the container and *in* your life.

Here is the picture! God is so full of love that love is just oozing out of Him and into the life of anyone who is related to Him! This kind of love is actually treated as a by-product of having God in your life. It is not a case of you having to actually seek it because it just comes as a result of your walking with God. To be honest, the only thing you can do is put up a barrier to keep it from coming! Otherwise, God's love will just keep flowing into your life.

Verse seven ends by saying you cannot know this kind of love unless you have been born again! Another way to think of being born again is that of being *restored* to the image of God! Paul says elsewhere, "Put on the new man which has been created or restored by God in righteousness and true holiness." (Ephesians 5:24)

Why is this important? It is because you must first have a right relationship with God before you can enjoy the many blessings of God! The right relationship is the result of accepting Jesus Christ as your personal Lord and Savior! That is when a person is born again!

It is important to understand the born-again experience does *not* take away the old sin nature which causes us to behave like the world. That eradication will not happen until death or the Rapture. But being born again does *add* a new nature or a new man. We learned in a previous study that the new nature/man is one of Christ living in me! Christ is the very image of God! (Colossians 1:15) Being the image of God in me, He is now committed to restoring me to how God originally designed me! It is correct to say that I am not yet what I'm going to be, but let me hasten to add that, thank God, I'm sure not what I used to be! Hallelujah for this improvement!

"If any man is in Christ, he is a new creation! Old things have passed away and behold, all things have now become new!" (2 Corinthians 5:17)

The only way we can have this supernatural love for one another is if the God of love lives in our hearts! That is a fill-in-the-blank.

This is another reason why you need to be born again! You are cheating not only yourself, but you are also cheating your spouse, your children, your parents along with everyone else if you have not been born again! Being born again gives you access to the storehouse containing the love of God—a storehouse for not only loving God but also loving others!

Salvation brings the God of love into our hearts. That allows God to love others through us with the very same love that He Himself loves us!

You may be thinking, "But my love can never come close to how God loves." Here is the Bible's answer to your doubt. The word in chapter four that describes how God loves (*agape*) is the same word (*agape*) that describes how you can love God *and* love others! It is the *same* word!

It is not a case of God saying, "As God, I can love on this level, but you can only love on this level." There is no difference because *true love is God Himself loving others through us!*

It is not loving because of what you get in return! Rather it is a case that you assign value to someone and you then love that person with an unconditional love!

How do you love others? How about your family? How about your fellow church members?

Do you love like the world loves or like God loves?

Notice again: "We love"—we now have the ability to love just like God Himself loves—"because He first loved us."

One of the greatest hymns of the Christian faith was composed in less than five minutes. That hymn is now more than one hundred years old.

This song was written by George Matheson. George had been blind for more than twenty years when he wrote this song. It had been a very difficult twenty years.

Those years began with George losing his eyesight, then his fiancée left him, also. All of his plans turned to ashes, and his life was ruined.

Twenty years later his sister was scheduled to be married. George Matheson did not attend his sister's wedding. He instead stayed home and brooded about his twenty years of blindness. It had been twenty years since he had seen the beautiful smile of his mother. It had been twenty years since he had seen a sunrise or a sunset, seen a spring or a fall and none of that seemed fair to him.

But it was then the presence of God came upon him in a very special way. He took a pen and wrote blindly on a sheet of paper for less than five minutes. The poem became a song. The song is now in every hymnbook.

This is what he wrote:

> *"O Love that wilt not let me go,*
> *I rest my weary soul in Thee;*
> *I give Thee back the life I owe,*
> *That in Thine ocean depths its flow*

May richer, fuller be.

O Joy that seeketh me through pain,
 I cannot close my heart to thee,
I trace the rainbow thro' the rain,
And feel the promise is not vain
That morn shall tearless be.

O Cross that liftest up my head,
I dare not ask to hide from thee;
I lay in dust life's glory dead,
And from the ground there blossoms red
Life that shall endless be."

In his despair, he wrote about "life that shall endless be!" (eternal life) and that ended his despair!

And it all began with that "love from God which was so great that it will not let me go."

I am talking about the God where love begins but does not end.

16

WHAT IT MEANS TO LOVE LIKE GOD!

For I So Loved You!

Shortly before his death, a man by the name of Dr. Ludlow wrote an autobiography. This doctor had experienced a motherless childhood because his mother died at the same time he was being born. He would often hear the other boys talk about their own mothers. Their talk would always leave him with a feeling of loneliness which he could not describe. When he became old enough, his father told him how his mother had died.

It was time for Dr. Ludlow to be born. The physician said to the father, "Your wife is very sick. We may be able to save her, but the child must die. Or we can save the child, and let your wife die. Which shall it be?"

The father said, "She is the one to decide that."

They went to her and explained the situation. The mother smiled at them and said, "Let the child live."

Years later Dr. Ludlow said, "So my mother went out of life when I came into it. She gave herself for me."

Two thousand years ago in the Garden of Gethsemane, another Person had to make a similar decision. If He lived, we would die, but if He died, we could live.

Which choice would you have made if that person had been you? Would you have died for your spouse and children? I am sure the answer is yes! But would you have died for someone who hated you, abused you, cursed you, even wanted to kill you? Would you die for even your worst enemy?

Let's read our text in 1 John chapter four again. Verse seven says, "My beloved friends, let us continually love one another with an *agape*, selfless kind of love. This kind of *agape* love comes from God or, more literally, originates with God as its source." Verse nineteen adds the thought, "We love because He first loved us." Let's add a third verse that everyone can quote from memory. John 3:16 says, "For God so loved the world that He gave His only begotten Son that whosoever believes in Him should not perish but have everlasting life."

That's the kind of love I want to experience from God. It's also the kind of love I want to experience from God's people. Lest I forget, it's also the kind of love that God's people want to experience from me!

It is this God-kind of love that is the goal of our church. Read with me the goal at the bottom of your study sheet. *"Helping believers grow together in Him through love and forgiveness."* Underline the word love because the love in that statement is not human love, but it is the love of God that God will pour out in our hearts toward one another.

The goal may sound impossible, but I want you to know it is a very real possibility. This goal can even become a reality in a church like ours.

What does that mean? First, let me make a couple of introductory remarks about the big picture. We live in a world which uses the word love to describe practically everything. As a result, the word has almost lost its meaning in everyday conversation.

For instance, a man may say, "I love my wife," but five minutes later he may also say, "I love chocolate ice cream." I must ask, which does he love more, or does he love both of them the same? And if he does love them the same, would he dare admit to it?

One young man wrote a letter to his girlfriend. "My darling sweetheart (isn't that nice?), I love you so much that I would swim the whirling rapids of Niagara to be where you are. I love you so much that I would walk across the burning sands of the Sahara to be by your side. I love you so much that I would defy a whole army all by myself, to show you how much I love you." Then he added a P.S. "Honey, if it doesn't rain, I'll do my best to get over tomorrow night.'"

Even in our churches, the word has lost its meaning.

I read about a pastor who was leaving his church for another church. He was one of those liberal preachers who refused to preach against any sin. He didn't want to upset anyone!

A young man came up to him and said, "Pastor, I am so sorry we are going to lose you. When you came to us three years ago, I was a young man who did not care for God, man, or the devil. But since listening to your beautiful sermons I have learned to love all three of them!"

The word love has lost much of its meaning in the way that we live, talk, and think.

But yet when we read John 3:16 we are suddenly reminded that there is one love which soars like an eagle above all of the other loves. "For God so loved the world that He gave His only begotten Son that whosoever believes in Him should not perish but have everlasting life." Aren't you glad you have personally experienced the love of God in your life?

God says, "I am going to make it possible for you to love one another just like I love you."

Here are three Bible truths to write down.

1. God Loves a World of Less Than Perfect Humanity—So Can I!

Truth #1: God loves a world of less than perfect humanity—so can I! We begin with the objects of God's love. John 3:16 says, "For God so loved the world . . . " What kind of world did God so love?

We have this idea that God loved us because we were so lovable that God could not keep Himself away from us.

We picture God as being the young man who sees a beautiful young lady walking down the sidewalk. This young man immediately falls in love with her because she is very attractive, looks like she would be nice to spend time with, appears to be intelligent. Surely there is not a single thing wrong with her!

The young man then does everything to win her heart. He sends her flowers, takes her out to eat, and buys her jewelry! Maxes his credit card to win her heart!

We see ourselves as being the beautiful young woman that God is trying to win for Himself, but that is not so according to the Bible!

When the Bible says, "For God so loved the world," it does not mean the world of wonderful, kind, generous people who deserve God's very best. It means instead, the world of rebellious, sinful, God-hating people who deserve God's very worst!

We must begin by understanding what you and I are to God. The book of Romans chapter five gives us clarity as what you and I are to God.

The first description is revealed in the word "helpless" in verse six. Add the word "helpless" to your study sheet under point one. Romans 5:6 says, "In due time," which is another way of saying in God's time or at the perfectly appointed time, "when we were without strength"—powerless, weak, down on the mat and unable to pick ourselves up. Christ died for what kind of people? The ungodly. The word "ungodly" means "the people who are not godly."

We are described as helpless. It is the idea that we are *not able* to help ourselves. We're like the bedfast person who cannot feed himself or bathe himself or go to the bathroom by himself! We're like the blind man who must be led every step of the way. We are utterly helpless when it comes to lifting ourselves up to God so that we might meet His holy standards.

We're like a worm which can never raise itself to a man's level! That is why Isaac Watts wrote:

> *Alas, and did my Savior bleed*
> *And did my Sovereign die,*
> *Would He devote that sacred head,*
> *For such a worm as I?*

John 3:16 says, "For God so loved the *worms* and those worms are you and me!" Would you die for a worm? That is what the plan of salvation is all about!

Based on our identity as being nothing but worms, it would not be a surprise if John 3:16 read, "For God so *hated* the world that He condemned the world."

Let's move on. The second description is revealed in the word "ungodly" in this same verse. That's a fill-in-the-blank. Christ died for what kind of people? The ungodly. The word begins with the two letters "un." Those two letters negate the letters that follow. In other words, those two letters mean the opposite of the letters that follow.

For example, the word unattractive means the opposite of attractive. The word unknown means the opposite of known. Likewise, ungodly means we are just the opposite of godly. *We are the very opposite of everything God is.* Whatever God thinks, we think the opposite. If God says turn left, we turn right! Whatever God hates, we love! Whatever God loves, we hate!

Why? Because we are ungodly or the opposite of God in our nature!

We must ask ourselves, would you die for someone who is the very opposite of everything you are and everything you believe in?

The third description is revealed in the word "sinners" in verse eight. The verse says, "God makes known His own love for us in that while we were still sinners Christ died for us." Let's add the word "sinners" to our study sheet and then let's also add the definition of sin. The English word "sin" comes to us from the Greek word *hamartia*. *Hamartia* has been defined as "missing the mark" as in missing the bull's-eye of God's righteousness.

God says, "If you want to know Me then you must hit the mark—the bull's-eye—of My righteousness or holiness." God's standard is a standard of 100% righteousness or holiness.

God is so perfect that there are no B's, C's, or D's in His grading scale. There are only two possible grades: A+ or F. Either 100% perfection or you have sinned and fallen short of the glory of God.

I remember once talking a teacher into changing the grade on my report card from a B+ to an A-. I saw my B+ grade and did not like it one bit. I asked the teacher, "What was my average?" She said, "It was a ninety-four." I said, "A ninety-four was an A- in last year's class." She said, "A ninety-four is a B+ in my class." Guess what she did? She decided that I was trying hard to do my best. She decided to encourage that behavior by changing my grade to an A-.

That is something no one will ever be able to do with God. God's grading scale is one of either perfect righteousness or zero righteousness. Either A+ or an F.

The angels in heaven have always hit 100% perfection. That is why they are allowed to live in heaven!

The demons and Satan were once the angels in heaven, *but they failed one time.* That one failure turned their grade from an A+ to an F. That was why God kicked them out of heaven. The Bible says, "God then created hell for the devil and his angels." (Matthew 25:41)

But here is the problem: not one person in the entire history of mankind has ever hit 100% perfection except the God-man Jesus Christ!

Question: Would you die for a creation that is never, ever going to be worthy of you?

The fourth description is revealed in the word "enemies" in verse ten. The verse begins with the words, "For if while we were God's enemies." An enemy is a person who is fighting you every inch of the way. An enemy is at war with you. An enemy is planning how to kill you and remove you as a threat.

Now pay attention! We are inclined to love people who love us, but *God loved a people who hated Him!* God loved a people who were at war with Him and His Son, Jesus Christ!

Governor Pilate asked at the trial of Jesus, "Why? What evil has this Jesus done?" But we cried out, "Crucify Him! Crucify Him! He is worthy of death!" We then beat Him, we spit upon Him, we mocked Him, we drove the nails, and we then crucified Him!

Fathers, would you die for someone who raped and murdered your own daughter? Mothers, would you die for someone who ruined your son's mind with drugs and alcohol? Children, would you die for someone who is right now abusing your dear, sweet mother in a nursing home?

But that is exactly what God did when God so loved the world because it was His own enemies that He loved! For God so loved a world which so hated Him! That is how much God loves you!

Jesus looked down from the cross, and He prayed, "Father, forgive them for they know not what they do." In other words, "Don't send a million angels and destroy them for what they have done."

In so doing, God shows us how much He can love! He loved His own enemies in order to make them His friends! He then says to us, "If God so loved us, we ought also to love one another."

This kind of love originates in the heart of God. *Everyone that loves like God also loves the helpless, loves the ungodly, loves the sinners, loves even the enemies . . .* and "everyone that loves like God loves can know that he has been born again of God and knows God."

Truth #1 is God loves a world of less than perfect humanity—so can I! Let me say it again, so can I! With God's help, I want to do just exactly that, how about you?

How else can we know how much God loves us?

2. God Loves the World Enough to Give It His Best Effort—So Can I!

Truth #2: God loves the world enough to give it His best effort—so can I! Based on what we have just studied, it is important to ask ourselves, how far does God's love go? Does God's love go into the White House? Does God's love go into the abortion clinic? Does God's love go into the house of prostitution? Does God's love go under the bridge where the homeless live?

A family had a pet snake known as a boa constrictor. One night the parents put their little girl to bed. During the night, the snake crawled out of its box, made its way into the girl's room, wrapped itself around the girl's body, and literally choked the life from that little girl.

On the next morning, the parents walked into the room and found the snake wrapped around their little daughter's body. The father became so angry that he grabbed the snake, threw it outside, and shot it dead.

I want you to know God could have done the very same thing to every one of us when we nailed His only begotten Son to the cross!

Imagine how God felt watching His Son die! Imagine how Jesus felt when they pounded the nails through His hands and feet! Someone said, "He could have called 100,000 angels to come to His aid," and that would have been true. He could have said, "Tom Swartzwelder is not worth it" and that would have been true! He could have said, "Cast Tom and the rest of them into hell!" But, thank God, He did not do that, but He chose to die alone on an old rugged cross for you and me!

Imagine a scene such as this. Jesus is standing on Mount Calvary just minutes before being crucified. A soldier asks Jesus, "How much do you love me?" Jesus says, "I love you this much." He then spreads out His arms and lets that same soldier nail Him to a cross.

How far does God's love reach? How far does God's love extend? After all the sins I have done, does God still love me?

John chapter six and verse thirty-seven says, "All the Father has given to Me shall come to me. I guarantee the one who comes to Me will never be cast out." The offer of salvation is extended to "everyone who comes to Me." Fill in the blank. NO ONE IS REFUSED AT THE CROSS!

Jesus preached a "whosoever will" gospel! That "whosoever" included the thief on the cross, the adulteress at the well, a cheating tax collector named Zacchaeus, a murdering sheriff named Saul, more than one demon-possessed man, a lawyer named Nicodemus, Mary Magdalene out of whom He cast seven demons, hot and cold Peter, and even a nine-year-old Tommy Swartzwelder!

The simple axiom correctly states, "The elect are the whosoever wills, and the non-elect are the whosoever won'ts." The classifications are always in balance!

Billy Graham's sermons ended with the same song over and over again.

> *Just as I am without one plea*
> *But that Thy blood was shed for me,*
> *And that thou biddest me come to Thee,*
> *O, Lamb of God, I come, I come!*

> *Charlotte Elliott*

God keeps reaching out! Jesus wept over Jerusalem and said, "How often I would have gathered your people to Me just like a mother hen gathers her little chicks to herself, but you would not allow it!" (Matthew 23:37) "God strongly wills or strongly desires that all men should be saved and come to a firsthand knowledge of the truth." (1 Timothy 2:4)

Aren't you glad God gave you His best effort? You are born again because God gave you His very best effort!

God asks the same from you. God loves the world. He wants you to give your best effort to bring the world to Him. God loves His enemies! He wants you to give your best effort to love your enemies! God also loves the church. The Bible says that Jesus, "loved the church so much He gave Himself for it." (Ephesians 5:25) He wants you to give your best effort to make this church the best church it can be!

My father pastored for around thirty years. He taught me in my early years, "Love your enemies until *your* death." His message was twofold. First, you will likely make enemies if you preach the entire Bible! Second, never stop loving the people to whom you have been called to minister! I don't like admitting it, but those words have not been easy. After more than forty years of ministry, I still struggle with this issue. But he was right. God loves the world enough to give it His best effort—so can I! I must lay aside my personal hurts and allow God to love *everyone* through me!

Oh, dear God, help me to become the Good Samaritan to everyone I meet! Unfortunately, I can provide names of people I would prefer not to love. It would be easier to call down fire from heaven upon them! But God has called me to do something much different. God has called me to love them as God has loved me. "So, dear God, help me to become the Good Samaritan to *everyone* I meet!"

God, when they disappoint me like I have disappointed You—help me to love them. When they ignore my advice like I have ignored Your advice—help me to love them. When they say unkind words against my ministry like I have sometimes said unkind words against Your ministry—help me to love them. When they play church like I have played church—help me to love them even then.

God loves the world enough to give it His best effort—but how can a weakling like me do the same? 1 John 4:16-17 says, "And we have come to know and to believe the love that God has for us. God is love, and the one who remains in love remains in God, and God remains in him. In this, love is perfected with us so that we may have confidence in the day of judgment, for we are as He is in this world." (1 John 4:16-17, HCSB)

"As He is . . . so are we!"

God is love, and He wishes to reproduce that love in our hearts through the Holy Spirit! The whole passage makes it abundantly clear that perfect love or fullness of love is given to the person whose life is surrendered to the Most High God. The concept of God flowing through us includes love flowing through us, too!

Such a person has already surrendered the right of self-preservation to his God. Such a person recognizes he has been "bought with a price and is no longer his own." (1 Corinthians 6:19) Such a person has accepted a higher calling than a worldly calling. He knows he is here to let God love others through him.

Dr. Bernardo of London was known as a great philanthropist. He told the story of standing one very cold day at his front door when a little, ragged boy came up to him and asked to be taken into the orphan's home.

The good doctor pretended to be a mean man. He asked, "How do I know that you are telling me the truth? Do you have any friends to speak for you?"

The little boy said, "Friends! No, I ain't got no friends. But if these here rags," and he then held up his tattered garments, "won't speak for me then nothing else will."

Dr. Bernardo then picked up the little boy and carried him into his house!

For God so loved the world that whoever, including little orphans in tattered rags, comes to Him can be saved!

3. God Loves the World with an Enduring Love—So Can I!

Truth #3: God loves the world with an enduring love—so can I! In other words, God will make it possible for us to stay in this work for the long haul.

The word "enduring" has the idea of "how long will it last?" Man has a bad tendency to say, "I love," then change his mind a few months later.

I recall marrying a young couple who seemed to be deeply in love. I required them to go through three counseling sessions. We discussed everything I knew about a Christian marriage. Both of them said they wanted a Christian marriage. They stood in front of a large audience and repeated their wedding vows. The divorce was finalized less than one year later. It turned out the groom was already seeing someone else during our counseling sessions. He was seeing someone else even before the wedding! His love did not even make it to the wedding!

How long will the love of God last for you? The answer may surprise you. The answer depends on who you are and what your relationship is to God.

There are only two kinds of people in the world. First, there are those who are God's enemies because they are still rejecting Jesus as their personal Savior! Second, there are those who are now reconciled to God. They have waved the white flag of surrender and received Jesus on His terms to be their Lord and Savior!

If you are still God's enemy—if you have never turned away from your sin and put your faith in Jesus—I want you to know that _today_ God loves you with all of His heart!

2 Peter 3:9 says, "God is not willing that any should perish!" The cross is proof of that! Jesus died for all men, and all men includes you!

But if you die without Jesus, things _will_ change! *God's love for you will effectively stop at the grave.* The only thing left for you will be that of standing before a holy and righteous God! The justice of God will demand that you pay for your sin!

Someone disagreed and said, "God loves me too much to throw me into hell." That person fails to see that God's love for the sinner stops at the grave.

The only reason the unbeliever is not in hell today is because of the love of God. That love is presently holding back the judgment of God! But after the unbeliever dies, there will be no more love. Only the final judgment!

There is no love in hell! There is no love at the final judgment for the one who has rejected Jesus! The Bible says there is only "weeping and wailing and gnashing of teeth."

But as long as there is breath, there is still love. And where love exists, there is also still hope!

How do I know? Look at the cross! Jesus was not crucified alone but with two criminals. Both criminals were guilty of crimes worthy of death. One criminal used his final moments on earth to blaspheme the Love of God being displayed on the middle cross. The second criminal used his final moments on earth to seek forgiveness. He prayed, "Lord, remember me when You come into your kingdom." Jesus replied, "You shall join Me later today in paradise."

That is exactly what happened! Imagine the joy of that moment! The word "priceless" is the only word which comes to my mind. The second criminal was saved, rescued from hell, only minutes from a Christless eternity! The first criminal chose to live for eternity in a place where there is no love. The second criminal chose to live for eternity with the God of love!

It is possible we would have given up much earlier when it came to loving those two criminals! But it is evident Jesus had not given up! His love endured to the very end of their lives! From the cradle to the grave Jesus loved people! He *never* stopped loving! His love endured to the end of life itself!

That brings us to a very important fill-in-the-blank. Wouldn't it be great if we could follow His example and love others to the end of life itself? That is possible if we can stay focused on the *value* of the individual rather than the *works* of the individual. The biggest issue is not what the individual has done but something even more basic: the value of the individual himself.

Three words describe the value of every individual. These words are fill-in-the-blank on your study sheet.

The first word is "eternal." Everyone I meet will live forever. The person seated next to you will live forever. The first person you meet tomorrow will live forever. That person must receive Jesus or face an awful eternity without Jesus!

The second word is "image." Man was not made in the image of a toad or a frog. Man is not a product of evolution, but man was created in the image of God. It is true that image has been distorted by sin, but it does not change the fact that man has value.

The third word is "brief." James 4:14 says, "What is your life? It is just a vapor, a mist, a fog that appears for a brief time then passes away." Some things never change, things like the young far too quickly become old. When one is young, he thinks that old age is a lifetime away. He is correct in that line of thinking, but what he does not realize is how quickly a lifetime will pass.

I remember the first year of my retirement. I was feeling really good about retirement until someone pointed out that I had already gone through the stage of childhood. Also, I had already gone through the stage of leaving Mom and Dad and starting a career. Furthermore, I had already gone through the stage of raising a family. And I had already gone through the stage of planning and saving for retirement. Now I was in the stage called retirement. The person said, "Tom, there is only one more stage for you, and that is death." Up until that moment, there had always been another stage for me, but now there was not another stage! That was an eye-opening experience! That's why you need to consider how brief your life is and not waste it.

Who did Jesus come to seek and save? He came to those who will live eternally, who are made in the image of God, and who have only a brief time to prepare for eternity.

Those three words should shape how we approach our fellowman. It is critical that humanity experience the love of God! But that won't happen if we turn our love on and off like a light switch! It won't happen if we pick and choose which race or class we wish to love. It won't happen unless we are fully committed to providing an *enduring* love!

Rest assured, a Christlike love is an enduring love! It has now endured on Planet Earth for some six thousand years. I have every reason to believe it can endure through me for the rest of my days!

Lest I forget, what about those of us who are right now reconciled to God? How long will God's love toward us last?

I have good news. As a matter of fact, I have great news!

Who shall separate us from the love of Christ? Shall tribulation, or distress, or persecution, or famine, or nakedness, or danger, or sword? As it is written, "For your sake we are being killed all the day long; we are regarded as sheep to be slaughtered." No, in all these things we are more than conquerors through him who loved us. For I am sure that neither death nor life, nor angels nor rulers, nor things present nor things to come, nor powers, nor height nor depth, nor anything else in all creation, will be able to separate us from the love of God in Christ Jesus our Lord. (Romans 8:35-39, ESV)

Paul's list includes everything imaginable. The skeptic read what Paul wrote and said, "But, Paul, what about this and what about that?" and he mentioned several more possibilities. Paul added the thought "nor anything else in all creation." He then said to the skeptic, "Does that satisfy you?" I want you to know Paul's statement ought to satisfy every single one of us!

The Bible makes it plain that this preacher is now being loved by God and will be loved by God *forever*! "For nothing shall ever separate me from the love of God which is in Christ Jesus!"

My family, my mother, even you may stop loving me, but my God will never stop loving me because I am a believer in His Son!

"For nothing—absolutely nothing—shall ever separate me from the love of God which is in Christ Jesus!"

A father and son were standing on top of a hill. The father was pointing out various places to the east, west, north, and south. Then he swept his hand around the entire horizon and said, "Son, God's love is as big as all that!"

The little boy smiled from ear to ear, and he said, "Then we must be smack dab in the middle of God's love."

I want you to know that is exactly where you are if you have been born again! *"Smack dab in the middle of God's love."* You are in the center of God's love for all eternity because nothing can ever separate you from the love of God!

17

L-O-V-E CAN BE SPELLED J-E-S-U-S!

Love Never Fails

A Sunday School teacher asked her class of five-year-old students to draw a picture of love. One drew a picture of Mommy washing dishes, a second drew a picture of the family having evening dinner, and a third drew a picture of Daddy playing with them. But a fourth drew a picture of a man dressed like people from the days of the Bible.

The teacher asked, "What did you draw?"

The student answered, "I drew a picture of Jesus."

"Why did you draw a picture of Jesus?"

"Because when I think of love, I think of Jesus because no one can ever love like Jesus."

How do you define the word love? What is the love of God truly like? Let me suggest the simplest definition of all. The four letters l-o-v-e can be spelled with the five letters J-e-s-u-s!

1 Corinthians chapter thirteen is recognized as the love chapter of the Bible. That's your first fill-in-the-blank, too.

> *If I speak human or angelic languages but do not have love, I am a sounding gong or a clanging cymbal. If I have the gift of prophecy and understand all mysteries and all knowledge, and if I have all faith so that I can move mountains but do not have love, I am nothing. And if I donate all my goods to feed the poor, and if I give my body in order to boast but do not have love, I gain nothing. Love is patient, love is kind. Love does not envy, is not boastful, is not conceited, does not act improperly, is not selfish, is not provoked, and does not keep a record of wrongs. Love finds no joy in unrighteousness but rejoices in the truth. It bears all things, believes all things, hopes all things, endures all things. Love never ends. But as for prophecies, they will come to an end; as for languages, they will cease; as for knowledge, it will come to an end. (1 Corinthians 13:1-8, HCSB)*

Keep in mind this phrase from verse eight, "Love never ends or fails."

Let's clarify something before we go deeper into our text. Some of you may be using a King James Version that uses the word charity instead of love. The word charity has changed in its meaning over the last four hundred years and would not be the right word to use today. The actual Greek word is *agape*. We translate *agape* with the English word "love" or "sacrificial love" such as the love of John 3:16. Our English word "love" *includes* charity, but it also includes much more than acts of charity. Thus, we're talking about love in its many different aspects in this chapter.

Love is very hard to define, and therefore, it is not well understood. I read about a man who claimed to be in love with a woman. She refused to marry him, so he threw acid in her face and blinded her. He was sent to prison for several years. He left prison, proposed a second time and the woman married him. That's a strange view of love.

We also use the word "love" in many different ways. To a woman, love may be a diamond ring. She says, "I love my diamond ring." Indeed, she really does! To a man, love may be a sports activity like hunting or fishing. He says, "I love fishing." To a child, love may be a bicycle or a computer game. The child says, "I love my gifts at Christmas."

But there is one way you can define love so that all of us can understand its meaning. That way is to take this abstract word, wrap it in flesh and bone and think about love as a person rather than an idea or ideal.

All of us know what love is, but there has only been one person who can be truly described as the personification or the embodiment of love. That person is Jesus Christ.

If we substitute the name "Jesus" for the word "love," we have a beautiful description of not only what love is but also of what Jesus is.

You could read the passage like this: "Jesus suffers long and is kind; Jesus envies not; Jesus vaunts not Himself, is not puffed up, and does not behave Himself unseemly. Jesus seeks not His own, is not easily provoked, and thinks no evil. Jesus rejoices not in iniquity but rejoices in the truth. Jesus bears all things, believes all things, hopes all things, and endures all things. Jesus never fails."

Isn't that a beautiful picture of Jesus? Every detail fits Him perfectly! It is as if love came down from heaven, took upon itself human flesh, and they called its name Jesus!

Charles Wesley wrote a song about love becoming human flesh. He wrote,

> *Love Divine, all loves excelling,*
> *Joy of heaven, to earth come down,*
> *Fix in us Thy humble dwelling,*
> *All Thy faithful mercies crown.*
> *Jesus, Thou art all compassion,*
> *Pure, unbounded love Thou art;*

Visit us with Thy salvation,
Enter every trembling heart.

Wesley's point is that love has come down from heaven in the form of a man! I agree! That is why l-o-v-e can be spelled J-e-s-u-s.

Wouldn't that be a wonderful picture of you, too? As we read verse four, can we substitute your name in place of the word love? As we read verse five, can we put your name in front of everything on that list? As we read verse six, can we put your name in front of everything on that list? Then we come to an even harder test which is verse seven. Can we put your name in front of everything on that list? Then we come to the ultimate test—to the first three words of verse eight. Can we take away the word charity or love and replace it with your name? *When we think of love and what love is, can we also think of you?*

This discussion of love can be divided into four categories. Each one is a fill-in-the-blank on your study sheet.

1. The Love of Jesus Knows How to Handle People.

Category #1: The love of Jesus knows how to handle people. The church at Corinth had one of the greatest problems that any church can have, and that is people problems.

Let me share a little secret with you. Most church problems are not doctrinal. The sign over the door (the name of the church's denomination) settles most of the doctrinal issues. I have experienced very few doctrinal problems in my forty years of ministry. It is my experience that Catholics attend Catholic churches, Pentecostals attend Pentecostal churches, and Baptists attend Baptist churches. We normally attend the church with which we have the most agreement!

Also, most church problems are not financial. There may be a squabble over budget priorities, but it's unlikely to rise above the level of a squabble. Quite honestly, there's usually not enough extra money for a really good squabble! At least that has been my experience! I will also note the Lord has a way of taking care of the finances if the people truly love Him.

The greatest problem, and this is a fill-in-the-blank, is people getting along with one another. It is probably the first issue that comes to our mind when we discuss the importance of love. Our first reaction is, "Do I have to love people? Aaaagh!" To paraphrase Ben Franklin, "Does thou love people? Then do not squander people for that is the stuff life is made of!" But it's also the reason so many of us want to crawl in a hole and pull the hole in behind us. Many of us retire to get away from people! Why? People have problems that often turn the people themselves into problems.

Thankfully for all of us, this is the first issue which Paul addresses! Verse four says, "Love suffers long, is kind, and envies not." One would think those three issues alone would drain love of all of its energy, but as we shall see later, love still has the strength to deal with three other big issues.

Jerry Vines, the former president of the Sothern Baptist Convention, said, "The Corinthian Christians were well-acquainted with the gifts of the Spirit, but they failed to understand the graces of the Spirit." One of those graces was love.

The Corinthians unlovingly thought, "I'd like to have his spiritual gift. I'm jealous of that person because I don't have the gift he has. I deserve the spotlight just as much as he does!" This mentality created many problems throughout the church. It also indicated very few people were like Jesus because l-o-v-e can be spelled J-e-s-u-s!

One of the most important principles in Christianity states that no one can be used effectively by God unless you can first get along with people. Why? Because meeting the needs of people is what God's work is all about! Our ministry does not occur in a vacuum. Sometimes we may wish that it did, but the reality is that it does not! No ministry can succeed unless it occurs in a laboratory of people.

John D. Rockefeller was asked what he considered to be the most valuable skill in his employees. He quickly replied, "The ability to get along with people!"

Some people really struggle with this issue. Some even say, "It's not my nature to get along with people." If this statement describes you, it is critical that you pay close attention to the next statement. *God says He can improve my nature by filling me with His love!* This is a fill-in-the-blank, so I will repeat it. God says He can improve my nature, even transform my nature, by filling me with His love!

Notice how God's love changes us!

Verse four begins in my mind with the words, "Jesus is exceedingly patient with people." The King James Version says, "Love suffers long" which is another way of saying love is able to endure difficult people for a very long time. The idea has nothing to do with surviving a long wait at a traffic light. The idea instead is one of being able to survive difficult people.

Which would you rather experience? A difficult traffic light or a difficult person?

To suffer long is to be patient with people who upset you and perhaps even go a step further and treat you badly. Love is able to endure a lot and absorb a lot. That includes abuse, criticism, lies, and all manner of wrong treatment.

It is interesting to me that this word patient is the same Greek word in Galatians 5:22 where Paul says, The fruit of the Spirit is love, joy, peace, and what comes next? Patience or long-suffering. The Holy Spirit's presence in our lives enables us to be patient with our fellow man even when our fellow man is less than desirable.

Was Jesus good at doing this? Yes, He was! He lived for thirty-three years with people who defied God in their daily lives. He endured the many ups and downs of the apostles. He endures my inconsistencies, too!

Let me give you four questions to consider. First, do I realize how patient God is with me? Try to honestly answer that question! Second, am I patient with those to whom it is difficult to minister? Third, have I tried to be understanding? Fourth, am I as patient with others as I expect them to be with me?

I wonder if this item is listed first because it is the hardest one for most of us. But it is very important we understand that this is a *conquerable* issue for all of us through the power of the Holy Spirit!

Verse four continues, "Love is kind." The previous thought was about what you can absorb from others, but this part is about what you dispense or give back to those same people. Love endures so much but pays back with kindness. To be kind is to do good to those who are irritating you.

Kindness and gentleness are synonyms in this verse. A gentle soul is also a kind soul! This kindness mellows our hard nature into something which becomes a blessing instead of a curse.

One item which continually infuriated the Jews was that they could not stop Jesus from doing good! One great example happened at His arrest in the Garden of Gethsemane. There was a brief skirmish in which Peter cut off the ear of a servant named Malchus. Excuse me for my sanctified imagination, but I can see Jesus looking at the handcuffs then saying, "Wait a minute. There is something I must do." He then reached down to the ground, picked up the ear, and reattached it to Malchus's head.

No one has ever loved His enemies like Jesus! No one has ever been kinder to His enemies than Jesus. I pale in comparison with His effort!

There are two questions I need to consider for myself. First, do I unconsciously wear a smile or a frown? This is important because what you do unconsciously gives us a glimpse into your soul! Second, do I look for opportunities to help others? That is one mark of a kind heart.

Improvement number three is in the next part of verse four and states, "Love is not envious." This is a very important part of knowing how to handle people. It begins with your heart having a right spirit, and that right spirit is then able to deal with people.

To envy is to want what others have. To envy not is to be pleased with the success of others. Sometimes their success may even come at your own expense. The Apostle Paul was able to beat this problem in his own life. He wrote from prison in Philippians 4:11, "I have learned to be content in whatever circumstances I find myself!" In other words, *I live independently of my circumstances.* I will not allow my circumstances to change either me or my attitude toward people.

Someone said, "But I am not like the Joneses, and I want to be like the Joneses!" Sometimes we are so envious it eats us alive!

But think again of the words, "Love is not envious." Let's change that to Jesus is not envious. How much did Jesus have? Very little! Did Jesus try to keep up with the Joneses? No.

There are two points I want to share in this regard about the life of Jesus. First, Jesus always had enough to get by! When I was a young man, I heard a statement that I accepted as a rule for my life. Here is that statement. "All I need in life is a pathway through it." That statement has kept my attitude right for many years in the area of material possessions. It's also a fill-in-the-blank. "All I need in life is a pathway through it."

That leads me to the second point. Jesus stayed focused on God's will for His life. There is an interesting phrase in the Bible which says, "Jesus set His face toward Jerusalem." (Luke 9:51) He was determined to accomplish God's goal for His life rather than keep up with the Joneses!

Everyone struggles with envy, but being like Jesus will overcome envy.

Think for a moment. Have I thought that God does not love me? Am I jealous of another's success, money, good looks, or popularity? Do I grieve at the prosperity of others? Have I spent more time in envying others than in an attempt to improve myself?

The reality is that when you truly love Jesus, you won't care who gets the credit!

I may have done something really dumb in 1996, but I have always been content with what I did. Every position in our accounting department was being eliminated. Most of the twenty-four employees were offered positions in the same city or in our headquarters in Columbus, Ohio. My boss turned down a lateral move which would have allowed him to remain in the same city.

As a result, the job was then offered to me. I discussed the offer with my boss. During the discussion, my boss said he had reconsidered and probably had made a mistake. I passed on this information to the hirer. I suggested that he might want to talk to my boss again before making a final offer to me. Which he did!

After more deliberation, my boss chose to move to Columbus and I got the job. Needless to say, many people did not understand my logic. The job represented a significant promotion and pay increase for me! But I did it anyway because I wanted what was best for him! Quite honestly, I liked him. He was my golf buddy. Like Paul, I was a fool for Jesus's sake! In my own simplistic way (perhaps naïve way) I was convinced Jesus would take care of me. And, yes, Jesus is still taking care of me more than twenty years later.

When I am like Jesus—filled with the love of Jesus—I will be in a right relationship with others.

2. The Love of Jesus Overcomes Our Superiority Complex

Category #2: The love of Jesus overcomes our superiority complex. Some people suffer from what is commonly referred to as an inferiority complex, but it is obvious to psychologists and common-sense people like me that a *superiority* complex also lies deep within the majority of us. Such a complex can be traced back to our basic need for something called significance. We need, sometimes desperately need, to know we are important to someone or something. No one wants to be an oxygen thief, but everyone wants to contribute in some way. *Plus, we want to be recognized for our contribution.*

But that hunger creates a lot of problems!

This is a fill-in-the-blank. It is important to realize that love not only changes my relationship to others, but it even changes my relationship to my own inner being.

Verse four continues, "Love vaunteth not itself." I prefer to say it like this, "love is not boastful . . . does not brag . . . does not use a megaphone to announce its accomplishments."

I once worked for a man who often said, "If I don't promote myself, no one else will." His attitude created relationship problems with his staff! He used us to exalt himself! I believe the man left out the biggest promoter of all time and that is God. God does the best job of promoting people that I have ever seen. He certainly succeeded with Joseph, Moses, Joshua, and Daniel in the Old Testament!

The psalmist testified, "For promotion cometh neither from the east, nor from the west, nor from the south. But God *is* the judge: he putteth down one, and setteth up another." (Psalm 75:6-7, KJV) The Bible urges us to put our trust in God rather than in man!

Please notice love has no superiority complex. Neither does Jesus. Love does not promote itself—does not brag about its abilities or achievements to promote itself. Neither does Jesus. Jesus said, "My will is not to do My own will but the will of Him that sent Me." (John. 4:34)

I once worked for a man who would brag about the size of his income tax refund. He would even get upset if anyone in the department got a bigger refund than him. He never understood that his philosophy was actually costing him money. He could have banked that money throughout the year and gained interest on it! But, no, he wanted the biggest tax refund of anyone! And he wanted everyone to know about it!

Verse four continues, "Love is not puffed up." Someone said, "Pride is an inflated idea of one's own importance!" That is very true! It is important to understand that love, though, has no pride to hinder it.

The spirit of pride and the spirit of arrogance are the exact opposite of the spirit of God's love! They are the exact opposite of J-e-s-u-s!

"Vaunts itself" has the idea of how we look before others, but "puffed up" has the idea of being internal or within us. Being puffed up is how we really feel about ourselves. The man who is puffed up sees himself as being elevated from where he once was and where was that? That was on the same level as all of us. But he is now puffed up which means he sees himself as being above us.

If we were truly honest, the epitaph on many tombstones would say, "Here lies a man who was in love with himself."

Do you remember the old fable about two swans and a frog? The frog asked the swans, "Would you like to see the wonders of my pond?" The swans said they would, and the frog showed them his pond.

The swans then asked, "Would you like to see the wonders of our sky?" The frog said, "Yes, I would, but I can't fly."

The swans said, "We will hold a stick in our beaks. You hold onto the stick with your mouth, and we will fly you around."

Soon the three of them were flying through the sky. The three of them passed over a village. A woman looked up and said, "Have you ever before seen anything like that? Who in the world could think up an idea as brilliant as that?"

The frog opened his mouth and said, "I did," and that was the end of the frog.

The end for many of us is when we say, "I did" or "I think" or "I have." The Bible warns us, "Pride goes before destruction and a boastful spirit before a fall." (Proverbs 16:18)

Here are some excellent review questions. I don't know who wrote this list, but he did a great job. The first question is, have I talked too much—especially about myself? Do I realize that boasting is often a sign of inner weakness and insecurity? Have I refused to admit when I was wrong? How often do I use the word "I"? Must I always be in the limelight?

I hope you take the time to seriously consider these questions. It's hard to change into the person you could be if you don't first take the time to identify the person you already are!

The superiority complex continues in verse five. "Love does not behave itself unseemly or inappropriately." Remember, love is always a gentleman or a lady. Love has good manners! It does not talk rudely or crudely. It does not use expressions which offend people. It does not cause people to turn away and try to escape!

Ask yourself these questions. Have I been vulgar and crude in actions and conversations? Have I purposely disobeyed the normal rules of courtesy? Do I enjoy making fun of other people?

Can you imagine Jesus failing in any of those questions? I can't. Jesus does not behave Himself inappropriately.

Notice also that, "love seeks not its own benefit." Love is not selfish. Love is not about my being number one but about others being number one.

Was there a selfish bone in our Lord? No! He was instead always giving Himself to others!

Our superiority complex insists on having its own way, but love does not insist on having its own way!

Nor did Jesus insist on having His own way! The Bible says:

> *"Make your own attitude that of Christ Jesus, who, existing in the form of God, did not consider equality with God as something to be used for His own advantage. Instead, He emptied Himself by assuming the form of a slave, taking on the likeness of men. And when He had come as a man in His external form, He humbled Himself by becoming obedient to the point of death—even to death on a cross." (Philippians 2:5-8, HCSB)*

But our superiority complex goes the opposite direction.

Ask yourself, have I acted like a spoiled child? Do I fail to consider the needs and desires of others? Do I try to work deals for my advancement? Do I camouflage my own desires as the needs of others? Must I win every time? Am I a poor loser?

Here is the conclusion, and it is a very powerful conclusion. When I am like Jesus, that means filled with the love of Jesus, I will then be in a right relationship with even myself.

3. The Love of Jesus Conquers the Enemy of Sin.

Category #3: The love of Jesus conquers the enemy of sin. That means love is very powerful! Love changes us on the outside, changes us on the inside, then strengthens us in our battle with sin. The same three truths can be said about Jesus, too! Jesus changes us on the outside, changes us on the inside, then strengthens us in our battle with sin! Love encompasses the entire person!

1 John 4:4 says, "The One who is in you is greater than the enemy who is in the world!" The One who is in you is Jesus Christ. The enemy who is in the world is the devil.

Some people wonder if there is a real devil. I can safely say if you are still wondering, well, the devil probably already has you cooked and ready for his evening meal!

I had a relative who got into a fight with the devil in her kitchen. She was praying to Jesus, but the devil kept interrupting her prayer. She tried singing to Jesus, but the devil kept interrupting her singing. She finally became so upset that she threw her skillet at the invisible devil and yelled, "Get out of this kitchen! There ain't room enough for both of us in this kitchen!"

I don't think I ever met that relative. But the devil was very real to her! I want you to know that the devil is also very real to me.

Let me show you what love does to the attacks from the devil. The rest of verse five and all of verse six deals with the attacks from the devil.

The Bible says, "Love is not irritable or easily provoked." Those words have the idea of being roused to anger, probably roused to actually perform an act of anger. The Bible may say love is not easily provoked, but it should go without saying that most people *are* easily provoked. This includes Christians who know very little about love!

We could say that love rolls with the punches. Some people, though, fly off the handle over everything, and I do mean everything. When someone sins against them, they sin back! They automatically retaliate! Their philosophy is, "If you hit me, I will hit you back harder!" Sometimes they imagine a problem and retaliate when they were never wronged. Such people may sing like a nightingale in the choir, but they are not filled with love.

There is something we need to acknowledge at this point in our study. It is a fill-in-the-blank. Write: the devil will make certain that conflicts arise in my Christian life. Mark my words: Those conflicts will happen! The devil will make certain those conflicts happen!

I had a bad experience in the eighth grade in my shop class. The other boys wanted to start a fight between another boy and me. They pushed me toward him so he would have to retaliate. They punched me in the chest and dared me to fight. I chose not to fight. The other boy chose not to fight, too. I know because he never threw the first punch. I think he was as scared of me as I was of him!

That happens to most children, but it also happens to us adults. Someone says something or looks at us cross-eyed or, heaven forbid, doesn't agree with our way of thinking. Our anger is aroused just like that of the creature Godzilla! We're ready to breathe fire if anyone gets too close!

But the Bible says love rolls with the punches!

Do you remember how Jesus acted in His trials? The Bible says Jesus answered them not a word! He could have called 10,000 angels, even 100,000 angels, to wipe out all of His enemies, but He chose to answer them not a word! That response was an act of His will!

A Puritan wrote, "I am determined so to be angry as not to sin; therefore, to be angry with nothing but sin." Don't vent your anger on others; vent it on sin!

Do your own self-examination on this issue. Are my feelings easily hurt? Am I touchy? Do I become resentful when things don't go my way? Do I lose my temper to cover up my own weakness? Do I justify losing my temper by saying it makes me feel better, but forget the effect upon other people? Do I let little inconveniences and annoyances irritate me?

Maybe you fail in this area, and the devil eats your lunch. Remember, though, what the Bible says. "God's love is not easily provoked . . . is not easily stirred to anger." The Holy Spirit can teach you to love, and love can give you victory in this area.

The Bible goes on to say, "Love thinks no evil." That expression is not very clear. The key word is the word "thinks." Maybe you are good at controlling your temper. But how good are you at controlling your thoughts? Some people's favorite expression is, "Get Out of My Head." One fault in human nature is that we have problems controlling our thoughts.

Love does not dwell on the evil done to you by others. Literally, the idea is, love does not keep track of the wrongs done against you.

One man did just the opposite. He wrote in a notebook all of the wrongs which had been done to him over the years. The only thing that effort accomplished was to turn his heart into a bitter heart. He reached a point where those things could no longer be forgotten or buried in the past. His number one goal is getting even with the people who wronged him.

Story number two! A young married man told his friend, "Every time my wife and I get into an argument she becomes historical." The friend said, "You mean 'hysterical.'" The man said, "No. Every time we get in an argument, she reminds me of everything I have ever done wrong."

Jesus could have said, "You whipped me with the cat-o-nine tails, you put a crown of thorns on My head, you drove nails through My hands and My feet, so into hell you go!" But He didn't keep count of their sins. He prayed instead, "Father, forgive them for they know not what they do."

Someone said, "But I can't do that!" Consider this! After Jesus was crucified, a man named Stephen was executed for preaching about Jesus. Stephen was stoned to death instead of crucified like Jesus. The stones were used to crush the life from his body. Stephen's final words were,

"Lord, do not record this sin against them." (Acts 7:60) He was able to say those words because l-o-v-e can also be spelled J-e-s-u-s. He was able to do what Jesus Himself was able to do!

Look closely at the review questions and put a mark next to the one that bothers you the most. Am I always trying to find faults and imperfections in other people? Am I suspicious of other people? That's a good one. Do I throw cold water on others' enthusiasm? Is my pessimism really resentment and envy?

Let's take our first look at verse six. "God's love does not rejoice in iniquity." There is an old saying, "Good news travels fast in this community. Bad news travels twice as fast."

Love does not take joy in the sin of others. The natural tendency is to hear about someone's sin and immediately spread it! We hypocritically say, "I'm saying this in love . . . " or "I shouldn't be saying this but . . . " In so doing we are indicating that so-and-so is a bigger sinner than we are! Surely, we would not do what that person did! Surely, we would never stoop so low!

In so doing, we lower our brother and elevate self. Can you imagine Jesus doing anything like that?

Notice that, "Love rejoices instead in the truth." Love upholds the truth, even promotes the truth rather than grabs hold of the rumor or a lie.

A man filled with love will have nothing to do with lies, but he will make certain that the truth prevails. He will follow the Bible instruction to, "buy the truth and sell it not." (Proverbs 23:23)

A western politician became very upset about something the local newspaper said about him. He rushed down to the newspaper and demanded to speak with the editor. The editor asked, "What do you want?" The politician said, "You are telling lies about me in your newspaper, and you know it!" The editor said, "You have no cause for complaint. What would you do if I told the truth about you?"

The person who is filled with the love of Jesus knows there's plenty of not-so-good stuff to be told about him, too! The old saying is still true, "Point one finger at me and you'll have three fingers pointing back at you!"

How well do you do in this area? Here are the review questions. Do I try to degrade others to elevate myself? Do I tease to belittle people? Have I ever been glad at the misfortunes of others? I have, and probably you have, too. I'm not proud of it, and I prefer that it not happen again. Am I happy to hear others speak ill of someone I do not like? Ouch! Have I engaged in or encouraged gossip? Do I have a "get-even" attitude when others do me wrong? Can I laugh at my mistakes when I know I am wrong? Or do I grieve and resolve not to repeat the same mistakes?

Don't forget! The love of Jesus conquers the enemy of sin.

4. The Love of Jesus Is Not Limited by Circumstances.

Category #4: The love of Jesus is not limited by circumstances. Verse seven deals with the problems brought about by our circumstances. Notice the wording. "Love bears all things, believes all things, hopes all things and endures all things." That sounds like love gets the victory over the many circumstances of life.

Love may look weak, but it actually conquers every foe.

First, love bears all things. The theologian Charles Hodge pointed out that this may mean one of two things. First, it may mean bearing in silence all the troubles of life, or second, it may cover up all things as in the sense of covering your faults and failures, even saving you from disgrace and embarrassment. The Bible says, "Love covers a multitude of sins." (1 Peter 4:8)

Others may lose their composure, insult you, even hurt you but you never lose if you keep on loving!

Verse seven adds, "Love believes all things." Love is optimistic toward others. Love is not naturally suspicious because it expects the best from people. It does not automatically question motives (even though all people are also sinners prone to sin).

I recall someone saying, "Optimism is the only reality." That is a good way to approach life!

You can't be full of love and full of pessimism at the same time!

I made a choice many years ago. I chose to be optimistic about people and later proven wrong rather than be pessimistic about people and then still proven wrong, just wrong about different people. The fact remains that people are people! I made a choice not to treat people as a failure but to give them the chance to succeed. Some later succeeded while others never stopped failing!

But I have done what I can do for both the successes and the failures!

"Love also endures all things." Love does not weaken under stress and pressure. Why? Because there is a special strength in love. That supernatural strength comes from God Himself. Do you remember the title of this message? "L-O-V-E can be spelled J-E-S-U-S!" Verse eight says, "Love never fails." Let's read it another way. "Jesus never fails."

Let's see how well I stack up on this issue. First, do I try to see some good in every person? Am I willing to make allowances for small mistakes? Do I do my best, or am I content with mediocrity? Do I hold grudges?

No one ever said life was easy because life is certainly not easy! One of my favorite sayings is only two words long, but it says so very much, "Life happens." Circumstances change. Good times come then bad times come then hopefully the good times come again.

Solomon wrote, "To everything there is a season." He then wrote about a time to cry and a time to laugh. He knew such times in spite of his great wealth and wisdom! That means "life happens" to all of us!

But the lesson is clear! The love of Jesus is *not limited* by circumstances. Hallelujah for that truth! In every circumstance of life keep on loving! When in doubt, keep on loving! When friends desert you, keep on loving! When it seems that all hope is gone, keep on loving!

"Love (Jesus) never fails."

You have to believe in something! Believe in Jesus who is also love!

It happened on a cold Sunday morning in February. A wealthy man was walking quickly through the snow. He noticed a little boy standing on the sidewalk. The boy's eyes were focused on one particular spot on the sidewalk.

As the wealthy man approached, the boy pointed to the place on the sidewalk and said, "Please don't step there, sir. That's where I slipped and fell down."

When you are filled with the love of Jesus, you will be surprised at how far you will go. How do I know? Because John 3:16 says, "For God so loved the world that He gave . . ."

God so loved that He went all the way for you.

That is what the love of God is truly all about.

18

THE FUNDAMENTALS OF FORGIVENESS

How to Forgive – Part 1

Sometimes you hear a story that stays with you for the rest of your days. You may only hear the story once, but the story leaves a permanent impression. Let me share one of those stories with you.

This story happened on a Sunday night in my father's home church. My father was a young man serving as the Sunday School Director, Adult Bible teacher, and the Music Director in his church. The church service was scheduled to begin at 7:00 p.m. At 6:50 p.m. Brother X entered the building and started toward the front of the church. He passed Brother Y on the way. The two of them always got along, but something bad was about to happen.

One brother said something the other brother did not like. I do not know what was said. It is said the two issues most argued in the workplace are religion and politics. Both of these men, though, practiced the same religion so we can mark that possibility off the list. Maybe the disagreement was regarding politics or the economy or something as simple as the weather.

The first statement triggered a rebuttal. The rebuttal triggered another rebuttal. That rebuttal triggered still another rebuttal. The two men raised their voices, put their finger in each other's faces, and were shooting each other with their fingers. They expended all of their bullets!

Everyone in the church heard the argument. Everyone in the church was shaken by what they heard.

Seven o'clock arrived. The church service began. But it was an awful beginning. The choir was not looking at their songbooks. They were instead looking back and forth between the two men and wondering when round two would begin. The congregation was not singing either. Everyone was on edge. The Holy Spirit was even on edge. He was not free to do His work in the hearts of the people.

Someone was called on to pray. That person struggled in his prayer. The choir struggled in its special music. Nothing was going right.

Then the choir finished and came down to join the congregation. As they did so, the two men rose from their seat and walked toward each other. The choir stopped. Everyone stopped. No one moved. Everyone watched these two men and wondered if a fight was about to begin.

The two men met in the center aisle. Both men were crying. Both men said, "I am sorry. I sinned against you. I did not mean what I said. I really do love you. Please forgive me."

The two men hugged each other, and everything became right with the world. The choir was happy. The congregation was happy. The pastor was happy. The Holy Spirit was happy. Everyone was happy.

What had begun very badly ended very well for everyone. A dead church service became a lively church service.

Sometimes incidents like that happen at church, home, work, and everywhere we go. Things happen that we wish did not happen. Things escalate and may even get out of control. We're headed for the precipice, and unfortunately, we are taking a relationship with us!

We need to know how to deal with those things when they happen, and keep them from becoming even worse.

That brings us once again to our goal at the bottom of today's study sheet. Everyone read it with me. *"Helping believers grow together in Him through love and **forgiveness**."*

For some time, we have been studying how to make that goal a reality in our lives and also in the life of our church. We have now come to the final word in our goal. It is the word "forgiveness."

Your study sheet points out that forgiveness is far too often the missing piece in the puzzle of successful relationships. The inability to forgive hurts family, friends, marriages, churches, neighborhoods, factories, government, management . . . in short, anywhere a human being exists.

Forgiveness, along with the lack of forgiveness, is a really big issue!

All of us are acquainted with the words of Alexander Pope who said, "To err is human, to forgive, divine." Most of us are much better at the first part—"to err is human"—than the second part—"to forgive, divine." But the truth is the second part will determine the fate of so many relationships! And relationships are a very important part of life!

That means we must—absolutely must—succeed in this final part of our goal. *We must know how to forgive, so we don't ever lose the people we love so very much.*

So how are we going to approach this subject? Most of us have heard a sermon or two on this subject. But none of us have ever done an in-depth look at it.

I want us to do this study right since forgiveness affects so much of our personal lives as well as our church life. I have developed sixteen questions that need to be answered from the Word of God. We will examine these sixteen questions over the next three sessions.

1. What is Forgiveness?

Question #1 What is forgiveness? Let's do a quick word study of two Greek words translated "forgiveness" in our English translations. The first word is *aphesis*. This is the word in 1 John 1:9 which says, "If we confess our sins, God is faithful and right to forgive (*aphesis*) our sins and to cleanse us from all unrighteousness." The Greek word *aphesis* means to "send away" or "carry away" as in the sense that the debt is no longer attached to you. *The debt has been sent away from you.* It has been discharged from your account!

Therefore, I have no grounds to hold anything against you. It is not a case of 50% of your wrongdoing is sent away, and 50% is still attached to you! Rather it is a case of 100% of your wrongdoing has been sent away, and 0% is still attached to you. That's why 1 John 1:9 says God's forgiveness results in us being cleansed from *all* unrighteousness. All means 100%.

This is the same Greek word that appears in Ephesians 1:7. That verse says, "In Jesus, we have redemption through His blood, even the forgiveness or the sending away of our sin."

We can conclude that *aphesis* has the idea of 100% satisfaction. The issue has been 100% settled, and it is time to move on. There is no reason to talk about the past anymore because the past has been sent away. That's shouting ground for the Christian! It means my sinful past has been sent away. Of course, we know where our sinful past was sent! It was sent to the cross of the Lord Jesus Christ! The Bible says in 1 Peter 2:24, "Jesus, in His own self, carried our sins to the tree called the cross." He nailed our sins to His own cross! Thank God for that!

The second Greek word is *charizomai*, and it has the idea of "graciously providing forgiveness." The key word in that definition is "graciously." *Charizomai* is Paul's favorite word for forgiveness. It emphasizes that *forgiveness is not something you earn* but something that originates in the grace of God. Ephesians 4:32 says, "Be kind to one another, tenderhearted, and forgive (*charizomai*—graciously forgive) one another as Christ has forgiven you!"

The point is that both Greek words make it clear that forgiveness is not a halfway thing, but it is an all-the-way thing. There's no such thing as being 50% forgiven or even 99% forgiven. You are either 100% forgiven or you are not forgiven.

That last statement is a fill-in-the-blank. Let me say it again and make sure we stay together in this study. You are either 100% forgiven, or you are not forgiven.

Forgiveness has the idea of erasing a wrong, so the wrong can never come back to haunt you. The wrong is now gone. That is hard to say, but it is true. The wrong is now gone.

Let's pause here and make one thing crystal clear. The Bible has an abundance of material on this subject called forgiveness. That makes it very obvious that forgiveness is indeed possible. It is possible that *humanly speaking* there may be a limit to how much we can forgive, but *divinely speaking* there is no limit to how much we can forgive.

Gandhi taught in his philosophy, "Forgiveness is only for the strong. The weak can never forgive." But the Bible says all can forgive!

The reason all can forgive is because of where forgiveness takes place. This is a fill-in-the-blank. Corrie Ten Boom said, "Forgiveness is an act of the will, and the will can function regardless of the temperature of the heart." That was her way of saying, and saying correctly, that *forgiveness is not a decision based upon emotion, but rather it is a decision based upon the will.*

Someone said, "I don't feel like forgiving." God's reaction to that attitude is, "Who cares if you feel like forgiving? Forgiveness is not based upon your feelings. It is based upon doing what is right. *Your will has to overcome your feelings and do what is right.*"

Let me give you an example. You may not believe this, but I often misbehaved when I was a little boy. Dad would then spank me for my misbehavior. And, no, those spankings did not warp my personality! Dad would often say, "This will hurt me more than it hurts you." As far as I was concerned, those words were a lie because he never cried a single time, but I sure did.

His point, though, was well taken. Spanking me brought discomfort to my father, but *his will overcame his discomfort.* His will was stronger than his feelings. His will convinced him to do what was right!

The same principle holds true in the category of forgiveness. This is a circle the right word on your study sheet. Forgiveness IS NOT—I repeat is not—an action based upon your emotions. It is an action of the will based upon doing what is right.

The best example of that is how God deals with us whom the Bible describes as His enemies. Experience teaches us that it is much easier to forgive a friend than to forgive an enemy! But God did not forgive us as His friends; He forgave us instead as His enemies and then turned us into His friends.

The German Lutheran pastor Martin Niemoller spent time as a political prisoner in a German concentration camp in World War II. He later said, "It took me a long time to learn that God is not the enemy of *my* enemies. God is not even the enemy of *His* enemies."

The Bible talks instead about God being a God of love, mercy, grace, and patience. All of those things draw us to His forgiveness. God is continually reaching out to His enemies and trying to turn them into His children.

God's forgiveness is always complete forgiveness! When God forgives, He truly forgives!

Aren't you glad He has 100% forgiven you?

2. On What Basis Does God Forgive?

Question #2 On what basis does God forgive? On what basis does God forgive sinners like us? The answer is that God forgives for Christ's sake.

The King James Version says in Ephesians 4:32, "And be ye kind one to another, tenderhearted, forgiving one another, even as God for

Christ's sake hath forgiven you." The newer translations more correctly translate the ending phrase as, "God has forgiven you in Christ or through Christ." The point is that my forgiveness takes place in one specific location, and that specific location is "in Christ." Our forgiveness is based upon what Christ has done for us on the cross!

Imagine me going to God and saying, "God, forgive my children for my sake." God will laugh and say, "No." Suppose the Roman Catholic Pope goes to God and says, "God, forgive this Catholic's sin for my sake." God will laugh and say, "No." God will say, "My forgiveness is based upon one reason alone! I will forgive for Christ's sake and no one else's sake! My forgiveness is not located at Walmart! Rather My forgiveness is located in Christ and Him alone!"

What has Christ done that is superior to me? What has Christ done that is superior to the pope? First, He lived a perfect life. The Bible says He "did no sin neither was deceit found in Him." (1 Peter 2:22) That makes Him much different than us!

Second, He did what He was predicted to do. The Bible says He fulfilled Old Testament prophecy in His birth, life, death, and resurrection. The best part is there is still more prophecy to fulfill in the future!

Third, He offered a perfect sacrifice. Isaiah 53 says, "It pleased the Lord to bruise Him. The Lord has laid upon Him—upon His cross—the iniquity, or sin, of us all." That means your sin and my sin have been transferred to His account!

Fourth, He rose from the dead as the "firstfruits" of the new creation. The term "firstfruits" means Jesus is the first or the prototype of what is to come after Him in the resurrection! He is the first to come off the resurrection assembly line! The Bible says, "Jesus is the first to come out of the ground in a glorified body. His resurrection will then be followed by the complete harvest in which we as believers get resurrected at His second coming." (1 Corinthians 15:20-22) The Bible even goes so far as to say, "We shall be like Him for we shall see Him as He is!" (1 John 3:2)

Now answer me this: Can any of those things be said about you, me, our parents, the president, the pope, your favorite television preacher or anyone else you know? No! The Bible makes it plain that Jesus Christ did what no one else can do! That's why the Bible says, "But this man, after He had offered one sacrifice that would take away sin forever, then sat down at the right hand of God the Father!" (Hebrews 10:12) Remember this: we were nothing but wicked, vile, helpless, depraved sinners when Christ came to save us!

The basis of our forgiveness is totally in Him! That's why we call Him our Savior! It is because He and He alone is our Savior!

3. How Much Did God Forgive When He Saved Me?

Question #3 How much did God forgive when He saved me?

I read about what happened at the conclusion of a revival meeting. A deacon came forward with an old man who had accepted Christ and wanted to be baptized. Someone in the audience yelled out, "Pastor, I don't mean to interfere with your business, but I just want to say you've got hold of an old sinner and just one dip won't do him any good. You'll have to anchor him out in deep water overnight!"

I share that story because all of us were bad sinners when God saved us! There were no good sinners in the eyes of God, only bad sinners who had broken God's holy law and deserved to go to a devil's hell. That's not saying much in our favor, is it?

Here is something you may not know, but it will make sense if you think about it. This is a fill-in-the-blank. When God saves you, He immediately forgives all of your sin—that includes past sins, present sins, and future sins. Please remember Jesus died two thousand years ago for the sins of everyone. All of the sins of the Old Testament saints were in the past. All of the sins of the New Testament saints (including me) were in the future. *Salvation, through the cross, handles all of those sins at the same time.*

This teaching may confuse you. You may think, "Why do I seek forgiveness for today's sin if it has already been forgiven?" A full answer takes more time than we have here. It is very important, though, that you understand the difference between the forgiveness of *salvation* and the forgiveness of *daily living.* They are *two separate issues* in the Bible.

The analogy of footwashing in John chapter thirteen provides a very clear explanation. "Jesus said to him, 'The one who has bathed does not need to wash, except for his feet, but is completely clean. And you are clean, but not every one of you.'" (John 13:10, ESV) (The King James Version is misleading in verse ten because it misses the distinction between two Greek words. The modern translations recognize that distinction and correctly use "bathe" or "take a bath" to distinguish the first action from the second action of washing one's feet or hands.)

The complete bath represents salvation. That makes sense! The bath represents a complete, once-for-all cleansing from sin. Through this process, the repenting *sinner* becomes a believing *saint* in the eyes of God (Ephesians 1:1). At that time God justifies the sinner and clothes him with the righteousness of Jesus Christ (2 Corinthians 5:21). God regenerates or recreates the believer "in Christ" (Ephesians 2:10) and seals him with the Holy Spirit (Ephesians 4:30). Much more is done, also. Suffice it to say, it is a complete salvation! The believer's destiny is now settled for eternity. His salvation is so certain that God even refers to him in the here and now as already glorified (Romans 8:30) even though the actual glorification awaits our resurrection and bodily change (Philippians 3:21). When I think about those truths, I find myself saying, "Even so, come, Lord Jesus!"

Psalm 103:12 says in a wonderful way, "As far as the east is from the west, so far hath he removed our transgressions from us." (KJV)

Someone asked an old-time saint, "Does the devil ever bother you about your past sins?" The saint said, "He sure does." "What do you do?" I just tell him to go east."

The person asked, "Does the devil come back after doing that?" "Yes, he does." "Then what do you tell him to do?" "I tell him to go west."

"When the devil comes back, what do you then tell him to do?" The saint said, "I just keep him going from east to west."

Here is the point. If I face west, put a stake in the ground at this very spot then go west and circle the entire earth I will return to this very stake. At that time, I will still be facing west. In other words, I can keep going west and *never stop* going west! The same is true about going east! That's how far God has removed my sins from my account! You can never get to the place where you can find my sins!

What does the word forgiveness mean? We learned in our first question that forgiveness means "sending away." God has sent away my sins as far as the east is from the west. Thank God, the old account was truly settled long ago!

A Scottish doctor was known for his skill and humble spirit. He eventually died. His accounting books were examined. The examiners saw that words had been written with red ink over several customer accounts. The words read, "Forgiven, too poor to pay."

The wife was not like her husband. She wanted every dime she could get. She said, "These accounts must be paid." She sued the people for the money.

The matter went before a judge. The judge reviewed the books and said, "Is this your husband's handwriting in red ink?" She said, "Yes, it is."

The judge said, "There's not a court in the land that can obtain the money if he has written 'forgiven' on that account."

I want you to know that's what Jesus did for me. He took the book that contained my sins and wrote, "Forgiven" with the red ink of his blood on every page.

A man said, "My sins are too great for God to forgive me." The preacher said, "Your sins are indeed very great, greater than most men, but I want you to know God's grace is greater than your sin!"

It is important that the believer recognize the order as first, we become saints at salvation then second, *following* salvation, we are expected to act like saints.

Jesus taught the same order in John chapter thirteen. The bath of salvation comes first, followed by a daily cleansing or washing for those times when we fail or sin as saints. The first washing is a complete bath! The second washing is for the feet only. Please remember that wearing sandals in Bible times resulted in dirty feet, feet covered in dust! The dirty feet picture the daily defilement that comes upon us from walking in this ungodly world.

The believer's salvation may have been perfected, but he *himself* has not yet been perfected! Unfortunately, he will still sin during his earthly walk. *That sin, of course, has zero effect regarding his salvation. That sin, though, does have an effect on another category we call the believer's fellowship with the Lord.* Fellowship is a good term because it describes the communion which exists *after* salvation between the saint and the Lord.

Our daily sin hinders and sometimes even disrupts our fellowship with God. It casts a cloud between God and me. It's similar to a parent having a disobedient child. The disobedient child still belongs to the parent, but the fellowship is sure disturbed! The cure is to confess that sin to God and seek God's forgiveness. 1 John 1:9 says, "If I confess my daily sins, God is faithful and right to forgive me of my sins and to cleanse me from that sin's unrighteousness." Jesus gave us a parallel teaching in the Model Prayer. He taught us to pray, "Forgive us of our sins in the same manner that we forgive those who sin against us." (Matthew 6:12)

Let me summarize this answer with a fill-in-the-blank. I only ask *once* for the forgiveness of salvation, but I have asked *zillions* of times for the forgiveness of my daily sins! *In other words, there is only one bath, but there are zillions of times to wash my feet!*

Here is the bottom line. How much has God forgiven me? Completely! Based on God's complete forgiveness of me, I am now supposed to completely forgive you! Isn't that great? Complete forgiveness will allow our fellowship with each other to continue on and on until Jesus comes!

4. What Is the Standard of Forgiveness?

Question #4 What is the standard of forgiveness? The author C. S. Lewis once said, "To be a Christian means to forgive the inexcusable because God has forgiven the inexcusable in you." Lewis was right on the mark!

The Bible gives us the standard in Ephesians 4:32, "As God in Christ forgave you." How much did God forgive me? He forgave me with complete forgiveness! Thorough forgiveness! Nothing lacking forgiveness! No exceptions either. Every sin was included whether it be past, present, or future!

The Bible provides a great story to teach God's standard of forgiveness.

> *Then Peter came to Him and said, "Lord, how many times could my brother sin against me and I forgive him? As many as seven times?" "I tell you, not as many as seven," Jesus said to him, "but 70 times seven. For this reason, the kingdom of heaven can be compared to a king who wanted to settle accounts with his slaves. When he began to settle accounts, one who owed 10,000 talents was brought before him. Since he had no way to pay it back, his master commanded that he, his wife, his children, and everything he had be sold to pay the debt. "At this, the slave fell facedown before him and said, 'Be patient with me, and I will pay you everything!' Then the master of that slave had compassion, released him, and forgave him the loan. "But that slave went out and found one of his fellow slaves who owed him 100 denarii. He grabbed him, started choking him, and said, 'Pay what you owe!' "At this, his fellow slave fell down and began begging him, 'Be patient with me, and I will pay you back.' But he wasn't willing. On the contrary, he went and threw him into prison until he could pay what was owed. When the other slaves saw what had taken place, they were deeply distressed and went and reported to their master everything that had happened. "Then, after he had summoned him, his master said to him, 'You wicked slave! I forgave you all that debt because you*

*begged me. Shouldn't you also have had mercy on your fel-
low slave, as I had mercy on you?' And his master got
angry and handed him over to the jailers to be tortured until he could pay everything that was owed. So My heavenly
Father will also do to you if each of you does not forgive
his brother from his heart." (Matthew 18:21-35, HCSB)*

The entire passage begins with Peter's question about how often he
should forgive someone who sins against him. The text does not say how
Jesus felt about the question, but I imagine Jesus was quite frustrated
with Peter's attitude.

Peter was likely licking his chops and thinking about retaliating the
next time it happened. Boy, did Jesus burst his bubble!

Jesus teaches a very valuable lesson about forgiveness by turning the
spotlight on us! How much has God forgiven us? Ephesians 4:32 says,
"As God in Christ forgave you!" In so doing, Jesus makes it plain that
the act of forgiving others *begins* with our remembering how much we
have been forgiven by God! Indeed, God has forgiven us of many more
sins than our brother has committed against us! After all, every one of
our sins occurs in direct opposition to God! But only some of our brother's sins are pointed directly at us! Clearly, our debt to God is greater
than our brother's debt to us!

The Bible story tells us about a man who owed ten thousand talents
to the king. This was an enormous sum. Quite honestly, it was a ridicu-
lous sum that defies calculation. For example, the Roman government
collected approximately one thousand talents annually from the region
we know as Israel. That means this man owed ten times the annual collection of taxes for the entire country! It is, therefore, clear that Jesus is
using an exaggerated amount. No one ever had a debt this high.

Why would Jesus use such an outlandish figure? The number is in
keeping with His instruction to Peter to forgive four hundred and ninety
times or seventy times seven. Poor Peter could not count that high because he did not have that many fingers and toes! Jesus mentioned such

a high total because it was not feasible for anyone to keep track in that manner.

The point is Peter needs to concentrate on the act of forgiving rather than keeping track of the many times he forgives.

This poor debtor owes so much money he can never hope to pay it back. Indeed, his debt is so great it can't even be counted. Ten thousand talents are an incalculable sum!

The debtor recognizes his situation. He has no chance to save himself based upon any future business decisions. The stock market cannot bail him out! He has no rich uncles to pay off a debt so great as this! His income tax refund will likely be confiscated by the authorities as a down payment on his debt. Winning the lottery would even leave him short! Quite clearly, he is in a pit so deep he will never be able to climb out.

The debtor pictures you and me in our debt of sinfulness. We owed a debt so great that we had no hope of ever paying it. Where would we begin? Who could we turn to? Is there any way to turn our filthy rags into clothes of righteousness? *Quite clearly, we were in a pit so deep we would never be able to climb out.* We owed God an unpayable debt. Brother, we were in bad, make that awful, shape!

Our only hope, along with the debtor's only hope, was for the *entire debt to be written off.* "Written off" is another way of saying the debt is forgiven or "sent away" from our account.

Verse twenty-seven says, "Then the lord of that servant was moved with compassion, and released him, and forgave the debt." The English word translated "forgave" is the same Greek word we talked about in Question #1. It is the Greek word *aphesis*. We noted earlier that the Greek word *aphesis* means to "send away" as in the sense that the debt is no longer attached to your account. The debt has been sent away from you. In this case, the king chooses to dismiss or cancel the debt.

The story should have ended with the freed servant joyfully running all the way home. He should have been spreading cheer everywhere because his debt is no more. He is a free man! His debt has been canceled! Millions of dollars in debt are no more! He gets a free start in life!

Unfortunately, this servant does just the very opposite. He goes to someone who owes him a tiny sum of perhaps a thousand dollars, perhaps one ten-thousandth of what he had owed. In other words, this man owed practically nothing!

The not-so-forgiving servant sounds like a New Testament version of Scrooge. He also sounds like a lot of Christians who want to be forgiven by God, but they don't want to give the same kind of forgiveness to someone in the church or at home or at work.

Unfortunately, I have known employers who would never accept an employee's apology, who kept rubbing the employee's nose in a mistake which happened years ago. That employee couldn't get the same pay raise as everyone else because the boss remembered one time when that employee had failed.

I served as a witness in one meeting where the boss ripped an employee for what he had done several years earlier. The employee responded, "We've talked before about that mistake. I apologized for doing that. I was wrong. But I haven't done it since. Why do you keep bringing it up?"

The employee just wanted to have the debt forgiven, but he never found forgiveness in that boss. Sad to say, he eventually suffered a nervous breakdown and left the company all because of a rotten boss who did not know how to forgive.

The forgiven servant said, "Pay me that one thousand dollars!" The person said, "I can't." The forgiven servant then had the man arrested and dumped into prison. The law said this man would have to stay in prison until some family member paid his debt.

Wow! What a forgiving fellow! Forgiven of an enormous, even humongous debt he cannot pay, but he won't forgive someone else in the very same situation—wanting God to bless him but not wanting to be the same blessing to others.

What a man! I submit to you the wealth of a man isn't in *how much* he has but in *what he does* with what he has.

The king eventually heard about what had happened. He arrested the mean servant and said in verse thirty-two, "I forgave you a great sum that you could never repay. Shouldn't you have passed on the same grace and forgiven this other man of his tiny, pitiful debt to you? Here is what I intend to do to you, a worthless human being. I am reinstating the amount of money you owe me. I am handing you over to the inquisitors—another word for inquisitors is torturers—until you pay everything that is owed me. Based on the size of your debt, it is unlikely you will ever leave the prison alive."

Look closely at the last verse in the chapter. "Jesus said, 'That's how My heavenly Father will treat you if you don't forgive your own brother from your heart.'" And all of God's people said, "Ouch!"

Think through with me what just happened. We are sinners and owe God an unpayable debt. But God forgives our debt by sending it away to the cross of Calvary where Jesus died for our sins! God then sets us free from our debt.

Now think: How well do we now forgive? God's standard of forgiveness is very high! This is a fill-in-the-blank. He forgave us more than we will ever need to forgive anyone. Would you agree with me on that statement?

Here is a warning for all of you husbands, for all of you wives, for all of you employers, for all of you employees, for all of you parents, for all of you church members!

Don't place yourself above God in the area of forgiveness. *It is God and God alone who has set the standard. You have no right to change the standard.*

God has forgiven you of a debt you can never pay. It is time for you to go forth and do likewise.

19

HOW TO SET THE PRISONERS FREE!

How to Forgive – Part 2

Preparation: Prepare actors and a chair for the skit.

Have you ever met anyone who was really touchy? There was a woman who was both touchy and suspicious. Her neighbors were very careful not to offend her. They constantly thought of her when they made their plans. But one day they totally forgot about this very touchy woman. They planned the annual neighborhood picnic. They invited everyone in the community, but they somehow forgot to invite her.

Someone finally realized the mistake. The neighbors went to the woman's house and invited her to the party. But she said, "Me? Go to your picnic? It's too late for that! I've already prayed for rain!" Bless her heart! At least, she had faith in her prayer and believed it would rain!

But think instead about people who are the very opposite of that touchy woman. It was said of King Henry VI of England, "He never forgot anything but injuries." It was said of Cranmer, "If you want to get a favor from him, do him a wrong." What a compliment to his character! Emerson said about Abraham Lincoln, "His heart was as great as the world, but there was no room in it for the memory of a wrong." Spurgeon gave us this advice, "Cultivate forbearance till your heart yields a fine crop of it. Pray for a short memory as to unkindness."

Everyone faces issues in life which help shape our character. One of the most important issues is in the area of forgiveness.

Robert Frost wisely wrote, "If one by one we counted people out for the least sin, it wouldn't take us long to get so we had no one left to live with. For to be social is to be forgiving."

Let me pose two questions to you. The questions are on your study sheet. Would you rather attend a forgiving church or an unforgiving church? Circle the word you prefer. Second, would you rather attend a loving church or an unloving church? Circle the word you prefer.

We each have the power to make that happen in our own church. Let's commit ourselves again to our goal at the bottom of your study sheet. *"Helping believers grow together in Him through love and forgiveness."*

Let's continue our study in the area of forgiveness. I have titled this section, *"How to Set the Prisoners Free"* because that is exactly what forgiveness does. Forgiveness sets the prisoners free! All of the prisoners!

Let's fill in some blanks.

1. Do I Want Reconciliation or Revenge?

Question #1: Do I want reconciliation or revenge? The biblical goal is forgiveness and reconciliation. But the most important question is, what do *you* want? What is *your* goal? It is entirely possible you may have a different goal. Your mouth may say, "I want reconciliation and forgiveness." But your heart may say, "I want revenge and to get even."

You have to make a big, big decision. I am afraid far too often we want revenge. I am just wondering, have you ever chosen revenge over reconciliation?

Oscar Wilde used to say, "Always forgive your enemies; nothing annoys them so much." In so doing, he used forgiveness as a way to get even. That is not really forgiveness. It is just stirring the pot more!

Sometimes we cry out for justice when we actually mean, "God, prove me right," or we pray, "Lord, make the miserable dog more miserable until she apologizes." We then try to get even.

The emperor Sigismund took a different approach when he conquered a kingdom. At that time, his enemies were totally defeated. He could have easily exterminated them, but he instead chose to admit them to his own kingdom. He reasoned, "Do I not destroy my enemies when I make them my friends?" His kingdom then became stronger!

One pastor said, "Most of us want to get even, and we can get even. Jesus told us how." He then read where Jesus said, "You were taught to love your neighbor and hate your enemy. But I say you should love your enemy and bless those who curse you." (Matthew 5:43-44)

The pastor said, "Here is how to get even. Pray for the obnoxious, pray for the thoughtless, pray for the insensitive, pray for the hardhearted, pray for the rude, and pray for the mean. But be careful about your prayers. *That kind of praying not only changes other people but sometimes those prayers backfire and change us! And that's really getting even!"*

We may have been offended, insulted, and sinned against. We must now decide if we want to love our brother and seek reconciliation, or do I want to hate my brother and get even?

This is a fill-in-the-blank. The way of love chooses reconciliation; the way of hate chooses to get even.

Dale Carnegie told the story about being in Yellowstone Park and watching the rangers feed the grizzly bears. He said, "One night the ranger brought garbage to attract the grizzlies. Those grizzlies can whip any animal in the West except the buffalo and the Kodiak bear. But those grizzlies would always allow one little animal to eat with them. The bears would growl at the other enemies and send them scurrying away. But not this animal because this animal was a skunk."

Carnegie said, "It was obvious the grizzlies resented the skunk and would love to have their revenge, but they did not. And you can guess why. The cost of getting even was just too high!"

What about you? Do you want to get even? I pray the answer is, "No, thank you." Every minute we spend plotting revenge robs us of our own peace of mind. It's simply not worth it! But it is worth it to gain our brother!

2. Will an Unforgiving Spirit Affect My Prayer Life?

Question #2: Will an unforgiving spirit affect my prayer life? Yes! It will affect your prayer life, but it will also affect *more* than your prayer life!

One day a visitor was watching an old farmer plowing with a mule. After a while, the visitor said, "I don't like to tell you how to run your business, but you could save yourself a lot of work by saying, 'Gee and Haw' to that mule instead of just tugging on those lines." The old farmer pulled out his big handkerchief and wiped his face. Then he said, "I reckon you're right, but this animal kicked me five years ago, and I ain't spoke to him since."

The moral of the story is obvious: a grudge is harder on the one who holds it than the one it is held against. That's why the Apostle Paul said that we are to "forgive any man if we have a quarrel against him. Just like Christ forgave us, we are to forgive each other." (Colossians 3:13) If our Lord can extend mercy to you, surely you can be merciful to those who offend you.

Two brothers had a quarrel then refused to speak to each other. The mother did everything she could to reconcile the two brothers, but it was not to be. It really bothered the mother, and she became very sad. One brother saw what had happened to his mother. He decided to cheer her with a beautiful gift. But to his surprise, she refused the gift. She said, "I don't want any gift until you have become reconciled to your brother."

1 Peter 3:8 says, and this is a fill-in-the-blank, "Husbands, treat your wives right so your prayers to God will not be hindered." The opposite is equally true: "Treat your wives wrong, and your prayers to God *will be* hindered!" That's more than a threat. That's the truth!

One wise man said, "If momma ain't happy, ain't nobody happy!" Likewise, if God ain't happy, ain't nobody else happy either!

Jesus taught, "Therefore, if you are presenting your offering at the altar, and there remember that your brother has something against you, leave your offering there before the altar and go; first be reconciled to your brother, and then come and present your offering." (Matthew 5:23-24, NASB)

Reconciliation and forgiveness go hand in hand! You can't have reconciliation unless you have an agreement on what is wrong, an apology for the act of doing wrong, and forgiveness from the offended party. The Bible makes it clear that an unforgiving spirit hinders our prayer life. It grieves the Holy Spirit and makes it more difficult, nigh impossible, to pray in the Holy Spirit! We may try praying, but the Holy Spirit keeps reminding us of a problem that needs to be resolved.

God is saying, "Leave your offering at the altar and make an attempt to be reconciled to your brother."

3. How Can I Develop a Forgiving Spirit?

Question #3: How can I develop a forgiving spirit? This question is for all of you who know in your heart that you should forgive, but you have trouble forgiving. You also know an unforgiving spirit is not good for either you or the people around you. How then can I develop a forgiving spirit?

Someone wrote, "Those who have hurt you in the past cannot continue to hurt you now unless you hold on to the pain through resentment. Your past is past! Nothing will change it. You are only hurting yourself with your bitterness. For your own sake, learn from it, and then let it go."

Forgiveness does not come easily to any of us. D. L. Moody told about a man who thought he was going to die. The dying man called another man to his bedside and said, "I forgive you for what you did to me." Then he said, "But if I get well, the old grudge still holds." That story is being repeated in many lives today.

It is probably true that the three words, "I have sinned" are the hardest three words to confess. (Confess in the biblical sense means I actually mean it.)

Saying and practicing the three words, "I forgive you" may qualify, though, for second place! Forgiveness is not easy.

Robert Jordan said, "Any fool knows men and women think differently at times, but the biggest difference is this. Men forget, but never forgive; women forgive, but never forget." In plain English, we all have our own struggles.

That brings us to a fill-in-the-blank. I believe Martin Luther King, Jr. was right when he said, "Forgiveness is not an occasional act, it is a constant attitude." He used the word *constant*, meaning it is non-stopping. It is also an *attitude* meaning it is a style of living or a mental approach to life. It is like looking at the world through rose-tinted glasses. The tint makes everything look different. The same is true with your attitude. Forgiveness should be a constant attitude that shapes the way you approach everyone you meet.

Are there any suggestions that might help us actually *practice* forgiveness? Yes, there are. Let me mention four. These suggestions should help you develop an attitude of forgiveness with your spouse, family, coworkers, plus brothers and sisters in Christ.

First, rank your suffering in comparison to Christ's suffering on the cross. I am sure you knew the first suggestion would begin with the cross. It seems everything in our discussion has to do with the cross. The cross has a way of putting everything in perspective!

Has anyone ever suffered like Jesus? He alone bore the weight of the entire world! "God the Father laid upon Him the sin burden of us all!" (Isaiah 53:6) How does your suffering compare with His degree of suffering? It goes without saying that our suffering ranks a far-distant second to His suffering! This is important! If Jesus could endure such suffering and *still* offer salvation to the world, I can surely do something of far lesser value!

Second, count your blessings before you count your curses! This step will change your focus from "Woe is me!" to "Blessed is me!" It is easier to approach forgiveness from the vantage point of being blessed than the vantage point of being cursed. You are very blessed! But only occasionally cursed. Keep the two in proper perspective!

Third, begin your prayer time with a prayer for the offender. Perhaps it would be best to put yourself in the shoes of the offender. What would that person need or feel? The offender could be in anguish, too! Asking for forgiveness can sometimes be very depressing—so depressing that the offender gives up doing anything for the Lord! Such a withdrawal from Christian service is not our goal! Reconciliation is our goal! Jesus taught, "Pray for those who offend you." (Matthew 5:44) It's easier to heal *and be a healer* if you are first praying for the person!

Fourth, pray every day for a forgiving spirit. Jesus taught this recipe in the Model Prayer, "Forgive our debts to others in the same manner that we forgive those who are indebted to us." (Matthew 6:12) God often uses prayer as a means of creating a submissive spirit within us. Prayer has a way of transforming our character! Prayer allows the Holy Spirit to mold me and make me after His will into the forgiving person that He wants me to be!

Those four suggestions can be put into practice by every one of us. This is another fill-in-the-blank. Never forget that a forgiving spirit is often made possible by a loving spirit! That is why our goal is written as, *"Helping believers grow together in Him **through love and for-***

giveness." A loving spirit is a great help in the development of a forgiving spirit!

4. What Happens if I Don't Forgive?

Question #4: What happens if I don't forgive? The first instinct is to say, "Nothing happens!" Unfortunately, that is not so. One of the best-known stories in the Bible is the story of the prodigal son in Luke chapter fifteen. The English author Charles Dickens once described it as the "greatest short story ever told."

The story begins with a father who had two sons. Most people know about the one son (the prodigal or wasteful son) but are ignorant about the second son (the elder brother). The elder brother is actually the one critical to this discussion, but I am getting ahead of myself.

The younger son decided to leave home. He had the audacity to ask for his share of the inheritance before his dad even died. The younger son took his money and abandoned the family. He went to a distant country, and the Bible says he engaged in "riotous, sinful living." He quickly went through all of his money and ended up living in the hog pen with the hogs. Nothing could have offended a Jew as much as being with the hogs because the law of Moses did not allow the consumption of bacon or ham.

Finally, he came to his senses, and he said, "There's plenty of food back home. There's also a soft bed back home. There's also a roof over my head back home. But wonder if Dad will forgive me? I'll never know the answer unless I try." The younger son left the hog pen, returned home, and said, "Father, I have sinned." He had left the house with his head held high; he returned, though, with his chin touching the ground.

The best part of the story is that the father forgave the son. In spite of every evil done by the younger son, and it was plenty, the father forgave the son. The father celebrated his son's return by killing the fatted calf and hosting a big celebration.

That is the first part of the story. But do you remember how the story begins? It begins with the statement that the father had not one but *two* sons!

Let me read you the rest of the story. This is my own version.

> *Now the elder brother was working in the field when the younger brother came home. The elder brother finished his work and started toward the house. As he came near, he heard laughter, music, and dancing. He asked one of the servants to explain the reason for the celebration. The servant replied, 'Your younger brother has returned home. Your father has slaughtered the fattened calf and is hosting a celebration.' The elder son did not like what he heard. He instead became angry, pouted, pouted some more, kept pouting, and refused to attend the celebration. Someone told his father. His father came to him and pleaded with him to join the celebration. The elder brother said, 'Father, I did not leave home like my younger brother. I did not deprive you of your money by asking for my inheritance. I instead stayed home and have obediently worked for you all of these years. In that whole time, you never even gave me a young goat so that I could celebrate with my friends. But now my younger brother has come home—the one who blew half of your money on prostitutes, drinking, gambling, and all manner of riotous living—and what have you done? You slaughtered the best calf for him!' The father said in closing, 'Son, you are my son, too. You have always been with me, and everything I have left has always been yours. But it's time to celebrate. Your brother was dead and is alive again; he was lost and is found.' (Luke 15:25-32)*

Let me bring the story forward to the current century. The younger son abandoned the house of God known as the Father's house. He has now returned. This is the first time he has been in church in many years. The elder brother, though, has always been in the house of God, maybe every time the doors are open. He may even have a perfect attendance record for the last twenty years. But he has a big, big problem.

Let's act out what it means to be the elder brother. Brother _____ is going to play the role of the elder brother. (Note: Have the elder brother come forward grumbling about, "This is taking too much time" and be seated in a chair beneath the pulpit. At the same time, the deacons will assemble at the front on both sides of the auditorium. The script is as follows.)

- Pastor to the congregation: What do we do at the end of a church service? We give an invitation and invite sinners to come to Jesus. Let's sing a verse of "Just As I Am" and see how the elder brother fits into what God is doing.
- The congregation remains seated and sings the first verse of "Just As I Am."
- Deacon 1 approaches the pastor with a weeping man: "Pastor, this man has been attending my Sunday School class for several weeks. He wants to get saved."
- Pastor: "Then get him saved! Lead him in the sinner's prayer."
- The deacon and the seeker kneel at the front. The deacon leads the seeker through the sinner's prayer. During this time, the elder brother is very fidgety and keeps checking his watch. The elder brother is very annoyed.
- The seeker (now saved) rises. The pastor asks him if he has accepted Jesus. The seeker answers yes. The pastor asks the audience, "Are you happy for him?" The audience answers, "Yes."
- The seeker returns to his seat and happily shakes hands with people along the way. Deacon 1 joins the other deacons.
- Deacon 2 approaches the elder brother.
- Elder brother to the deacon: "Why does our church service always go this long? I believe we could get a bigger crowd if we had shorter services. You guys should have taken that man to another room and talked with him. All of us could

then have gone home and done something more important than sit here and waste our time." Deacon 2 shakes his head in sadness and joins the other deacons.

- Deacon 3 carries an offering plate containing a check. He walks past the elder brother to collect the day's offering. The elder brother stops him.

- Elder brother to the deacon: "If you guys don't start doing it my way I'm going to take my check back. Do you hear me? Are you going to do it my way?" The deacon shakes his head no. "I will take my check from the offering plate and tear it in two!" The elder brother removes his check from the offering plate and tears it in two. The elder brother continues, "We'll see how long you can pay the bills without me!" Deacon 3 shakes his head and joins the other deacons.

- Deacon 4 approaches with a handful of bulletins. The elder brother stops him.

- Elder brother to the deacon: "I was on vacation for two weeks, and you changed something in our church without asking me. I've been here for thirty years! Thirty years! It isn't fair what I have to put up with." Deacon 4 shakes his head and joins the other deacons.

- Deacon 5 approaches with a sign which says "World Missions." The elder brother stops him.

- Elder brother to the deacon: "Why do I keep hearing all this talk on world missions? I believe missions starts at home and those other people can take care of themselves. This church has a lot of financial needs. We need new carpet, new plumbing, new lighting, new vans, new air-conditioning, and a new sound system! By the way, my Sunday School classroom was too cold this morning, and it's ninety degrees outside! I'm telling you that we need to put our church first!" Deacon 5 shakes his head and joins the other deacons.

- Deacon 6 approaches and is stopped by the elder brother.
- Elder brother to the deacon: "When is so-and-so going to apologize to me? Twenty-five years ago, so-and-so told me off, and do you know what that so-and-so said? He said (long pause) . . . Well, I don't remember what he said, but it was sure wrong, and I've never forgotten it. You deacons need to meet with him and tell him to apologize to me." Deacon 6 shakes his head and joins the other deacons.
- Deacon 7 approaches and is stopped by the elder brother.
- Elder brother to the deacon: "When are you guys going to start listening to me? My daddy was a preacher, and I've seen churches make all kinds of mistakes. For example, I told you we should have built that gymnasium another way. It should have been wider and longer and higher. Anyone could have seen that! And what about that new Sunday School teacher? He got mixed up about the rider on the white horse in that Bible book called Revolution. I don't think we can trust a teacher like that. I'm not going to mention his name, but you know who I'm talking about, right?" Deacon 7 shakes his head and joins the other deacons.
- Elder brother to the congregation: "I wouldn't say this to just anyone, but between you and me our preacher is waaaaaaay too shallow for this church. He's also the most long-winded guy I've ever listened to. And if your deacons would get out there and do their job and visit people and call people on the telephone, we'd have a lot more people in this church."
- Elder brother shakes his watch. "If we don't end this thing by noon, I'm out of here. The line down at Cracker Barrel is getting longer by the minute!"
- Deacons approach as a group. One asks, "We've been talking, and we would like to know. Who are you? What is your name?"

- The elder brother rises and says, "Don't you know my name? My name is the elder brother."
- All exit and return to their seats.

How many of you want to be the elder brother? I hope the answer is no one. Don't raise your hand for my next question, but how many of you have been the elder brother at least once in your life? Probably most of us.

The elder brother is the person who thinks the church owes him something. It's usually based on how long the person has been in the church as if seniority means one gets extra privileges in God's church. Or it can be based on how much you give. If you believe your giving is substantial, it is easy to think the church ought to do it your way. After all, you see yourself as being the one who is paying the bills. Or if you're really gifted in some area, you may get the idea that you ought to be treated with a degree of reverence. Or if your family has been a big part of this church's history. You get the picture!

My father pastored Baptist churches for thirty years. He once had an elder brother who was actually a woman. The church approved a budget to redo the church auditorium. The auditorium was in really bad shape. The inside walls were even bowed.

This elder brother went into a first-class rage that extended for weeks. Do you know what she said? She said, "This church sits on property belonging to my family. That means this property will revert back to my family if this church ever ceases to be a Baptist church. My father built this building with his own two hands. You don't have the right to touch a single nail in this building."

She was mean when she said it, and she even looked mean!

Do you know what happened? The elder brother and dad had war, but the church put its foot down and redid the auditorium. The new auditorium was so beautiful that it actually became the pattern for the renovated auditorium in my wife's home church.

Here's the end of the story. It took a long time, but eventually, the elder brother became a loving sister. She became a dear friend for the next two decades. But she missed a lot of blessings along the way!

I wonder if the elder brother in Luke chapter fifteen ever became a loving brother instead of a jealous brother. What do you think? Do you think he ever learned how to forgive? Or maybe he left the house and moved away?

Jesus said, "If you forgive people for what they do wrong to you, your heavenly Father will also forgive you. But if you don't forgive people, your Father will not forgive what you do wrong." (Matthew 6:14-15) In other words, you'll be a miserable person. After all, the Bible says, "The way of a transgressor is hard." (Proverbs 13:15) Reconciliation is always preferable to misery!

A pastor visited an elderly woman in a hospital. She was near death. The conversation turned to the squabbles in her family. The woman said, "I told my brother I will never forgive him. He accused me of taking more than my share of mom's things when she died. He said, 'I want the berry spoon.' But I'm not going to let him have the berry spoon."

The mother had died forty years earlier. But they were still fighting over the berry spoon!

I can't imagine fighting forty years over a berry spoon or a piece of china or a gun or a piano.

Listen to me! *Sometimes it's just time to move on.* Life is too short to spend it on small things like berry spoons.

The elder brother chose to brood—isn't brooding fun? I hear it beats everything on earth! I am sure brooding is the number one goal for all of us, right? Our life's ambition is to brood.

No, to be honest, none of us want to brood because brooding is a miserable life.

The elder brother, though, chose to brood even though he could have enjoyed the celebration. He probably wanted his younger brother to crawl home on broken glass and be locked in jail for thirty days with no water or food. "It would do him good!" was his line of reasoning. "My younger brother has disgraced my father. He has ruined the family name. He no longer deserves to be a part of this family."

The elder brother was probably like the parent who beats his child until his anger is exhausted. How wrong and yet how often it happens!

The younger brother has ruined his life in the faraway country with *riotous living.* But the elder brother is ruining his life at home with *brooding death.* I say that because brooding is not living. Brooding is dying.

I wonder who should be pitied more: the younger son who is miserable in the hog pen, or the elder brother who is miserable at home. Neither one is enjoying life.

There is a big lesson that we need to discuss at this time. Here it is!

When you forgive someone who has injured you, you actually set *two* prisoners free. The first prisoner is the person who has offended you. *The second prisoner is you.*

That's why the title of this chapter is "How to Set the Prisoner**s** Free." The word "prisoners" is not singular but plural. It means there are usually two prisoners that need to be set free, and one of them is you.

Let me share a story that explains it very well. A man was dying. No one liked this man. No one ever spoke to him. He even made it plain he did not want anyone to speak to him. He was a very angry, bitter man.

He had been hurt seriously by a good friend in his younger days. The injury bothered him for the rest of his life. Now he was old and dying.

The dying man said, "I'll remember getting hurt to my dying day. I go over it every morning. I think of it every night. I've cursed him a hundred times each day. But I see now that my curses have eaten into my soul. My hate has hurt nobody but myself. God knows it turned my life into hell."

He was an elder brother.

He was also one of *two* prisoners who needed to be set free.

But it was now too late to do him any good.

Let me give you a word of advice. *Don't ever allow yourself to become the elder brother.* It will hurt you even more than the original injury itself. Your hurt will then become the hurt of your spouse, your family, and the people close to you. It's not worth it.

Don't ever allow yourself to become the elder brother.

There was a wealthy businessman in Boston who was also a very committed Christian. He married a woman and gave her a beautiful home. But she later became an alcoholic. One day she left the house never to return. She left behind a note which said that she was an embarrassment to her husband. She was damaging her husband's Christian testimony. So, she left home never to return.

The husband immediately hired some private investigators to search for her. They left pictures of her in the big cities. They even left pictures with the funeral homes along with these instructions, "If this lady should ever come to you, buy the finest clothes that money can buy, give her the finest casket possible, bank it with flowers and send for me."

Time passed. One day an undertaker in a distant city called the husband. The husband went to the city, went to the funeral home, and looked down upon the face of his dead wife. He said, "Nellie, if you only knew how much I loved you, then you would have come back to me."

When the funeral was over, the husband went to the tombstone company. He bought a very expensive tombstone. They asked what words he wanted to have inscribed on the tombstone. He said, "I want you to engrave just one word. It is the word 'forgiven.'"

This man could have become very bitter. He instead chose to keep loving.

May we do the same.

20

A DOG'S SERMON ABOUT FORGIVENESS

How to Forgive – Part 3

Sir Walter Scott had a problem with the verse where Jesus said, "If someone slaps you on the right cheek, turn your left cheek to him, also. Don't get into a fight with him." (Matthew 5:39) God, though, taught him the meaning of that verse in a very unusual way.

One day Scott was out for a walk. He noticed he was being followed by a stray dog. Scott picked up a rock. He threw the rock at the dog to chase it away. His aim was usually bad, but this time his aim was surprisingly good. The rock hit the dog and broke its leg.

The dog then did a strange thing. The dog limped up to him and licked the hand that had thrown the rock. Sir Walter Scott said, "That dog preached the Sermon on the Mount better than any preacher."

I say this to my shame, but my pets often do a better job of forgiving than I do. How about your pets? But I can't live with those results because *forgiveness is the key to maintaining a good relationship with everyone I love* including my spouse, my children, my friends, and especially, my church.

I confess to all of you that I need help in this area called forgiveness. Am I the only one who needs help? I think not.

That's why forgiveness is mentioned in our goal. Look at the bottom of your study sheet. Please read our goal with me. *"Helping believers grow together in Him through love and forgiveness."*

The Bible gives us plenty of help regarding forgiveness.

Let's see what the Bible has to say. It's time to fill in some blanks.

1. What Happens if I Forgive?

Question #1: What happens if I forgive? The Bible uses a very unique word to answer that question. Galatians 6:1 says, "Brothers and sisters, if a brother is caught in the trap of sin, it is the responsibility of the more spiritual people to restore that brother with a gentle attitude. Be careful, though because that same sin may try to trap you." The King James says, "restore such a one in the spirit of meekness."

The word "restore" perfectly answers the question of what happens when I forgive someone. The English translation "restore" comes to us from the Greek word *katarizo*. We get our English word "artisan" from that same Greek word. The word expresses the idea of an artisan or a skilled craftsman who is an expert at repairing or renewing an object to its original design.

The same Greek word is used in Matthew 4:21. Jesus passes by and sees James and John, the sons of Zebedee. The Bible says James and John were sitting in their fishing boat *katarizo* their nets. In other words, they were restoring or repairing their nets.

Galatians 6:1 says you and I have been called to a ministry of repairing people or restoring people. We don't specialize in repairing fishing nets. We specialize instead in repairing people.

Forgiveness includes the act of repairing people because forgiveness is all about restoring relationships. Some sort of action has broken the relationship. The relationship now needs mending. That goal will be accomplished through forgiveness. This is what Jesus meant when He said, "Through the process of reconciliation, you will gain your brother." (Matthew 18:15)

Forgiveness and reconciliation mean the broken leg is now made whole. The cripple is now able to walk. The blind is now able to see. The dumb is now able to speak. The depressed is now able to smile. The outcast is now home. The sick is now well. The two have now become one just like it was always intended to be.

Through the act of forgiveness, I find myself ministering both to the other person *as well as to me.* Think back to the title of the previous message, "How to Set the Prisoner<u>s</u> Free." The word "prisoners" was plural because I am also one of the prisoners! I have been hurt, and I need to be set free from my hurt.

Through forgiveness, I am restoring not just a broken bone but also a broken relationship.

2. What Happens if I Apologize and Ask for Forgiveness?

Question #2: What happens if I apologize and ask for forgiveness? This question represents a change of direction. Most of our study has been from the vantage point of the offendee, of the person who has been sinned against. But now we turn our attention to us as the offender, as the one who is in the wrong.

We live in a fast-paced world. We're moving so rapidly that sometimes we don't recognize how we come across to people. We may not have meant to be cruel, but we apparently came across that way. Someone has been hurt.

Or it may have been a case where we actually intended to be cruel. Or we may have lost our temper with someone like our spouse. Everyone knows how husbands and wives fuss! Quite honestly, what we did was clearly not right. It does not matter if we intended for it to happen. *Making it right is all that now matters.*

The Bible says, "Let not the sun go down upon your anger." (Ephesians 4:26) In other words, settle your anger while it is still daylight so you can sleep well tonight. The same principle is true in the area of forgiveness. It's a lot easier to apologize before bedtime than to toss and turn the entire night thinking about it!

What happens if I apologize and ask for forgiveness? Let me mention three items. These are fill-in-the-blank.

First, I have honored my Lord by doing what He told me to do. My apology is an act of obedience to my Lord and Savior. Second, I have honored myself by doing what I know is right. I truly want to practice what the Bible says. That means I have a higher standard than most people. My standard is one of doing what is right! Third, I have honored the process by doing the only thing I can control. I cannot control the other person's reaction. I can only do what I can do. In so doing I have made it possible for us to achieve a good outcome.

Many years ago, a Christian professor named Stuart Blackie taught at the University of Edinburgh. On one occasion he was listening to the students present oral readings in the class. One young man stood to begin his reading. The professor noticed this student held his book in the wrong hand. The professor rebuked the student for violating the policy. He harshly said, "Take your book in your right hand and be seated!"

The student held up his right arm. Everyone could then see the student did not have a right hand! Everyone became uneasy. They wondered what would happen next.

The professor made his way to the student, put his arm around him, and began crying. He said, "I never knew about it. Please, will you forgive me?" The young man accepted the apology. It made a lasting impression on that young man.

A preacher told this story some months later in a large church. The preacher finished his message. A young man came forward, turned to the audience, and raised his right arm. His arm ended at the wrist. He said, "I was that student. Professor Blackie later led me to Christ. *But he could never have led me to Christ if he had not made the wrong right.*"

I share that story to remind you that God is the One multiplying the results of our lives! It is always best to do what God says to do when God says to do it and how God says to do it!

Forgiveness is part of doing what is right.

3. Can Forgiveness Be Experienced in a Difficult Situation?

Question #3: Can forgiveness be experienced in a difficult situation? I will admit this question is a little bit awkward. I thought about rephrasing this question but finally decided that it says what needs to be said.

Sometimes we think we're past the point of reconciliation. That may indeed be true, but, then again, it may *not* be true. Your problem may fall in any number of categories: family, work, neighbor, church and so on. It may be a very difficult situation!

But is it an impossible situation? The answer is most likely no. That means we need to keep praying about the situation. Jesus taught us, "Man should always pray and never give up." (Luke 18:1) The situation may look hopeless to us, but it may not be hopeless to God.

Let's think through what happened to Jesus on the cross because the cross represents the most difficult situation of all time for forgiveness to take place. During his time on the cross, Jesus prayed for a spirit of forgiveness to surround His cross. The prayer, "Father, forgive them for they know not what they do," demonstrates the merciful heart of a loving God.

Visualize the scene in your mind. The insensitive Roman soldiers drove the nails through the feet of Jesus then proceeded to gamble for His meager clothing. The crowd and religious leaders toured the site and mocked Him as He suffered. The criminal on the right and the criminal on the left fired insults at Jesus. Surely no good can come from this difficult situation. But still, Jesus prayed, "Father, forgive them."

Could such a remarkable feat actually be done?

Through God's grace, such a feat actually *was* done in the life of one thief. One of the thieves repented and made the request, "Lord, remember me when You come into Your kingdom." (Luke 23:42) Who could have expected something as thrilling as that? One of the Roman guards watched Jesus die then announced in awe, "Truly, this was the Son of God!" (Matthew 27:54) Who could have expected something like that? Nicodemus, a member of the Sanhedrin Court, openly aligned himself with Jesus *after* He died. (John 19:39) Who could have expected something like that? Lest we forget, this difficult situation was then followed by the *entire book of Acts* as proof of what God is able to do!

4. Does Forgiveness Require Mentally Forgetting?

Question #4: Does forgiveness require *mentally* forgetting? The short answer is no. But forgiveness does mean *practically* forgetting. There is a big difference between mentally forgetting and practically forgetting. Mentally forgetting may not be humanly possible in all situations.

Lewis B. Smedes wisely said, "Forgiving does not erase the bitter past. A healed memory is not a deleted memory."

This problem is one area where it actually helps to have a bad memory!

The old-time preachers often talked about the "sea of God's forgetfulness." There is plenty of scriptural support for that expression. Jeremiah 31:34 says, "I will forgive their iniquity and I will *remember their sin no more.*" That is God Himself speaking! Evidently, God is able to compartmentalize His thoughts much better than you or I!

The prophet Micah writes, "Who is a God like you, pardoning iniquity and passing over transgression for the remnant of his inheritance? He does not retain his anger forever because he delights in steadfast love. He will again have compassion on us; he will tread our iniquities underfoot. You will cast all our sins into the depths of the sea." (Micah 7:18-19, ESV)

Psalm 103:12 says, "As far as the east is from the west, so far hath he removed our transgressions from us." (KJV)

It has been said that to forgive and *not* forget is to bury the hatchet with the handle sticking out. That may be true in some cases, but that may also be the best you can humanly do! The damage simply goes too deep! However, burying the hatchet with the handle sticking out is much better than still waving the hatchet! A buried hatchet can do no more harm, but a waving hatchet is a danger to all! In this case, we should be pleased with such a result, even though it falls short of the most desirable result of forgiving *and* forgetting.

The word "forget" can mean one of two things. First, you truly do forget. That is what we know as "mentally forgetting." The wrongdoing is now in the past and can never be restored to the present. It has been removed from our memory!

Second, you may still remember the wrongdoing, but *you don't bring it up again nor allow it to influence the way that you think.* The second definition is more in line with the way God forgets. We know God knows all things. Psalm 139:2 says God even knows our "downsitting and our uprising." That means God even knows when we go to bed and when we rise in the morning! Should we also remind ourselves that He "knows the way that I take"? (Job 23:10) Yes, God knows all things. God never really forgets in the sense that He can no longer remember it. Therefore, the question becomes, *will God keep reminding us of the wrongdoing after He forgives? The answer is no!*

God's forgiveness is of such a high degree that it should always be viewed as a settled transaction. God covers our sin with the blood of His own dear Son. Covered sin = forgiven sin = settled sin!

We studied earlier about one of Paul's greatest failures. John Mark abandoned Paul's first missionary journey and returned home to his mother. John Mark matured, though, and wished to join Paul on his second missionary journey. Paul, however, refused to accept Mark's apology.

I can picture Paul telling Barnabas, "Mark left us once. He'll leave us again! Leave him home with his mother!"

The disagreement became so divisive that Paul and Barnabas chose to go their separate ways. Paul took Silas on his second missionary journey. Barnabas took his nephew John Mark on his own missionary journey.

Who turned out to be right? Barnabas! Who turned out to be wrong? Paul! Evidently being an apostle does not guarantee a 100% success ratio!

Time passed. John Mark eventually proved himself as a capable minister in the Lord's work. He served faithfully with Barnabas and Peter (1 Peter 5:13). As a matter of fact, he eventually wrote the second gospel known today as the Gospel of Mark. That gospel may be the earliest of the New Testament writings.

The Apostle Paul eventually recognized his mistake and forgave John Mark. Shortly before his death, Paul wrote from the prison in Rome, "Timothy, only Luke is now with me. When you come to see me, I want you to pick up John Mark and bring him with you. He is *profitable* or *useful* to me for the work of the ministry." (2 Timothy 4:11)

That is much different than saying, "I remember when you failed. Are you going to fail this time, too?"

How many of you want to be remembered for everything you have done wrong, especially for the things you did wrong when you were young? Some people say, "I'll forgive you, but I'll never forget." That's their way of saying I intend to keep the problem burning inside me, and yes, you will hear about this problem sometime in the future!

True forgiveness means you are able to extinguish the fire that is burning in your heart. Forgiveness treats the conflict *and* the person's apology as a settled matter. "We will speak of it no more" is the biblical spirit embedded in forgiveness!

It is as if you are meeting that person for the very first time! A clean slate exists for the two of you. It is time to move forward! What will the two of you write on that clean slate? Hopefully, the past is indeed a settled matter, and you can begin again.

Clara Barton has been credited with founding the Red Cross. Such an endeavor, though, was not easy! She was severely criticized. After all, the Red Cross was something totally new; people often criticize new things. One day a friend reminded her of a very specific criticism. The friend said, "Clara, surely you remember that criticism." Clara said, "No. *I distinctly remember forgetting that criticism."*

Let me ask you a question. How does anyone distinctly *remember forgetting that criticism?* Such a statement is contradictory, but it is still possible. How is it possible? It is possible because *forgiveness is an act of the will.* That is a very important fill-in-the-blank. You may never *mentally* forget, but you can *practically* forget. You can treat it as a settled matter. That happens when we *will it to be so.*

5. How Often Should I Forgive?

Question #5: How often should I forgive? It may be better to change the question to, "How often *must* I accept his apology? Lord, at what point can I just punch him in the nose? Or send him an anonymous letter calling him every name in the book? Lord, if anyone deserves a bad time, he surely does!"

Have you ever experienced that sense of exasperation? I knew of one church where everyone kept waiting for so-and-so to mess things up. The mess-up would occur, the folks would do damage control then they would go back to waiting . . . waiting for so-and-so to mess things up again . . . which, of course, he always did. In this case, the person was very headstrong and usually leaped before he thought. By and by, he became better at staying within his lanes, but he never got fully trained!

The Apostle Peter asked our Lord, "How often do I have to forgive my brother and sister for what they say about me and do to me? Is seven times enough?" Jesus responded, "Seventy times seven is the minimum number of times to forgive your brother and sister." (Matthew 18:21-22)

The Bible does not say this, but my sanctified imagination suggests that Peter then asked, "What happens when I reach four hundred and ninety times?" Jesus probably answered, "Come back at that time, and I'll give you further instructions." Of course, no further instructions were necessary.

The principle of forgiveness is clear. *We can stop forgiving others only if Christ stops forgiving us.* Since the latter will never occur, the former should never occur either.

Dr. Robert J. McCracken began his career pastoring a church in Canada. There was an old woman in that church who took a strong dislike to him. This woman was continually badmouthing McCracken to other people.

He dreaded the day when he would have to pay her a visit. Finally, the day came. He paced back and forth in front of her apartment building and tried to work up the courage to face her.

He got the bright idea that maybe she was not home, and he could simply leave his business card. He climbed the stairs and knocked on her door. Thankfully, there was no answer. He knocked again and heard a faint sound inside. He knelt down and looked through the keyhole to see if anyone was there. To his surprise, he saw an eye staring at him from the other side.

The woman said, "Pastor, this is the first time we have ever seen eye-to-eye." The pastor said, "Yes, and we had to get down on our knees to do it."

Getting down on our knees has a way of preparing our heart to deal with difficult people. That is so because it often prepares my own heart to deal with me!

6. What Happens if the Offender Does Not Apologize?

Question #6: What happens if the offender does not apologize? Should I ignore his sin and treat the matter as a solved matter? Question #6 implies the offender has been made aware of his offense, but for whatever reason, the offender defiantly refuses to make things right. In his mind he is right, and you are wrong. As a matter of fact, he might even insist on an apology from you!

For instance, a woman attended a college seminar about loving people of different races and backgrounds. She listened closely then went to the speaker and said, "I really appreciate what you shared today, but I wouldn't want the love for people that you have for me." The speaker asked, "Why not?" She said, "Because I want the joy of hating those who hate me!"

Some people are motivated by bitterness for an entire lifetime! Their sole purpose in life is to make others miserable. Other people won't apologize because, in their view, an apology is a sign of weakness! Still others are ashamed of what they have done and don't want to face the matter.

Most of us don't like to hear an apology which begins with the words, "*If* I have offended you." If "if" is the correct word for you to say, well, we have a big problem! That's a fill-in-the-blank, too.

We sometimes miss the connection between forgiveness and reconciliation. The two are linked at the hip. You may have a forgiving spirit that yearns to forgive, but actual forgiveness will not occur until reconciliation also occurs. *Reconciliation occurs when an apology is offered, and the apology is accepted.*

Suppose I pray, "Father, forgive the world for their sins so they can go to heaven." Will God answer that prayer? No. I may have a forgiving spirit, but such forgiveness requires an admission of guilt *and* an acceptance of Jesus Christ as Savior on the part of each individual.

It is rather foolish to say forgiveness has occurred when the matter has not been resolved or settled. As the injured party, you may choose to move on. As the offender, you may also choose to move on. *But moving on is not the same as forgiveness or reconciliation.* The decision to move on actually leaves one in an unhealthy state of affairs with the potential for more of the same conflict somewhere down the road.

The best material on this subject was written many years ago by Arthur Pink in his book *The Seven Sayings of the Savior on the Cross*:

Here we are plainly taught that a condition must be met by the offender before we may pronounce forgiveness. The one who has wronged us must first "repent", that is, judge himself for his wrong and give evidence of his sorrow over it. But suppose the offender does not repent? Then I am not to forgive him. But let there be no misunderstanding of our meaning here. Even though the one who has wronged me does not repent, nevertheless, I must not harbor ill-feelings against him. There must be no hatred or malice cherished in the heart. Yet, on the other hand, I must not treat the offender as if he had done no wrong. That would be to condone the offence, and therefore, I should fail to uphold the requirements of righteousness, and this the believer is ever to do. Does God ever forgive where there is no repentance? No, for Scripture declares, "If we confess our sins, He is faithful and just to forgive us our sins and to cleanse us from all unrighteousness" (1 John 1:9). One thing more. If one has injured me and repented not, while I cannot forgive him and treat him as though he had not offended, nevertheless, not only must I hold no malice in my heart against him, but I must also pray for him.

When I pray for my enemies I can pray for their health, safety, family plus I can also pray for them to reach a point of repentance and forgiveness.

During Jesus' crucifixion, His enemies did not want to be forgiven. In their view, they were crucifying someone worthy of death! But, lest we forget, Jesus knew Pentecost was coming. Acts chapter two was indeed coming! On that day Peter sought an apology (also known as repentance) by preaching, "With wicked hands, you have crucified and slain the Lord of Glory!" What happened? Instead of facing God's certain judgment, three thousand crucifiers repented and got saved. We can view their repentance as an apology. "Father, I have sinned!" was undoubtedly heard many times on that day. It may very well be true that Acts chapter two is the result of Jesus praying, "Father, forgive them for they know not what they do!"

Unfortunately, only three thousand apologized on that day. Many, many more could have apologized but did not! It is sad to say, but the rest of the city continued on the broad road which leads to a devil's hell. Jesus had prayed for them, too, but the prayer had been in vain. However, you can't blame Jesus! He did all that He could do to reconcile the world unto Himself. Sometimes the same sad conclusion will happen to us, too.

7. How Can I Forgive Myself?

Question #7: How can I forgive myself? One of the greatest dilemmas in life is being able to live with ourselves after we have messed up. Some mistakes are very costly. It may be a financial mistake in which you invest your money in a sure gusher, but it ends up being a dry hole. It may be a sexual transgression which costs you a marriage. It may be a career choice which turns out to be a disaster. By and by, you find yourself sitting in the ashes like Job of the Old Testament. You are so far down that there's no direction to go but up!

How can I live with myself after such a catastrophic mistake? It may be a sin, or it may just be a failure or mistake. The outcome is basically the same because the outcome is still catastrophic.

C. S. Lewis said, "I think that if God forgives us, we must forgive ourselves. Otherwise, it is almost like setting up ourselves as a higher tribunal than Him." There is no higher authority anywhere than God! You must accept God's conclusion by faith then move on with your life.

A young man was having a lot of problems getting along with other people, especially his own family. His wife was a fine person. She was

very attractive, affectionate, and supportive. But he was constantly criti-
cizing her. Everything she did was wrong.

Slowly it occurred to him that his marriage was being destroyed. He
went to a counselor. In his first session, he met trouble like a man—he
blamed his wife! This went on for several sessions.

Eventually, though, he became honest, and the truth came out. The
problem actually began before his marriage. He was in the military and
spent two weeks on leave in Japan. He was lonely. He fell into sexual
temptation and sinned. That sin had never left his mind.

He later got married. Years passed. The root of the problem was
simply this: He had never forgiven himself. He had sought God's forgiveness and was sure that God had forgiven him. But he had never
forgiven himself.

He hated himself. He would look in the mirror and hate what he saw.
He was afraid to talk about this with anyone. He did not feel he was worthy of having an honest woman.

He would often say to himself, "I have no right to enjoy my wife. I
have no right to enjoy my life. I must pay back the debt." He chose to
live in the prison of his own unforgiveness.

It's fill-in-the-blank time. First, face the facts. Second, change your
direction, and seek God's forgiveness. Third, build your life upon God's
forgiveness. Ask yourself, "Is God bigger than me? Yes, He is. Has God
forgiven me? Yes, He has." It's time to move on and pick up the pieces.

There are three things you should never do. First, you should never
put a question mark where God puts a period. Second, you should never
dig up what God has buried. Third, you should never live by feelings
when God says live by faith! You know by faith in the Word of God that
God has forgiven you. It is time to move on and be what God wants you
to be!

8. How Should I Handle Being Sinned Against?

Question #8: How should I handle being sinned against? By this
point in our study, everyone knows that forgiveness is not an easy thing
to do. I read somewhere that first prize for being the laziest man in the

world went to the guy who whittled with an electric knife! Forgiveness, though, demands the opposite from all of us. It requires the highest in diligence rather than the lowest in laziness!

I must *want* my brother to be my brother! I must *want* my sister to be my sister! How can I make that happen despite our broken relationship?

The Bible says:

> *"If your brother sins against you, go and rebuke him in private. If he listens to you, you have won your brother. But if he won't listen, take one or two more with you, so that by the testimony of two or three witnesses every fact may be established. If he pays no attention to them, tell the church. But if he doesn't pay attention even to the church, let him be like an unbeliever and a tax collector to you. I assure you: Whatever you bind on earth is already bound in heaven, and whatever you loose on earth is already loosed in heaven." (Matthew 18:15-18, HCSB)*

These are the gospel steps to obtain a workable reconciliation with your Christian brother or sister. These are fill in the blank.

First, accept your responsibility as the offended party to seek reconciliation by making the offender aware of what he has done. Someone has to step up and be a man in this situation; the Bible says it may as well be you! You obviously know there was an offense; in all fairness, the offender may not know there was an offense. So, you are the one who needs to be on the offensive. However, please notice that this is to be done privately. The injured person is not to damage the offender by alerting the entire community to what the offender has done. If possible, this entire matter is to remain private.

Second, it is likely the offender will agree with you. Most people don't want to deliberately hurt someone they know. The offender then offers an apology, and you graciously accept the apology. In so doing, you will gain or recover your brother or sister.

Third, in those cases where Step Two does not work, it is now necessary to take two or three witnesses and make another attempt at reconciliation. The witnesses should not think of themselves as lawyers on behalf of the injured party! Their purpose is to be witnesses and promote the need for reconciliation. It is possible the offender may apologize at this time. Hallelujah! Such an apology would end the process.

However, Step Three may not end in reconciliation. In Step Four it is now time to present the matter to the church for their review. The church has the right to judge the matter, determine if the injured party has a legitimate complaint, and if yes, whether the offender has made an apology. *If* it is determined the offender has wronged the injured party, *and* if the offender refuses to make things right with an apology, *then* the church is to discipline the offender.

My first experience using the Matthew 18 precepts occurred when I was a very young preacher. Someone in the church accused our Sunday School Director and me of teaching a doctrine that was contrary to the church. The accusation was damaging and had the potential to be very damaging if it was widely publicized. Following a Sunday evening service, I asked the offender to meet with me in private. He graciously did. I discussed what I had heard. He admitted to making the accusation. I then said he was incorrect in his statements. I carefully explained what I believed and what I preached. To my surprise, he said, "Then I was wrong. I'm sorry." We hugged, and the matter was never spoken of again.

I learned a very important lesson that day. I learned that peacemaking is not the same as avoiding conflict. "Blessed are the peacemakers" is about *making* peace where there is no peace. Peacemaking requires one to walk into a conflict without knowing the final outcome. It can be a pleasant outcome, or it can be an unpleasant outcome. But it is a necessary part of reconciliation.

The painting, *The Last Supper,* is recognized as one of Leonardo da Vinci's greatest works. It is said he got into a terrible argument with a fellow artist a short time before he began *The Last Supper*. Da Vinci decided to get even by painting the man's face on the body of Judas

Iscariot. Imagine having your face on the body of Judas Iscariot! The man would live in infamy for as long as the painting lasted.

Then da Vinci came to the face of Jesus. Something, though, seemed to be hindering his effort. He finally concluded that he could not paint Jesus until he first changed the face of Judas. He proceeded to change the face of Judas into someone he did not know. Only then was he able to paint the face of Jesus.

Someone wrote, "Oh, what blessings we will forfeit When forgiveness we withhold! Fellowship with God is broken, And our heart grows hard and cold!"

I don't want my heart to become hard and cold. How about you?

That's why we need to learn how to forgive.

21

HOW EFFECTIVE IS OUR GREENHOUSE?

More Than Last Thoughts . . .

A Plea for Re-Thinking Church

By this point, you have already absorbed a lot of material designed to make you think. Hopefully, this material will develop you to a higher level of service to the One who has purchased us with His own blood. You have read this material because you have an innate desire to give more to Him.

We have now reached the end of *God's Greenhouse: How to Grow People God's Way*. But I'm not quite ready to say goodbye and God bless you. Most of this chapter was originally written in 2008, but it is as relevant today as it was then. If we updated the survey data for the current year, the data would likely be the same, if not slightly worse due to the increasing average age of the church membership.

I truly believe, indeed, I believe *very* deeply, in what is written in these remaining pages. This is not filler material. From my perspective, it may be the most important material of all. It resonates very deeply within me. I pray you are able to make it work for you.

A little boy attended church for the first time. The ushers passed the offering plates down each row. When the ushers reached his row, the little boy said loudly, "Don't pay for me, Daddy. I'm under five."

Every parent can remember those days of discounted tickets for our children! I knew of one parent who was so cheap (he still owned his first dollar) that he got a discounted ticket for his seven-year-old child by *carrying him* through the line for the five-year-old children! He saved an enormous three dollars by lying about his son's age!

In time, though, even seven-year-old children look their age! The discounts ebb until they disappear altogether. The children's menu at the restaurant is replaced with an adult menu, and in some cases, we then stop going out to eat! The cost is suddenly more than we can afford.

The American process is based upon a premise that we eat more as we grow older. Therefore, the size of the meals and the cost of the meals are adjusted upward regardless of whether the person actually eats more. You may be an adult and eat like a bird, but you will pay the same price as the adult who eats like a horse!

We tend to grade spiritual maturity in the very same way—by age! If one has silver hair (or no hair) *and* has spent many years in church, we assume that he has now arrived at a state of spiritual maturity.

It is my experience, though, that many of our middle-aged and older adults have never grown past the baby stage described by Paul in 1 Corinthians chapter three. I sometimes find myself asking, who is to blame for their lack of growth? Sometimes it is the fault of the Christian. He never applied himself to be a fully committed disciple of Jesus Christ. On the other hand, many adults were never given the tools to develop to a higher level. In such cases, their churches had a very low definition of maturity.

Let me give two examples from the same church. I knew a deacon who had been a deacon for more than twenty years. He was a good man. He would be a good companion to have in a foxhole when the enemy is charging! This deacon told me very honestly, "I thought I was a good deacon until you came here as our pastor. Now I know how little I knew and how little I did." That statement was an adequate assessment of not only him but of his entire church. The church was showing the effects of an inferior process for maturing Christians.

Our church secretary had been the secretary for nearly thirty years. She told me very honestly, "We thought we had high standards until you came. Now we realize we had very low standards." Incidentally, twelve years after I moved on, that church had transitioned from a soul-winning church of one hundred and twenty attendees to zero attendees. The doors were now closed. What a tragedy!

Those same comments can be repeated in many ministries. How do things like this happen in God's churches? We pride ourselves on being a people who believe in the Bible, but the actual maturity level of most churches is pitiful, sad, and failing. Instead of the church beating down the gates of hell, we are in retreat and even declining in far too many places.

The reason this condition exists is that we have an inadequate view of spiritual maturity. We have a bad tendency to think in terms of age, effort, participation, and attendance. In reality, none of those items create maturity. *They may be signs of maturity, but in themselves, they do not create maturity.*

The story is told of a man who asked for a pay raise based upon his forty years of experience. The boss said, "No. You have done nothing more than experience one job for forty years. You are not experienced in anything else."

That illustration pictures many of our church members. We have not developed outside our teeny, weeny little world.

May I suggest that we redefine maturity in terms of completeness or well-roundedness? This helps us establish a very clear target. In these cases, clearer is always better! The five commonly accepted objectives of ministry, discipleship, worship, fellowship, and evangelism are manageable, definable, and measurable. Items such as prayer, tithing, and music would be better treated as subcategories in one of these five broader categories.

My personal philosophy toward ministry grew by leaps and bounds when I discovered the truth of Ephesians 4:11-13. I had read the text many times, but finally, it sank in! The entire context reads as follows:

> *"Christ personally gave to the church some people gifted as apostles, some people gifted as prophets, some people gifted as evangelists, some people gifted as pastors who also serve as teachers, for the purpose of <u>training</u> or equipping the saints to do the work of the ministry, in order that the body of Christ might be built to a higher level, until all of us reach the level of unity in the faith and a complete knowledge of God's Son, growing into a spiritually mature man that measures up to the full measure of Christ's fullness."*

That is a mouthful. I don't have time to explain every thought, but I want to give you something that is very, very special to me. It is so special that it may revolutionize the way you see this thing we call "doing church."

I underlined the word "training" because that one word changed my view of church. The word translated "training" is derived from the Greek word *katartismos*. It appears in the same sense in 2 Corinthians 13:11, Galatians 6:1 (translated restore), 1 Thessalonians 3:10, Hebrews 13:21, and 1 Peter 5:10. The complete word in this verse actually has the idea of "equipping or preparing for service." God gives us these gifted men who specialize in training us to do "the work of the ministry."

You can think of these people as the instructors in God's Greenhouse. They are the people who make the classroom experience a profitable experience. That is, if you listen to them and do what they say! (We developed the importance of the classroom experience in Chapter Fourteen, "The Teeter-Totter of Success.")

Do you remember how God's Greenhouse began? It began in 1 Corinthians chapter three. "Paul sowed, Apollos watered, and God gave the increase." Paul was good at sowing, Apollos was good at watering, and God did what only God can do and gave the increase. It worked marvelously!

Effective sowing and effective watering in God's Greenhouse do not happen by accident! Paul was really good at what he did. Apollos was really good at what he did. Both of them had been trained or equipped to do the work of the ministry! In turn, they trained or equipped others to do the same work of the ministry! In turn, those trainees trained others to do the same work of the ministry! This has continued down to the present day with the result that we are now the ones who are equipped to do the work of the ministry.

How can this training be done more effectively?

First, it means we need a better process to develop our people! The word process is in contrast to an event, especially an event that occurs only once. The word process denotes it is a continuing, repeatable system of development. It has often been said that great churches are a good church which has seen it all, done it all, and *keeps on doing it!*

Such a church continues its process week after week, month after month, and year after year. It knows what it is trying to do, keeps updating its tools (programs, procedures, staff), and keeps its eye focused on the process. ***This process trains the people then turns the trained people into trainers of more people*** (2 Timothy 2:2). There will be times when God moves your better-trained people to other churches for ministry. Praise the Lord! That is one way to determine if you have a God-honoring process. Such an "advancement" will create openings for those who are going through your current training process!

In addition, we need a way of measuring where we currently are and what is currently possible. The business world refers to it as a "best-practice study." It must be acknowledged that few church leaders truly know how to measure church performance. Accordingly, the pastor often gets much of the blame for poor church performance. This creates a vicious cycle of defeat for both the pastor and the church. However, it is my hopefully unbiased conviction that most pastors are not the problem! God did not send the pastor to be the problem but to be *part* of the solution. The church leadership needs to recognize that it can never identify the problem or solve the problem unless it has a way of *measuring the current performance of the church.*

Let's look closely at two charts. These charts are derived from a survey done by Ellison Research of Phoenix, Arizona which appeared in the November 2005 issue of *Facts and Trends* (a Southern Baptist publication). Though old, this remains one of the most enlightening surveys I have ever seen for two important reasons. First, it illustrates graphically what churches can do; second, it provides a means of *measuring my own church* versus other churches. Through this survey, I can identify and target the bull's-eye rather than continue shooting in the dark!

TABLE 1: What is offered per year by size?

Tool	Small %	Medium %	Large %
New membership training	50	64	87
Basics of Christianity	39	52	65
How to study the Bible	38	41	60
Evangelism/outreach training	29	43	62
Spiritual growth/renewal	33	34	53
Effective prayer	31	30	52
Spiritual gifts inventory	23	31	55
Marriage enrichment	16	33	56
Leadership development	21	25	45

Basics of church's denominational perspectives	21	25	33
Parenting/child development	9	15	55
Financial management	10	13	40
Skills and talents profile	9	17	34
Grief recovery	5	7	25
Recovery from substance abuse	6	6	15
Health/weight loss/exercise	4	5	19
Ministry in the workplace	5	4	7
Divorce recovery	3	2	16
Life skills	2	5	9
Totals	354%	452%	788%

TABLE 2: What is offered by denomination and perspective?

Tool	S. Baptist	Methodist	Lutheran	Pentecostal	Presbyterian	All Others	Mainline	Evangelical
New Membership	52%	58%	84%	62%	76%	66%	67%	61%
Basics of Christianity	36	39	58	55	41	53	48	49
How to study the Bible	32	45	55	37	50	53	56	38
Evangelism/outreach training	54	24	31	38	19	32	22	49
Spiritual growth/renewal	34	36	38	31	47	39	40	34
Effective Prayer	34	26	15	46	23	38	27	36
Spiritual gifts inventory	37	30	22	37	23	36	28	32
Marriage enrichment	36	20	16	37	12	28	17	34
Leadership development	22	22	20	38	29	31	22	27
Basics of church's denominational perspectives	17	36	43	26	45	22	38	23
Parenting/child development	25	12	10	16	25	20	14	21
Financial management	24	11	7	29	4	17	6	21
Skills and talents profile	18	14	22	16	16	21	18	16
Grief recovery	11	16	16	2	7	11	14	7
Recovery from substance abuse	8	10	10	8	7	7	6	8
Health/weight loss/exercise	12	9	12	4	12	8	7	8

Ministry in the workplace	6	2	2	6	2	7	3	6
Divorce recovery	8	8	4	5	2	5	3	6
Life skills	2	4	3	5	4	5	4	3
Totals	**468**	**422**	**468**	**498**	**444**	**499**	**440**	**479**
	%	%	%	%	%	%	%	%

Several denominational facts are worth noting. Lutherans have the highest percentage of new membership classes at 84%, compared to Southern Baptists who have the lowest percentage at 52%.

Southern Baptists also have the lowest percentage of classes teaching the basics of denominational beliefs with only 17%. This occurs in spite of Southern Baptists priding themselves as a "people of the Book." (I have the freedom to say this since I am a Southern Baptist.)

Only 49% of evangelical churches have classes oriented to evangelism/outreach training. Evidently, 51% of evangelical churches have missed the purpose of the Great Commission. Pardon me for asking, but is it possible they are not really evangelical?

Interestingly, not one of my pastorates provided evangelism/outreach training in the two years prior to my arrival. Not a single one! Yet isn't this supposed to be one of the highest priorities of God's church? How can this be? What is your own past and present experience? Is your current church accomplishing this goal? I am sure you would agree this is a revealing issue.

Genuine purpose-driven churches provide the necessary training because training provides the means of achieving their purpose!

Robert Gross, former president of Lockheed Aircraft Corporation, once shared with his supervisors, "It's one thing to build a product; it's another thing to build a company. Companies are nothing but men, and the things that come out of them are no better than the people themselves. We do not build automobiles, airplanes, refrigerators, radios, or shoestrings. We build men. *The men build the product.*"

The last statement can be paraphrased in the following way in church language: *"The men build the kingdom of God!"* Kingdom building is hard work! It requires skilled craftsmen just like any corporation. That's why we're called coworkers with God!

It is my firm conviction that every church (regardless of size) can establish a better training program. Just a cursory glance at this survey indicates that the majority of these classes are necessary to develop complete or well-rounded Christians.

I am especially proud of the training we provided in a pastorate that averaged one hundred and twenty people in worship. That's not a lot of people, but it proved to be enough! Based on this survey, it is interesting to note that we apparently provided more tools for personal development than even the large churches.

May I share with you how a purpose-driven emphasis (worship, ministry, fellowship, evangelism, and discipleship) can work in real life? Our purpose statement read as follows: "Our church's purpose is to help every member become complete in Christ by emphasizing personal development in discipleship, evangelism, ministry, worship, and fellowship."

Based on this purpose statement, we proceeded to develop opportunities to grow people! Some folk grew to levels they would never have attained otherwise. Interestingly, many of those opportunities are included in this survey. Let's take a look.

- New membership – We implemented a periodic four-hour seminar CLASS 101 called Discovering Church Membership. This seminar was patterned after Rick Warren's Christian Life and Service Seminars. It introduced new members to our church's goals and made them aware of our own expectations for them.
- Basics of Christianity – We provided a BASICS class during Sunday School for adult <u>beginners</u> in the faith. This class followed a one-year cycle designed to teach the Trinity, inspiration, deity of Christ, etc. I taught this class. Six people completed the

first year's cycle and rotated out. It was our practice to allow new students to rotate into the class at any time since the sessions did not build upon prior knowledge.

- How to study the Bible – Not provided.
- Evangelism/outreach training – We provided training on Thursday evenings using the Southern Baptist program known as the NET. In addition, we converted our midweek service to a Be A Missionary Wednesday service for all adults. Evangelism training happened every Wednesday night because this was a very weak spot for the current membership. Also, we provided a periodic four-hour seminar CLASS 401 Discovering My Life Mission developed by Rick Warren.
- Spiritual growth/renewal – We taught a periodic four-hour seminar CLASS 201 called Discovering Spiritual Maturity developed by Rick Warren. This included a process for establishing a daily quiet time with the Lord!
- Effective prayer – We intentionally programmed more prayer into our midweek service. Why? There was a significant performance gap between the effective prayer habits of the Social Security generation and the ineffective prayer habits of the younger generation. Also, we provided copies of the book *Praying Effectively for The Lost* by Lee E. Thomas and used it as a study text. Our Wednesday service concluded with small prayer circles. Last, our internet prayer chain included more than sixty email addresses.
- Spiritual gifts inventory – This was done through a periodic four-hour seminar CLASS 301 called Discovering My Ministry. It is provided by Rick Warren. *It is the best material I have ever seen* on this subject, but it does require extensive homework.
- Marriage enrichment – Not done. However, I routinely provided a four-sermon series each summer titled How to Deal with Family Problems.

- Leadership development – CLASS 501 (monthly Saturday morning leadership training) was developed in-house to meet this need. One session created a comprehensive listing of every ministry presently functioning in the church so we could help new people find a way to serve immediately! We listed a staggering 332 ministries that continually happen in a church averaging one hundred and twenty people.
- Basics of church's denominational perspectives – this objective was met in the Sunday morning BASICS class.
- Parenting/child development –Not done although we did provide free educational tutoring for students.
- Financial management – Not done. What potential, though, especially with this younger generation!
- Skills and talents profile – this profile was part of CLASS 301. That class helped students evaluate their Spiritual gifts, Heart, Abilities, Personality, and Experience (otherwise known as SHAPE). It taught, in essence, identify what you are good at and use it for the glory of God!
- Grief recovery – Not done. However, a larger Baptist church just a mile away included grief recovery in its training process.
- Recovery from substance abuse – Not done.
- Health/weight loss/exercise – Not done.
- Ministry in the workplace – This is admittedly a vague category. Our Wednesday night Be A Missionary theme equipped soul winners to share Christ in their place of employment. One Hospice worker used the CLASS 401 training to lead several patients to a saving knowledge of Jesus Christ! That ministry was as effective as door-to-door visitation!
- Divorce recovery – Not done.
- Life skills – Not done.

How well does your church do in providing these important ministries? Let's grade ourselves in the same ministries as the ministries in the above charts. Give yourself a score of 100% in each ministry category your church provides. Give yourself a score of 0% in each category your church does not provide. Add the results. Next, compare your own total with the totals in Chart 1 of the small church, medium church, and large church. (The large church category begins in the area of at least five hundred in regular attendance.)

As noted above, we provided personal growth opportunities in categories 1, 2, 4, 5, 6, 7, 9, 10, 13, and 17. Based on our grading scale, we achieved a 100% rating in ten categories. That's a total of 1,000%. By contrast, the large churches (Chart 1) only attained a 788% rating. This rating system is not intended to be really scientific, but it illustrates that a small church can do much of what needs to be done!

At the same time, it leaves me wondering why the large churches do not provide more opportunities than they do. Perhaps St. John's syndrome has taken root! St. John's Syndrome states, "Churches become less effective the longer they are in existence." Why? The church's original sense of purpose evaporates through time. In many cases, it is simply a matter of the leadership arriving at its own maturity but forgetting its responsibility to help others (usually the next generation) come to maturity.

It is important to realize that the opportunities in these charts are very focused opportunities. They do not minister to every person at every point in his Christian life; however, they do minister to a substantial number of people at various points in their lives.

We do not begin or sustain a ministry just to have a ministry; instead, we allocate resources only after determining that the ministry will grow the people in accordance with our five-fold purpose.

God's church will become a much better church if this purpose is accomplished in just a *minority* of our attendees. The impact upon the community can be monumental over time.

Once again, our goal is to grow people! This is exciting! Experience teaches that people experiencing personal growth are generally more excited about life because growth raises our self-esteem. Self-esteem is usually related to one's significance in life. Most people truly want to make a difference in this world! *What makes a bigger difference than a growing Christian?*

The church benefits, the individual benefits, the community benefits, and the cause of Christ benefits in ways that we cannot even imagine! Only eternity can reveal the results! God has placed a hidden treasure in each member. Our God-given assignment is to help the members locate and unleash that treasure!

Once again, it's time for reflection. Does your current process bring people to a complete or well-rounded stage of Christian living? Think about your leadership team, then about the teachers and other staff members. Are they as spiritual and effective as the prior generation? For example, due to the passing of the Greatest Generation, some churches are now struggling with very few prayer warriors. Answer the following questions:

- How successful are your people in personal soul-winning and recruiting adults for church membership (an evangelism or outreach issue)?
- Are your people like Jesus in their lifestyle in such areas as love, forgiveness, temptation, and attitude (a discipleship issue)?
- How faithful are your people in attendance, giving, and prayer (a worship issue)?
- Do your people create a sense of belonging for the new members (a fellowship/assimilation issue)?
- Have your people identified their ministry? Are they active in that ministry (a ministry issue)?

Next conduct a review of your newest adult members. Write down each name then identify the tool(s) which will help that person reach a complete, well-rounded stage of maturity within seven years. Businesses do something similar in their management training programs, so why not do the same with God's church? For instance, is the new member also a new convert? If yes, how will he prosper in a normal Sunday School class where most of the discussion takes place on a giraffe level rather than a sheep level? He will likely be confused! Maybe even discouraged! Perhaps an introductory course will work best for him. In Paul's words, "he needs the milk before the meat." He needs to grow from infancy into a not-so-infant stage then eventually a spiritual adult.

After all, babies begin their development by rolling over, then they crawl, then they pull themselves up, then they walk, then they go to school, then they grow up, and the little child somehow becomes an adult and starts the cycle over with his own family. It has been like that ever since the creation of Adam and Eve.

One dies and is replaced by one being born. Life's race for one is now over; life's race for another is just beginning. The pages of one life have been completed; the pages for the other life are still blank.

I would like to help the one being born to fill in those pages. *I would like to sow my life in his life.* I would like him to know my Lord and Savior Jesus Christ in the abundant life.

"Behold, a sower went forth to sow."

I am that sower.

So are you.

May God help you to build a greenhouse environment for your people that can truly be called "God's Greenhouse."

SECTION THREE:
STUDY MATERIAL

Free editable Microsoft Word versions of the study sheets may be downloaded at

loaded at

www.godsgreenhouse.net

CHAPTER ONE SIGNS

The signs should be displayed so they are visible to everyone in the auditorium. PowerPoint is one option. I recommend using PowerPoint in addition to visually displaying the signs in a collage. Of course, you can always hang the signs on a fishing line!

Here are the signs:

1. Temple of God
2. Truth of God
3. Family of God
4. Priesthood of God
5. Schoolmaster of God
6. Hospital of God
7. Witness of God
8. Salt of God
9. Servant of God
10. Flock of God

STUDY SHEETS

Today's Subject: Foundational Principles

Key Question: What does God expect our church to be? Let's find out!

1. _____ of God.
2. _____ of God.
3. _____ of God.
4. _____ of God.
5. _____ of God.
6. _____ of God.
7. _____ of God.

The first two letters in "gospel" are _____.

8. _____ of God.
9. _____ of God.
10. _____ of God.
11. Our central text for this very important series is 1 Corinthians 3:9, "For we are God's fellow workers, also known as God's coworkers. You, as God's people, are God's <u>field</u>. You are God's <u>farm</u>. You are God's <u>garden</u>. You are the place where God grows things. You are also God's building." The King James Version uses the word "husbandry." A husbandry is the practice of *cultivating crops*.
12. Our church is a place where God _____ people!
13. "_____ cannot do it without _____ and He has chosen not to do it without _____!"

How much do you want a church where people can grow?

Today's Subject: God's First Greenhouse

- Our central text for this series is 1 Corinthians 3:9, *"You are God's farm/cultivated field/ garden."* We could also translate this phrase, *"You are God's _____."*
- The Bible _____ with God's first greenhouse.
- The name _____ means "delight."
- Our first goal is to create an environment where _____ His children.
- Tom Bandy's diagnosis of many churches: "We have made many church _____ but not many _____."

THE CHARACTERISTICS OF GOD'S FIRST GARDEN

1. _____ fruit.
2. _____ begets like.
3. Every _____ supplied.
4. State of _____.
5. Authentic _____.
6. Absent _____.
7. _____ home.
8. _____ God.
9. Warning _____.
10. Tree of _____.

Today's subject: Characteristics of a Spiritual Greenhouse

- Our central text for this series is 1 Corinthians 3:9 *"you (speaking of us at _____ Church) are God's farm/cultivated field/ garden."* We could also translate this phrase, *"You are God's _____."*
- Our church is the place where God _____ people! But none of this is possible unless we first have a condition (<u>greenhouse environment</u>) where God is free to work in the hearts of His people. It is then that we experience a <u>true, lasting</u> revival!!!
- Each one of these people is a _____ for us to grow in God's greenhouse.
- Our first goal is to _____ an environment where God can grow His children.
- Am I growing as a Christian? Yes   No
- Am I helping anyone to grow as a Christian? Yes   No

LESSONS FROM A COMMON, ORDINARY GREENHOUSE

1. _____ owner.
   i. Jesus said, "Upon this rock _____ will build _____ church." (Matthew 16:18)
   ii. "My" means "our." YES   NO
   iii. When God finds a church that is growing healthy Christians, God sends that church plenty of _____ to work with.
2. _____. The Jerusalem church allowed God to be in the _____ of every single ministry!
   a. Is Jesus in the middle of this ministry? YES   NO

      b.   Will our ministry help create a greenhouse environment so that people can grow in our church? YES NO

3. _____.

4. _____. Churches do not have a growing environ-ment when they have continual _____.

5. _____.

6. _____.

7. _____.

8. _____-through. "Good news travels fast in this church, but bad news travels even _____!"

9. _____.

10. _____. Our greenhouse is for large plants called _____ and small plants called _____.

Does God trust us enough to invest His seed in our church?
All of it   Some of it   None of it

Today's subject: The Pneuma in the Greenhouse

1. Our central text for this series is 1 Corinthians 3:9, *"you (speaking of us at _____ Church) are God's farm/cultivated field/ garden."* We could also translate this phrase, *"You are God's _____."*

2. Our church is the place where God _____ people.

3. Plants need _____ in order to grow.

4. All of us have heard of a pneumatic tool (a tool which operates by _____ pressure). The word pneumatic comes from the Greek word *pneuma* which means _____ or _____. The same word is used for the Holy _____ (*pneuma*). *The Holy Spirit is the air in God's greenhouse! Without Him there is no life! (See 1 Corinthians 3:16 and Ephesians 2:22.)*

5. How to have the Holy Spirit present in a church service:

    1. Ask Him to _____ with you.

    2. Ask Him to _____ through you!

    3. Ask Him to remind you that He is a Person with _____. How can we disturb the Holy Spirit?

    - Unnecessarily _____ in church.
    - Not _____ one another in a holy manner.
    - Not having a _____ attitude.
    - Hindering the time of _____.

    4. Ask Him to show you the _____ in your brothers and sisters.

    5. Ask Him to speak to _____ in every service.

        He will do this through the:

        - _____
        - _____

- _____
- _____
- _____

Today's subject: Warning Signs

1. Our central text for this series is 1 Corinthians 3:9, *"you (speaking of us at _____Church) are God's farm/cultivated field/ garden."* We could also translate this phrase, *"You are God's Greenhouse."*
2. Our church is the place where God *grows* people.
3. Can God remove His presence from a local church? _____
4. The _____ represents God's light or presence in a local church.
5. The church at Ephesus closed because it was no longer a _____ church for God to grow people!
6. The key issue for churches in the 21st century will be church _____, not church growth. When congregations are healthy, they grow the way God intends. Healthy churches don't need _____ – they grow naturally.
7. What causes a greenhouse to fail?
    1. Wrong _____ by the workers. Is this a problem for me? Yes   No
    2. Wrong _____ are used. Is this a problem for me? Yes   No
    3. Wrong _____ are used (list them below). Circle those that are a problem for me.
        a. _____
        b. _____
        c. _____
        d. _____
        e. _____
        f. _____

4. Wrong _____ is pursued. Is this a problem for me? Yes No

"To develop an _____ where God can plant His seed and bring that seed to full maturity in Jesus Christ."

Today's subject: Key Ingredients to a Successful Greenhouse Environment

Text: 1 Corinthians 3:1-10, the key phrase is in vs 9: "We are God's
_____." The work cannot be done without _____,
but He has decided not to do it without _____!

1. Key Question: What kind of people does "*US*" have to be in order
   for God to do His work?
2. Remember this: We don't come here to boss but we come here to
   _____ and it is a wonderful privilege to serve Jesus at
   _____ Church!
3. Answer to Question A above: "US" is not based upon our
   _____ but upon our _____.

THE FOUR KEYS TO A SUCCESSFUL GREENHOUSE ARE:

1. _____ - the only thing which is more beautiful than a
   flower is a mature, Spirit-filled Christian who looks just like
   _____. The only way this goal can be achieved is to
   _____ them one by one and then to _____ them
   one by one!!! Do you think this is a good way to express our goal?
2. _____ are followed. If you want God to give the increase, then do the planting and watering God's way!

   - There is _____ substitute for doing it God's way. Most of
     our problems happen when we do it our own way!

3. _____ - this is not a playtime! The reality is everyone we touch will live _____ (Matthew 25:46).

- The enemy of every life is the devil; the hope of every life is
  Jesus Christ; we are the only ones who can share that hope
  with others!

4. _____ - there is an old saying, "Everything rises
and falls on _____."

*Above all, you must believe in what you are doing! If you do not be-
lieve, you will fall beneath the criticism of others, the unfaithfulness of
many, and the lack of support for the cause.*

*Secret to success: Never do it for the people because the people as a
whole will never truly appreciate the effort. Instead, <u>do it for Him!</u> He
always knows!*

Yes, Do it for Him!

*God's Greenhouse: an environment where God can plant His seed
and bring that seed to full maturity in Jesus Christ.*

Today's subject: A Kinder, Gentler Church

ACHIEVABLE GOAL: *"Helping Believers _____ Together In _____ Through _____ And Forgiveness."*

- _____ practiced this goal in his everyday life.
- What would you most like to be known for?

  _____

- He was:
    a. _____.
    b. Controlled by the _____.
    c. Full of _____.

FOUR IDENTIFYING CHARACTERISTICS OF A BARNABAS:

1. A _____ Christian.
    a. This is the way the Bible introduces Barnabas to us.
    b. TRUE or FALSE - Barnabas would see a need then respond to that need.
    c. The name Barnabas means "_____" of encouragement."
    d. Encouragement is translated from the Greek word *paraklete*.
    e. Would Barnabas be a good man to have in our church? _____

2. Made everyone _____.
    a. Everyone was _____ of Sheriff Saul
    b. _____ comes to Saul's rescue.

      c. Our city is full of Saul's who need a Barnabas to help them grow!

3.   Willing to take _____ place.

      a. The original order was 1. Barnabas then 2. Saul. Who eventually became the more important?

        _____

      b. John the Baptist: "Jesus must _____, but I must _____."

4.   _____ others.

      a. Barnabas and Paul disagreed over a young man named _____.

      b. Who was more forgiving? Barnabas   Paul

      c. Do I ever need a second chance? _____

      d. How many chances do I need? _____

      e. Late in his life Paul said, "Mark is _____ to me for the ministry."

Helping believers grow together in Him
through love and forgiveness.

Today's subject: What Has to Happen Before I Can Grow?

KEY QUESTION: *Which Comes First? Growth or Life?*

A. You cannot spiritually _____ that which is spiritually _____.

B. Jesus taught Nicodemus, "Unless one is _____ he cannot see the kingdom of God."

C. One of the greatest problems in Christianity today is we are trying to _____ who are spiritually dead.

D. There are two worlds: _____ and _____.

E. Can a man be dead spiritually but alive physically? _____

F. _____ follows life and that life takes place in the center of your _____!

G. KEY: *"Except a man be born again he cannot see, experience, comprehend or understand the spiritual kingdom of God."*

EIGHT ITEMS THE UNSAVED PERSON CANNOT EXPERIENCE:

1. The person and pleasures of the _____.

2. The importance of a _____ experience.

3. The power of _____.

4. The richness of the _____.

5. The _____ for his life. Do you feel you have wasted your life in obeying the will of God? _____

6. Being in God's _____. *Kosmos* has the idea of an _____ system.

7. _____ escape from the eternal judgment to come. "God gave the right to become children of God to as many as *received* Jesus!" All _____ can do is make an effort to tell them. Only

_____ can open their heart, and only _____ can believe for the salvation of their soul.

8. The _____ of seeing someone born again. "They that sow in _____ shall reap in joy."

Helping believers grow together in Him
through love and forgiveness.

Today's subject: How the Devil Turns an 'US' Church into an 'I' Church

- "Behold, how good and how pleasant it is for brethren to dwell together in _____!" (Psalm 133:3)
- One of the devil's names is Abaddon in the Hebrew language and Apollyon in the Greek language. Both of those names mean _____.
- Jesus taught in Matthew 12:25, "A divided kingdom is headed for destruction. A divided city cannot survive. A divided home cannot stand." Based upon that principle we can also say, "A divided _____ cannot stand either."
- The number one goal of the devil is to divide our church, and the devil will begin with _____.

THREE WAYS THE DEVIL WILL DIVIDE US:

1. _____.
   - a. _____: deep theologian.
   - b. _____: polished, eloquent.
   - c. _____: Pentecostal Baptist.
   - d. _____: just honorable mention!

2. _____ control. Three common-sense words: _____ _____ _____.
   - a. _____ - the meekest man in all the earth. Meekness means "keeping one's power _____ control."
   - b. _____ - "I die daily . . . least among all the apostles."

3. _____ priorities. The devil takes the way I'm made and turns it against the way you're made because we don't see things the same way.

    a. Another word for "priority" is _____.

    b. We believe in our ministry so much we think our ministry ought to be the _____ priority in the church.

    c. What would a one-hundred-piece puzzle look like if all one hundred pieces looked exactly like one piece?

        _____

    d. How effective would this church be if everyone had the same ministry as mine?

"All together the links make the chain,
All together the cents make the dollar,
All together the bricks make the wall,
All together the shingles make the roof,
All together Christians can do great things."

Helping believers grow together in Him
through love and forgiveness.

Today's subject: When Togetherness Becomes Real Togetherness

- "Growth is never by mere chance; it is the result of forces working _____." (James Cash Penney)
- Acts 2:44 - "and all who believed were _____."
- Ephesians 4:3 - "endeavor (the Greek word *spoudazo* means to do our best or work hard) to keep the _____ created by the Holy Spirit in the bond of peace."

FOUR ESSENTIAL TYPES OF TOGETHERNESS:

1. _____ togetherness.
   a. The Greek work *hypertasso* speaks of submission in the sense of a voluntary yielding of ourselves in love to someone else.
   b. _____ took a back seat to Elijah!
2. _____ togetherness.
   a. "Let all things be done _____ and in _____." (1 Cor. 14:40)
   b. Each one of us has a role in this church.
3. _____ togetherness.
   a. Doctrine is similar to the _____ of your body.
   b. Ephesians, Galatians, Philippians, and Colossians: The first half of those books is dedicated to _____ – to what you must _____. The second half of those books is dedicated to how you _____. It would be horrible to be sincere about the wrong belief!
4. _____ togetherness.

    a.   Was the early church inclusive or exclusive? (Circle one.)

    b.   Which plant best represents your personality? _____

    c.   Did you identify anyone today whom you can help? _____

"All together the links make the chain,
All together the cents make the dollar,
All together the bricks make the wall,
All together the shingles make the roof,
All together Christians can do great things."

Helping believers grow together in Him
through love and forgiveness.

Today's subject: How to Be an Effective Co-Worker with God

- My job title is "_____ with God."
- Jesus said, "Take My _____ upon you! _____ get in one side, and I will get in the other side, and we'll work together!"

FOUR SECRETS TO BEING AN EFFECTIVE CO-WORKER:

1. Sow yourself in the _____.
   a. The first words of the Matthew 13 parable are, "Behold, the _____."
   b. "The harvest is plentiful, but the laborers are few; therefore, pray earnestly to the Lord of the harvest to send out _____ into his harvest." (Matthew 9:36-37)
   c. "He who goes out weeping, bearing the _____ for sowing, shall come home with shouts of joy, bringing his sheaves with him." (Psalm 126:5-6)
   d. "Go ye into all the _____, and preach the gospel to every creature." (Mark 16:15)
   e. _____ positive can happen without _____ sowing!

2. Sow the _____. "My Word shall not return to Me void or empty. My Word will _____ whatever I please!" (Isaiah 55:11)

3. Sow _____ seed.
   a. Some seed will not produce but God _____ some seed will produce.
   b. Result #1 - _____ minded hearer.

  c. Result #2 - _____ minded hearer. Emotions are
    much more _____ than faith! Faith goes deep!

  d. Result #3 - _____ minded hearer.

  e. Result #4 - _____ minded hearer.

4. Sow _____ a harvest. "They that sow in tears shall reap in joy. He that goeth forth and weepeth, bearing precious seed, shall doubtless come again with rejoicing, bringing his sheaves with him." (Psalm 126)

  a. What is a hundredfold return?

  b. _____ _____ _____ _____ _____% return on invest-
    ment.

Helping believers grow together in Him
through love and forgiveness.

Today's subject: Where Togetherness Becomes Heavenly Togetherness – Part 1

- "Blessed be the God and Father of our Lord Jesus Christ who has blessed us with all spiritual blessings in heavenly places _____."
- This subject is not about "how to get togetherness" or "what is togetherness" but "_____ is togetherness?"
- True spiritual togetherness is both a vertical and horizontal relationship. It is with _____ and _____.
- This togetherness comes from _____ itself!

THREE ERRORS IN OUR VIEW OF TOGETHERNESS:

1. We are spiritually together because we are united in an _____.
2. A well-written church _____ will bring spiritual togetherness.
3. Togetherness is the result of us being _____ of the same church.

   DEFINITION: Spiritual togetherness must be rooted in the _____.

WHAT IS HEAVENLY TOGETHERNESS?

1. We have the _____.
   a. _____ lives in me! (Galatians 2:20)

    b.   We are members of His _____. (Ephesians 5:30)

    c.   Just as the cookie is now being absorbed into the body, we have been vitally _____ with the life of Jesus Christ!

    d.   No one can say, "I have more of Jesus than you do."

2.   We have the same _____.

    a.   "Jesus Christ has been appointed to be the head over all things to the _____." (Ephesians 1:22)

    b.   We're like the _____; Jesus is like the Head.

3.   We have the same _____.

    a.   God has made everything available which is necessary to do the work of God.

    b.   All of these blessings are located _____.

Helping believers grow together in Him
through love and forgiveness.

Today's subject: Where Togetherness Becomes Heavenly Togetherness – Part 2

- "Blessed be the God and Father of our Lord Jesus Christ who has blessed us with all spiritual blessings in heavenly places _____."
- Being "in Christ" is like _____ (name) inside the ark!

WHAT IS HEAVENLY TOGETHERNESS?

1. We have the same _____.
   - a. Christ lives in me! (Galatians 2:20)
   - b. We are members of His body. (Ephesians 5:30)
2. We have the same _____.
   - a. "Jesus Christ has been appointed to be the head over all things to the church." (Ephesians 1:22)
   - b. We're like the arm; Jesus is like the Head.
3. We have the same _____.
   - a. God has made everything available which is necessary to do the work of God.
   - b. All of these blessings are located in Christ.
4. We have the same _____.
   - a. God sees all of us as having the same title and that title is _____.
   - b. "For this reason I bow my knees before the Father, from whom every _____ in heaven and on earth derives its name." (Ephesians 3:14-15)
   - c. We enjoy a _____ and _____ relationship!

5.　We have the same _____.

　　a.　I have the same anointing as the _____ Christian I know.

　　b.　"We were all made to drink of _____ Spirit." (1 Corinthians 12:13)

　　c.　Lord means _____; Jesus means _____; Christ means _____.

6.　We have the same _____.

　　a.　God sees us as already being in _____.

　　b.　The _____ sees us as already being invincible.

　　c.　Sin sees us as no longer being under its _____.

　　d.　The world sees us as belonging to another _____.

*Helping believers grow together **in Him***
through love and forgiveness.

Today's subject: The Teeter-Totter of Success

- There are _____ rooms in God's Greenhouse that must be mastered by the sower.
- 1 Corinthians 12, 13, and 14 form a teeter-totter! You must include all three chapters in your own sowing ministry in order for your ministry to be truly effective.

KEYS TO AN EFFECTIVE SOWING MINISTRY

1. An effective sowing ministry begins with a _____.
   a. A _____ is a place for teaching, study and, learning.
   b. Chapter _____ represents the classroom experience.
   c. Chapter twelve is the classroom where we learn what God has _____. We sow that ministry in others!
   d. Everyone is _____ for Jesus.
   e. This special ability is called a _____.
   f. Whatever I am _____ at is what I need to do for Jesus.
   g. We receive this spiritual gift when God _____.
   h. _____ made the decision about my spiritual gift.
   i. My ministry will be a ministry worth sowing in the lives of the people I meet!
2. An effective sowing ministry requires a _____.

a. A laboratory is a place where you put your learning into
_____.

b. Chapter _____ represents the laboratory experience.

c. God has _____ for everyone to follow. The
_____ are like guard rails to keep me from hurting the
ministry.

3. An effective sowing ministry is completed with a _____.

   a. The purpose of a hallway is to _____ rooms.

   b. Our hallway is _____ and _____.

   c. Chapter _____ joins the classroom with the laboratory. It makes our sowing ministry worthwhile!

Helping believers grow together in Him
through love and forgiveness.

Today's subject: Where Love Begins But Does Not End

- "My beloved friends, let us continually love one another with an *agape*, selfless kind of love. This kind of *agape* love originates with God. Everyone who loves in this selfless way is born again of God and knows God in daily experience. The one who does not love in this way does not know God because God Himself is love." (1 John 4)
- "Through the action of _____ one another all men shall know you are my disciples." (John 13:35)
- Love and forgiveness are not only an _____ but they are also _____.

WHAT'S LOVE GOT TO DO WITH IT? EVERYTHING!

1. The _____ of love.
   a. "Love is of God" is another way of saying love _____ from God.
   b. God Himself is the _____ of love. He is the _____ of love. Without Him, there is no love!
   c. All of creation loves because He loved first!
2. The _____ of love.
   a. The word *distort* has the idea of _____ something from its original meaning.
   b. Sin _____ the arrow. Sin twisted or _____ the arrow.

    c. The devil has distorted love into _____. Lust can exist at the same time that you are "hating one another." That means lust is not love!

    d. The devil has distorted love for others into love for _____.

    e. The devil has distorted love for the opposite sex into love for the _____ sex.

3. The _____ of love.

    a. The only way we can have this supernatural love for one another is if the God of love _____ in our hearts.

    b. True love is God loving _____ through us!

Helping believers grow together in Him
through love and forgiveness.

Today's subject: What It Means to Love Like God

- 1 John 4:7, "My beloved friends, let us continually love one another with an *agape*, selfless kind of love. This kind of *agape* love comes from God or more literally originates with God as its source."
- 1 John 4:19, "We love because He first loved us."
- John 3:16, "For God so loved the world that He gave His only begotten Son that whosoever _____ in Him should not perish but have everlasting life."
- Are you a believer? YES   NO

WHAT GOD DOES AND WANTS US TO DO!

1. God loves a world of less than _____ humanity – so can I.
   a. We are _____ (verse six).
   b. We are also _____ (verse six).
   c. We are _____ (verse eight). The Greek word *harmartia* means "missing the _____."
   d. We are God's _____ (verse ten).
2. God loves the world enough to give it His _____ – so can I.
   a. No one is _____ at the cross!
   b. Jesus preached a "whosoever will" gospel!
   c. God has called me to love _____ as God has loved me.
   d. God is love, and He wishes to reproduce that love in our _____ through the Holy Spirit!
3. God loves the world with an _____ love – so can I.

a. There are only two kinds of people in the world: enemies of God and reconciled to God. TRUE or FALSE

b. God's love for His enemies will stop at the grave. TRUE FALSE

c. From the cradle to the grave Jesus loved people!

d. We can keep loving others if we stay focused on the _____ of the individual rather than the _____ of the individual!

e. The value of every individual:

  ○ _____.

  ○ _____.

  ○ _____.

Helping believers grow together in Him
through love and forgiveness.

Today's subject: L-O-V-E Can Be Spelled J-E-S-U-S

- The _____ (Greek *agape*) chapter of the Bible is 1 Corinthians 13.
- When we think of love and what love is, can we also think of you? _____

WHAT DOES LOVE ACCOMPLISH?

1. The love of Jesus knows how to _____.
    a. The greatest problem in churches is people _____ with one another.
    b. God says He can _____ my nature by filling me with His love!
    c. Exceedingly patient - Do I realize how patient God is with me? _____ Am I patient with those to whom it is difficult to minister? _____ Have I tried to be understanding? _____ Am I patient with others as I expect them to be with me? _____
    d. Kind - Do I unconsciously wear a smile or a frown? _____ Do I look for opportunities to help others? _____
    e. Not envious - "All I need in life is a _____ through it." Have I thought that God does not love me? _____ Am I jealous of another's success, money, good looks, or popularity? _____ Do I grieve at the prosperity of others? _____ Have I spent more time in envying

others than in an attempt to improve myself? _____
Have I ever wanted someone to die? _____

2. The love of Jesus _____ our superiority complex.
   a. We have a basic need for something called significance.
   b. Love changes my relationship to my own _____ be-
      ing.
   c. Not boastful or puffed up - Have I talked too much, es-
      pecially about myself? _____ Do I realize that boasting
      is often a sign of inner weakness and insecurity? _____
      Have I refused to admit when I was wrong? _____
      How often do I use the word "I"? _____ Must I always
      be in the limelight? _____
   d. Behaves properly - Love is always a _____.
      Have I been vulgar and crude in actions and conversa-
      tions? _____ Have I purposely disobeyed the normal
      rules of courtesy? _____ Do I enjoy making fun of oth-
      er people? _____
   e. Seeks not its own benefit - Have I acted like a spoiled
      child? _____ Do I fail to consider the needs and desires
      of others? _____ Do I try to work deals for my ad-
      vancement? _____ Do I camouflage my own desires as
      the needs of others? _____ Must I win every time? Am
      I a poor loser? _____

3. The love of Jesus conquers the _____.
   a. Love (Jesus) changes us on the outside, changes us on
      the inside, then strengthens us in our battle with sin!
   b. Not irritable - The devil will make _____ that con-
      flicts arise in my Christian life. Are my feelings easily
      hurt? _____ Am I touchy? _____ Do I become resent-
      ful when things don't go my way? _____ Do I lose my
      temper to cover up my own weakness? _____ Do I jus-
      tify losing my temper by saying it makes me feel better,
      but forget the effect upon other people? _____ Do I let

little inconveniences and annoyances irritate me?

_____

c. Thinks no _____ - Am I always trying to find faults and imperfections in other people? _____ Am I suspicious of other people? _____ Do I throw cold water on others' enthusiasm? _____ Is my pessimism really resentment and envy? _____

d. No rejoicing in _____.

e. Rejoices in the _____. Do I try to degrade others to elevate myself? _____ Do I tease to belittle people? _____ Have I ever been glad at the misfortunes of others? _____ Am I happy to hear others speak ill of someone I do not like? _____ Have I engaged in or encouraged gossip? _____ Do I have a "get-even" attitude when others do me wrong? _____ Can I laugh at my mistakes when I know I am wrong? _____ Do I grieve and resolve not to repeat the same mistakes?

_____

4. The love of Jesus is not _____ by circumstances.

a. Bears all things – _____ covers a multitude of sins!

b. Believes all things - You can't be full of love and full of _____ at the same time!

c. Endures all things - Do I try to see some good in every person? _____ Am I willing to make allowances for small mistakes? _____ Do I do my best or am I content with mediocrity? _____ Do I hold grudges?

Helping believers grow together in Him
through love and forgiveness.

Today's subject: The Fundamentals of Forgiveness

- Forgiveness is the missing piece in the puzzle of successful relationships.
- Alexander Pope: "To err is _____, to forgive, divine."
- We must know how to forgive, so we don't ever lose the people we love so very much.

HOW TO FORGIVE – PART 1

1. What is _____?
    a. The Greek word *aphesis* means to _____ as in the sense the debt is no longer attached to you.
    b. The Greek word *charizomai* has the idea of "_____ providing forgiveness."
    c. You are either _____% forgiven or you are not forgiven.
    d. Forgiveness has the idea of _____ a wrong so the wrong can never come back to haunt you.
    e. Corrie ten Boom: "Forgiveness is an act of the _____, and the will can function regardless of the temperature of the heart."
    f. Forgiveness IS or IS NOT an action based upon our emotions.
2. On what basis does _____ forgive?
    a. God forgives for _____ sake.
    b. Christ lived a _____ life.
    c. Christ did what He was _____ to do.

    d. Christ offered a _____ sacrifice.

    e. Christ rose from the dead as the _____ fruits of the new creation.

3.   How _____ does God forgive when He saved me?

    a. When God saves you, He forgives _____ of your sin.

    b. In John 13, salvation is described as a _____. It pictures a complete, once-for-all cleansing from sin. Daily cleansing is described as washing your _____.

    c. I only ask _____ for the forgiveness of salvation, but I have asked _____ of times for the forgiveness of my daily sins!

    d. My daily sins hinder my fellowship with the Lord but have no effect upon my salvation.

4.   What is the _____ of forgiveness?

    a. C. S. Lewis: "To be a Christian means to forgive the inexcusable because God has forgiven the inexcusable in you."

    b. Forgiving others begins with our remembering how much we have been forgiven!

    c. God forgave us _____ than we will ever need to forgive anyone.

Helping believers grow together in Him
*through love and **forgiveness.***

Today's subject: How to Set the Prisoners Free

- Everyone faces issues in life which help shape our character. One of the most important issues is in the area of forgiveness.
- (CIRCLE THE ANSWER) Would I rather attend a forgiving church or an unforgiving church? Would I rather attend a loving church or an unloving church?

HOW TO FORGIVE – PART 2

1. Do I want reconciliation or _____?
    a. Jesus said, "_____ your enemies and _____ those who curse you." (Matthew 5:44)
    b. The way of _____ chooses reconciliation; the way of _____ chooses to get even.
2. Will an unforgiving spirit affect my _____ life?
    a. "Husbands, treat your wives _____ so your prayers to God will not be hindered." (1 Peter 3:8)
    b. There are plenty of issues upon which people can _____ *without being disagreeable.*
3. How can I _____ a forgiving spirit?
    a. Martin Luther King, Jr.: "Forgiveness is not an occasional act, it is a _____ attitude."
    b. Rank your _____ in comparison to Christ's suffering on the cross.
    c. Count your _____ before you count your curses!
    d. _____ your prayer time with a prayer for the offender.

    e. Pray every day for a _____ spirit.

    f. A forgiving spirit is often made possible by a _____ spirit!

4. What happens if I _____ forgive?

    a. Luke 15's story is about the prodigal son and the _____ brother.

    b. The elder brother is the person who thinks the church _____ him something.

    c. Jesus said, "If you forgive people for what they do wrong to you, your heavenly Father will also forgive you. But if you don't forgive people, your Father will not forgive what you do wrong." (Matthew 6:14-15)

    d. When you forgive someone who has injured you, you actually set _____ prisoners free. The first prisoner is the person who has offended you. The second prisoner is _____.

Helping believers grow together in Him
*through love and **forgiveness.***

Today's subject: A Dog's Sermon about Forgiveness

- Forgiveness is the key to maintaining a good relationship with everyone I love including my spouse, children, friends, and especially, my church.

HOW TO FORGIVE – PART 3

1. What happens if I _____?
    a. Galatians 6:1 – "_____ such a one in the spirit of meekness or gentleness."
    b. Restore = Greek *katarizo* = English artisan = an expert at _____ or renewing an object to its original design.
    c. We have been called to a ministry of _____ people or restoring people.
2. What happens if I _____ and ask for forgiveness?
    a. I have honored my _____ by doing what He told me to do.
    b. I have honored myself by doing what I know is _____.
    c. I have honored the process by doing the only thing I can _____.
3. Can forgiveness be experienced in a _____ situation?
    a. The _____ represents the most difficult situation of all time for forgiveness to take place.
    b. A _____ said, "Lord, remember me!"
4. Does forgiveness require mentally _____?

     a. Forgiveness means practically forgetting.

     b. Covered sin = forgiven sin = settled sin!

     c. Forgiveness is an act of the _____.

5.   How _____ should I forgive?

     a. Answer: _____ X _____ = _____.

     b. We can _____ forgiving others only if Christ stops forgiving us.

6.   What happens if the offender does not _____?

     a. Don't begin an apology with the two-letter word _____.

     b. Reconciliation occurs when an apology is offered, and the apology is _____.

7.   How can I forgive _____? C. S. Lewis: "I think that if God forgives us, we must forgive ourselves. Otherwise, it is almost like setting up ourselves as a higher tribunal than Him."

     a. First, face the _____.

     b. Second, _____ your direction and seek God's forgiveness.

     c. Third, _____ your life upon God's forgiveness.

8.   How should _____ handle being sinned against?

     a. _____ your responsibility as the injured party to seek reconciliation by making the offender aware of what he has done.

     b. Most likely the offender will _____. The matter is settled.

     c. If the problem persists, take two or three _____ and try again.

     d. If the problem persists, take the matter to God's _____.

Helping believers grow together in Him
*through love and **forgiveness.***

BIBLIOGRAPHY

DeMarco, Ron. *Heaven's Grocery Store.* Bible.org, https://bible.org/illustration/heavens-grocery-store

Facts and Trends. Nashville: Lifeway Publishing, 2005.

Pink, Arthur W. *The Seven Sayings of the Savior on the Cross.* Grand Rapids: Baker, 1984.

Soria, Susan. *Preach On.* New Hope Baptist Church, Plano, Illinois. http://www.findglocal.com/US/Plano/132011994985/New-Hope-Baptist-Church.

Vines, Jerry. *Luther Rice Bible Study Series: 1 Corinthians.* Jacksonville: Luther Rice Seminary, 1984.

Warren, Rick. *The Purpose Driven Church.* Grand Rapids: Zondervan Publishing House, 1995.

ABOUT THE AUTHOR

Tom Swartzwelder received his B.A. in Bible from Tennessee Temple University in Chattanooga, Tennessee in 1979 and his Master of Divinity from Luther Rice Seminary in 1987. He has pastored Baptist churches for nearly forty years in both bi-vocational and full-time roles. Tom retired in 2018 from secular employment as Finance Director for a local HUD agency. He continues to pastor and write practical how-to-do-ministry resources for church leaders. His resources are available for free download at GodsGreenhouse.net. Tom married Ruth Ellen Wiseman on the eve of beginning his ministerial training at Tennessee Temple University. They are the proud parents of Ashley, Lindsay, and Elizabeth and are enjoying a growing number of grandchildren. They reside in South Point, Ohio.

63163685R00267

Made in the USA
Columbia, SC
09 July 2019